SCOTS

PICTS

STRATHCLYDE

Dumbarton

Stirling

Clyde

Edinburgh

Tweed

Melrose

Coldingham

Lindisfarne

Farne Is.

Bamburgh

BERNICIA

Coquet I.

N

RHEGED

Ruthwell

Bewcastle

Tyne

Jarrow

Monkwearmouth

Hexham

West

Carlisle

Whithorn

Tees

Escomb

Hartlepool

Whitby

Ure

Lastingham

DEIRA

Ripon

Ouse

York

ELMET

Aire

Goodmanham

Ribble

Ledsham

Humber

0 10 20 30 40 50 Miles

MERCIA

NORTHUMBRIA IN THE DAYS OF BEDE

Peter Hunter Blair

First published in London, 1976.

Copyright © Peter Hunter Blair, 1976, Pauline Hunter Blair, 1996.

Facsimile reprint Llanerch Publishers, Felinfach, 1996.

ISBN 1 86143 012 4

ALSO PUBLISHED BY LLANERCH:

NORTHANHYMBRE SAGA:
A HISTORY OF THE KINGS OF NORTHUMBRIA
John Marsden.

THE LIKENESS OF KING ELFWALD:
A STUDY OF NORTHUMBRIA AND IONA
AT THE BEGINNING OF THE VIKING AGE
W. G. Collingwood.

SCANDINAVIAN BRITAIN
W. G. Collingwood.

NORTHUMBRIAN CROSSES
OF THE PRE-NORMAN AGE
W. G. Collingwood.

LIVES OF THE NORTHUMBRIAN SAINTS
S. Baring-Gould.

A HISTORY OF THE KINGS
Simeon of Durham, trans. Joseph Stevenson.

SIMEON'S HISTORY OF THE CHURCH OF DURHAM:
(an account of the Monks of St. Cuthbert).
translated by Joseph Stevenson.

BEOWULF
translated by John Porter, illustrated by Nick Parry.

ALDFRITH'S BEOWULF
Paula Grant.

For a complete list of c.200 titles, small-press editions
and facsimile reprints, write to LLANERCH PUBLISHERS,
FELINFACH, LAMPETER, DYFED, WALES, SA48 8PJ.

For Polly

'Time will run back and fetch the age of gold'

CONTENTS

ILLUSTRATIONS

Front cover design based on an Eagle of St John
from Corpus Christi College, MS. 197: by
permission of the Master and Fellows.

PREFACE

THIS BOOK IS not to be seen as a history of the kingdom of Northumbria, but only as a series of impressions touching upon themes which seem to me important and interesting. I have written it in the hope that it may enable others to share in the pleasure which I have found in many years of study largely devoted to Northumbrian history. If there be passages in it where the heart beats more warmly than is thought fit for a scholar, I can only plead that a leopard, particularly an elderly one, cannot change his spots. The book is based throughout on firsthand study of primary sources, but I have eschewed the use of footnotes, believing that scholars will know where the evidence is to be found.

My thanks are gladly given to the presses of Oxford and Cambridge Universities for permission to use, in tribute to his memory, some passages of Colgrave's translations in *Bede's Ecclesiastical History of the English People*, ed. B. Colgrave and R. A. B. Mynors (Oxford 1969), *The Life of Bishop Wilfrid by Eddius Stephanus*, ed. B. Colgrave (Cambridge 1927) and *Two Lives of St Cuthbert* (Cambridge 1940), and to use also a passage from A. Campbell's translation of the *De Abbatibus* (Oxford 1967); to Faber and Faber for permission to use a passage of translation by Richard Hamer, and, for similar kindnesses, to Professor K. Jackson and Dr R. I. Bromwich. The translations of Aldhelm's *Riddles* are those of J. H. Pitman; those of Abbot Hwætbert, called Eusebius, are the joint work of my wife and myself, save in one instance where I have used the translation of E. von Erhardt-Siebold. Where no acknowledgement is made in the text the translations are my own.

For help in obtaining photographs and for permission to reproduce them I am grateful to the Cambridge University Committee for Aerial Photography (Plates 1, 3, 4, 5 and 6), to the Royal Commission on Historical Monuments (Plates 2 and 7), to the Department of Archaeology at Durham University (Plate 7), to Mr A. F. Kersting (Plate 9), to the librarians of Cambridge University Library (Plate 12), of the Vatican Library (Plate 13) and of the University Library at Utrecht (Plate 15), to the Trustees of the British Museum (Plates 14 and 16) and to the Master and Fellows of Corpus Christi College, Cambridge (Frontispiece). Plate 10 is from a photograph taken many years ago by Gibson and Son, formerly photographers of Hexham. The examples of cryptic writing on pp. 164–5 are taken from W. Levison, *England and the Continent in the Eighth Century* (Oxford 1946). For chronology I have followed Kenneth Harrison, *The Framework of Anglo-Saxon History* (Cambridge 1976).

PETER HUNTER BLAIR

EMMANUEL COLLEGE
CAMBRIDGE

NORTHUMBRIA
IN THE DAYS OF BEDE

CHAPTER ONE

To the North of Humber

My colour ever changes as I flee,
And leave behind me heaven and earth; no home
Have I upon the earth, nor in the skies.
No mortal fears an exile hard as mine,
Yet I with soaking drops make green the world.

(*Aldhelm*: tr. *Pitman*)

IT IS IN the changing colour of the homeless wanderer who gives green growth to the earth that the answer to the poet's riddle lies. He was not telling of the rain itself, but of the clouds which belong neither to earth nor to heaven, but are driven restlessly between the two. Poets of the Anglo-Saxon age, in riddling mood, often turned towards the natural world for their themes—cloud and wind, sun and moon, rainbow and river. Their approach, perhaps more in harmony with this present age, may yet sometimes seem strange to those who were born into the lingering aftermath of romanticism. No fate was so harsh as that of the exile, the homeless wanderer, who faced the hardships of winter deprived of the love of his kinsmen and the cheerful warmth of home and hearth. And no exile, says the poet, is as hard to bear as that of the wandering cloud, having neither the memory of a home in the past, nor the prospect of a home to come. The mood seems far from Wordsworth's.

Wanderers on land and those who fare by sea both know the bitterness of frost, of snow and of hail, that coldest of corn. Sometimes the scribe cannot write, his fingers so stiff with the cold that the pen slips from his grasp. The sparrow flies swiftly from the wintry storms of rain and snow, through the warm firelight of the hall and back again into the tempest. Hills offer homes to robbers and wild beasts. Souls in purgatory leap from the fiery flames into storms of hail and drifts of icy snow. Nature, to those who lived in

Northumbria after the Romans had left and before the Vikings
came, seemed, and certainly was, relentlessly harsh. Their writers
tell nothing of the pleasures which later generations of poets have
found in mountain, moor and sea. For Bede's contemporaries joy
was more likely to be found where man's own labours had
softened the hardness of nature herself, in the fire burning brightly
in the hall, in the church with candles ablaze to honour a saint.
Walter Scott's horses learned to stop at their master's favourite
view where he could look down upon Tweed's fair river, all but
encircling Cuthbert's first monastic home, and lift his eyes to the
Eildons beneath which King Arthur slumbered, awaiting the
trumpet call. But the delight of Dryhthelm, a monk of the
monastery at Old Melrose, was to stand in that same river Tweed
in the depths of winter while the icefloes swirled about him.

   We can, if we make the effort, catch hold of this realist antithesis
to the romantic mood, where greater suffering was welcomed
upon earth for the greater assurance which it brought of the
heavenly rewards to come; but it remains difficult for us to
visualise its physical setting, the Northumbrian kingdom as a
landscape inhabited by men and beasts. Scholar or schoolboy can
now see in morning-paper or classroom, the pattern of land and
sea, sunshine and shadow, caught by the satellite's eye ranging
across half Europe in a single glance. We can walk from one end of
the Pennine Way to the other, guided by a map which will enable
us to mark every tarn or lough, to note every twist of beck or burn,
to read the contours of every rounded valley or sudden crag.
Should we choose to walk from Humber to Forth, or from Mersey
to Clyde, we know whether there will be sand or cliff beyond the
next headland or if some river mouth will force us inland to bridge
or ford. The map has become so familiar that we are in danger of
mistaking the pattern for the reality, of forgetting that no map can
tell us when a river will come down in sudden spate, whether the
peat hags will be as soft as the quicksands by Holy Island, when the
mists will fall on Cheviot. Yet it is to the map that we must turn,
since the physical structure of the land remains unchanged, only its
surface diseased with the sores of industrial refuse. Hard volcanic
cores still break through the smoothly rounded Cheviots. The
bright colours of a geological map show plenty of limestone,

needed by the Gaulish cement-makers when they came to teach the Northumbrians a lost skill. The Glen has not greatly changed its course since men went there to be baptised by Paulinus. There are still places where garnets can be found. Despite the damage done to the sand dunes by encroaching tourists, Holy Island is still protected against the assaults of the sea by an extension of that same outcrop of dark basalt that defended the royal stronghold at Bamburgh against the attacks of Penda, king of Mercia.

Bede, sensing the importance of physical and human geography for the history of mankind, entitled the first chapter of his own *Ecclesiastical History of the English People* 'Of the situation of Britain and Ireland and of their earliest inhabitants'. There is much here that is both relevant and interesting—Britain's geographical position in relation to Germany, Gaul and Spain; the size of the island itself; its natural products of fish, fowl and cattle, its wealth in minerals; the seasonal changes in the hours of daylight and darkness. After describing the physical properties of the island, Bede then tells of the different races who live there, and closes his chapter with an account of the blessings which had been bestowed upon the neighbouring island, called by him *Hibernia*, a land where the snow seldom lasted for more than three days, a land abounding in milk and honey where no snake was able to live.

Yet when we look at this chapter more closely, in particular at the account of Britain's physical length and breadth and its position in relation to the European mainland, we find that much of its information is derived from writers who lived in Mediterranean countries and some of them, notably Pliny, centuries before Bede's time. Bede's contemporaries did not draw maps of their own island, nor did they make their own measurements to reach their figure of 4,875 miles for the whole circuit of the coastline. Modern geographers of repute hesitate to give any figure at all, but those not troubled by the problems caused by rising and falling tides may accept a figure of about 4,910 miles. In Bede's time men often accepted the authority of someone else, as did a writer of Tyre in Palestine who quoted Bede's opinion about the sources of the river Jordan rather than going to look for himself. We may indeed regret that no Anglo-Saxon Cobbett or Boswell wrote directly from his own observation of

places and people in the country in which he lived, but to have
expected as much would have been to misread the age and
overlook men's necessary preoccupation with the means of
maintaining life.

There is much to be learnt from Bede's account of the island of
Britain. He tells us that the rivers abounded in fish, particularly
salmon, and that seals were often caught. The salmon are still
caught, abundantly in a good season, in Northumbria's
rivers—Tyne, Coquet or Tweed—and nowadays their flesh is
prized more highly than the flesh or hide of seals, but Britain's
largest colony of grey seals is to be found on the Farne Islands, so
large that its population must be controlled by culling, lest disease
spread through lack of nourishment for such a throng. We learn,
too, that whales were sometimes caught. They may be less
common now, but a visitor to Coldingham Bay, not far from
Æbbe's monastery, may sometimes see a Norwegian whaler at
anchor there. For the whole of his life—a long one by Anglo-
Saxon standards—Bede lived close to the sea and this is why, no
doubt, he wrote of mussels, whelks, salmon, seals, dolphin and
whales. He described the scarlet-coloured dye which was made
from whelks; 'a most beautiful red which neither fades through the
heat of the sun nor exposure to rain; indeed the older it is the more
beautiful it becomes.' We may turn to another riddle, composed
like that upon the cloud, by Aldhelm:

> From twin shells in the blue sea I was born,
> And by my hairy body turn soft wool
> A tawny red. Lo, gorgeous robes I give,
> And of my flesh provide men food besides:
> A double tribute thus I pay to Fate.
>
> (*Tr. Pitman*)

The fruits of the sea will have supplied many of the meals in
Northumbria's coastal monasteries. Come spring or summer,
autumn or winter, the fish were always there, needing only to be
netted, as men still net the salmon off Berwick pier, or
Scremerston sands. They demanded no summer pasture, no
autumn feeding. In their times of greatest abundance they could be

dried, salted or smoked, and perhaps this was one reason why so many monasteries lay beside river banks or tidal estuaries.

Bede writes in general terms of rich crops and of good pasturage for cattle and beasts of burden, but he tells us nothing in detail of cows, sheep, goats or pigs. We may suspect, even if we cannot prove, that the inland parts of his country depended very much more upon cattle than upon corn—as they continued to do throughout the Middle Ages and long after, when the Cheviot sheep drove men from the Highlands of Scotland. Deer seem now to be returning to areas where they once roamed in large numbers, and visitors to Chillingham may see, if they are lucky enough to be in the right place at the right time, a herd of wild cattle believed to be of ancient lineage. We can be certain that there were many sheep in Bede's time and that Cuthbert was far from being the only shepherd, yet it was not until centuries later that the Cheviots acquired the grass mantling which they wear today.

Our own familiarity with a modern map of Britain implies familiarity with the names of its places and rivers, its greater and lesser boundaries, features which have been established for centuries and which are nowadays subject only to occasional change. We may easily forget that Bede had no map. The modern county of Northumberland has very lately retreated still further to the north from the river which first gave it a name, while neighbouring Cumberland has expanded into a revived Cumbria. Both names, the one English and the other British, have a long history whose beginnings lie in the obscure centuries after Britain had ceased to be part of the Roman Empire. Bede was born at a time of very much more radical change in nomenclature, when men were giving new names to new farms and villages, or adapting old names of ancient towns and strongholds, and beyond these local names new ways were needed for describing larger areas. The two main islands could still be called *Brittania* and *Hibernia* in books as they had been during the Roman occupation, but the old provincial names—*Brittania Inferior*, *Brittania Superior* and so forth—perished as they lost their significance, and so also did virtually all of the old tribal names. The Brigantes would have found no place on a map of Bede's Northumbria.

A man who wished to give a name to his new farm could do so as easily as he can give a name to his new bungalow today; but a historian learning to write about a country whose political geography had undergone a revolutionary change, had a much more difficult task. He could not turn to map or gazetteer to find out the name of this or that part of the country, and even if there had been copies of works compiled by Mediterranean geographers in earlier times, they would have had no relevance. When Bede came to write of large geographical areas, rather than of individual places, his usual way was to refer to the people inhabiting those areas; Saxons or Angles for the most part. For closer definition he used the points of the compass—West Saxons, South Saxons, East Anglians and so forth. All these names had the advantage of turning very easily into Latin. We cannot tell whether he originated this nomenclature himself or whether he borrowed it from other writers, but it was not equally suitable for all parts of the country. He and others wrote of East Anglians and of Middle Anglians, but no writer of his age ever referred to North Anglians—*Angli Septentrionales*. The northern limit of this method of naming lay along the Humber.

The rivers of Anglo-Saxon England were not usually frontiers. Because their banks frequently offered good land for settlement, they tended rather to unite than to divide the people through whose lands they flowed; but the Humber was never a river of this kind. It is a tidal estuary, nearly eight miles wide at its seaward end, and the sailor must make his way inland for some thirty-five miles before the estuary narrows to the width of a single mile. This was a barrier much too formidable to be bridged, taxing all the greatest engineering skills even of the modern age, a barrier to be crossed only by ferry, and even then with difficulty because of the fierce tides and shifting sandbanks. And this was not all. The Humber estuary engulfs the waters of a dozen or more rivers whose lower courses run across a wide expanse of flat, low-lying land, marshy and liable to frequent flooding before the days of drainage and protective banks. The Romans, needing easy access to their northern garrisons, had driven two roads northwards from Lincoln. One ran along the Lincolnshire uplands till it reached the Humber at a point where the ferry crossing which faced the traveller was almost two miles wide. The other made a wide sweep towards the west so as to avoid the marshland before swinging back to York. Marshland and estuary together cut deeply into the eastern side of England for close on seventy miles, and a little to the west of the marshland lie the foothills of the Pennine chain, rising swiftly to high and difficult ground. The Romans built their road along the belt of open land between the marshes and the hills.

We ought surely to think it of great significance that Bede could find no name, analogous with his nomenclature for the more southerly parts of the country, which he could use of the people living to the northern side of this barrier. Had he been able to regard them as the North English he would surely have called them so, but in fact he describes them, not once but several times, as 'those races who live to the north of the river Humber' (*illae gentes quae ad boream Humbri fluminis inhabitant*). This was a long and clumsy phrase for frequent repetition, but there was a part of it (*ad boream Humbri*) which could return very easily into the native English *be northan Hymbre*—and here Bede found, with only slight concession to the forms of Latin, the name he needed—*Northanhymbre*, the Northumbrians—embracing not one people, but several distinct races. When he tells us that the Northumbrian race was of Anglian origin, he does not mean that everyone who lived to the north of Humber was English, but only that the Germanic element was of Anglian rather than Saxon or Jutish origin.

The Humber estuary and its adjacent marshland formed the most important frontier in England during the seventh and eighth centuries. This was the Borderland, no less significant for its own age than the Border between England and Scotland for later ages. Sing of 'the night mail crossing the border', and we evoke long stretches of moor and fell from Tweed to Solway; homelands of the Steel Bonnets of the sixteenth century, lands of ballad, feud, romance and all the barbarism of the English and Scottish Marches. It was not so in Bede's day. The Tweed valley lay in the heart of his kingdom. Carlisle was not a border town. The Northumbrian Marches where battles were fought against southern enemies lay far to the south. The very name 'Marches' is as old as Bede, who used it of Northumbria's southern neighbours and lasting enemies, the Mercians whose name, *Mierce* in the vernacular, means 'the people of the Marches'. Here, then, lay one of the major differences in the political geography of Bede's times. The frontier did not lie between Tyne and Solway where the Romans had put it; nor between Tweed and Solway where the Middle Ages have left it; but across the northern edge of the Midlands, between Spurn Head and the Pennines. To one side lay the kingdoms of the southern English, who were sometimes called the 'Southumbrians', to the other the Northumbrians.

Who were these different races living to the north of the Humber? We can identify four; of whom two, the Britons and the Picts, had lived in Britain so long that we can regard them as indigenous. The two others were newcomers—the English, arriving in numbers at which we cannot even guess, from ancestral homes which lie not far from Europe's northern shores, where now are parts of Germany, Denmark and the Netherlands; and the Scots, who could see their landfall on the Mull of Kintyre from their native Ireland. This racial diversity needs emphasis because it is the foundation upon which Northumbrian history rests. The kingdom of Northumbria was ruled by English kings who won and maintained their supremacy so long as they could defeat British, Scottish or Pictish rivals in battle; but concepts deriving from modern nationalism have no contribution to make to an understanding of the kingdom's history and the achievements of its people. Nor should we forget that its historians were English, though many of those who contributed to its civilisation were not. With only a small population and very large expanses of uninhabited moorland and mountain, there was no need for any precise definition of boundaries. Supremacy did not rest upon the maintenance of fortified frontiers, but upon the victory or defeat of a warband, often fighting their battles far from their homes.

Physical geography did, however, impose some boundaries, even though they were not comparable with the Humber Marches. Bede knew that far to the north of his own monastery two long and wide arms of the sea penetrated deeply into the island, one from the east and one from the west; and he also knew that near the landward end of both arms of the sea there were naturally defensible strongholds. The eastern arm was the Firth of

Forth by which there lay a stronghold called *Urbs Giudi.* Although this name has now vanished from the map, it seems all but certain that the place to which Bede was referring was the great rock which dominates the crossing of the Forth where it shrinks from firth to river, and whereon Stirling Castle now stands, commanding what has long been recognised as the gateway to the Highlands. The western arm was the Firth of Clyde and its stronghold, which Bede called the Rock of Clyde, we now call Dumbarton. Today's traveller, following the modern highway will cover a bare thirty-five miles from Stirling Castle to Dumbarton Rock. This northern isthmus, traversed by frontier works built by Agricola and later refortified by Antoninus Pius, became the meeting ground of all four peoples of northern Britain. During the latter part of Bede's lifetime, the Firth of Forth lay between the Picts and the English, and the Firth of Clyde separated the Scots from the Britons, although Dumbarton itself, the British stronghold, lay on its northern bank. Returning once again to the map we have now followed Britain's eastern outline from Humber, past Tees, Tyne and Tweed to the Firth of Forth and crossed the narrow isthmus to Clyde; but what of the island's western coast? Here our physical map shows one deep indentation, the Solway Firth, and several of lesser size, Morecambe Bay, Ribble, the estuary of Mersey and the sands of Dee, but so far as we can see, none of these formed a boundary of any significance.

We shall find it profitable to turn from the physical map of seashore and river, lowland and upland, to two Ordnance Survey Maps which would have interested the scholars of York in Alcuin's day as they read Bede's *History,* or Virgil's *Aeneid*—a map of Roman Britain and a map of Britain during the Dark Ages, the ages which followed the withdrawal of the legions. On the former, a man might count within the area of the kingdom of Northumbria upwards of one hundred and fifty, perhaps even two hundred, red symbols denoting the sites of forts for legions or auxiliary regiments or smaller detachments, for signal stations along the coasts or at points of vantage inland, for camps used only for a brief season, or even as an exercise in military construction. The black symbols of the towns, villages, and farms of civilian life are few on this northern part of the map. For these we must look south of the Humber. On the second map, of the Dark Ages, Northumbria seems almost empty, at least in comparison with the first, yet south of Humber the black symbols, which are used to show where Anglo-Saxons were buried, lie thick as rooks on the stubble.

The civilised parts of Roman Britain, the lowland zone, fell to the newcomers, but are we to suppose that when the Roman garrisons withdrew from the northern zone, the uplands, they left Northumbria as an empty land? It might almost have seemed so to Widsith, the imagined and far-travelled bard of an Anglo-Saxon poet, had he followed the road north looking for Kipling's 'smoke from East to West as far as the eye can turn, and then, under it . . . houses and temples, shops and theatres, barracks and granaries, trickling along like dice', but yet finding all deserted. The abandoned frontier would have offered an inspiring theme to a Northumbrian poet in elegiac mood, surveying the visible remains of a departed civilisation whose stone buildings, sculptured monuments, temples and fortifications were fertile ground for reflections upon the fate of those who had made them and had once enjoyed all the wealth and prosperity they implied. The harshness of life, the fickleness of fortune, the suddenness of disaster, were as much a part of everyday life in Northumbria as anywhere else in Anglo-Saxon England. We may enter into the mood if we will, and anyone who stands upon the Wall by Cuddy's Crag on a winter's day may find it hard not to; but we must escape from it towards a more prosaic, less melancholy approach.

The abandonment of a heavily-fortified military zone is likely to have resulted in some reduction of its population, even though a few of its garrisons may have been recruited from Britain itself. It is also likely that, when there were no longer any soldiers to be paid their wages and the camp followers had dispersed, coined money would quickly go out of circulation. There would also be a loss of skilled men—stonemasons, armourers, carpenters and suchlike—and also of such material aspects of Roman civilisation as glass and mass-produced pottery. The knowledge of how to make mortar was lost, and had to be learnt afresh when Benedict Biscop wanted to build his new church at Wearmouth in the Roman manner. Nevertheless old buildings remained, to become useful quarries for Wilfrid's church at Hexham or the church of St Andrew at Corbridge. To look upon these buildings as the work of giants was a justifiable poetic conceit, for no one could well deny that the making of the Roman Empire had been a gigantic achievement; but the Anglo-Saxons were fully aware that the giants were the Romans. Bede writes of these Roman frontiers, of their cities, lighthouses, bridges and roads, all as familiar landmarks. 'They made a famous wall which is still to be seen. It is eight feet wide and twelve feet high, running in a straight line from east to west, as is plain for all to see even to this day.' Wallsend itself, or *Segedunum* as the Romans called it, lay a bare two and a half miles away from Bede's own monastery at Jarrow.

One or two Roman stations have yielded some slight signs of Anglo-Saxon presence, but in general we shall probably be right in thinking that most of them were abandoned and left to slow decay. Yet they remained as features in the landscape, 'cities visible from afar', to impress and to remind.

> Tumbled are the towers,
> Ruined the roofs, and broken the barred gate,
> Frost in the plaster, all the ceilings gape,
> Torn and collapsed and eaten up by age.
>
> (*The Ruin*; tr. Hamer)

Meaning less to the poet, but of immediate practical use to men the roads were still there, to lead warbands from Edinburgh to Catterick or from Glendale to Chester. Cuthbert could have travelled the whole way by Roman road from Melrose to Chester-le-Street where his provident, if thievish, horse nosed out a shepherd's loaf of bread from the thatch above their night's lodging (Plate 1).

We know the names of many, but by no means all, of the Roman military forts, yet so far as we do know them, not a single one has survived as a recognisable derivative still in use as a name today. It is only at two or three places, which had civil as well as military importance, that Roman names seem to have continued in use. The name by which Carlisle was known to Bede—*civitas Lugubalia*—differed scarcely at all from the form in use during the

Roman occupation. The same is true of Catterick which Bede called a *vicus*, perhaps with deliberate intent to emphasise its Roman origin. Some of its inhabitants sought baptism by Paulinus where the Swale flowed past. Both places had been towns rather than forts during the Roman occupation. Ptolemy would have found it difficult to recognise in the name York the direct lineal descendant of his *Εβόρακον*, the Roman *Eburacum*. The Roman name continued in use, at least among scholars writing in Latin, but the English, as is often their way with foreign names, adapted it to their own ear. They displaced what was for them the meaningless *Ebur* (originally perhaps a Celtic personal name) by an English word *eofor* which sounded rather like it, but meant 'wild boar', and so *Eburacum* changed easily into *Eoforwic*. It remained for the Scandinavians similarly to adapt the English form to their own *Jorvik* whence there was another easy transition to York. The history of the place-name would be a strong indication, even if there were no other, that York had never ceased to be inhabited. Other Roman sites may have been used by the English. The son of Penda, king of Mercia, was baptised at 'a famous royal estate' called *Ad Murum*, described by Bede as lying twelve miles from the eastern sea. Anyone who walks inland along the twisting course of the Tyne for twelve miles from its mouth, and it is difficult to believe that Bede had never done so himself, will arrive at Newcastle, the site of a Roman fort adjacent to the Wall and, perhaps more important, of the lowest Roman bridge across the river itself. Whatever else may have vanished with the Romans, at least their buildings remained, buildings solidly constructed of durable materials which could have survived the onslaughts of winter weather for centuries. The massive columns at the heart of Roman York were still standing in the seventh century and the Italian bishop who came to preach to the English in Northumbria would be likely to find York in no worse state than some of the Italian cities which had suffered during the incursions of the Lombards (Plate 2).

Why did the English come to this part of Britain when there was plenty of land, richer in its soil and much easier of access, further south? We shall never be able to give a full and certain answer to this question because, with the end of Roman rule, we return for a century or two into a prehistoric age, an age, that is, from which virtually no contemporary written records have survived, save perhaps the writings of Patrick and Gildas. It may be that none were kept. The point needs emphasis. Many relatively minor episodes in the history of Roman Britain—the erection of a new building, the repair of an old one—can be dated with precision to a particular year from an inscription cut to mark the occasion, as the foundation stone of a new building may be inscribed today. After the end of Roman rule in Britain we shall not again meet with such precision for close on three hundred years, when we find the inscription which recorded the dedication of St Paul's church at Jarrow on 23 April 685. It is this lack of contemporary written evidence, preserved in contemporary manuscripts, which leaves the age in darkness and opens the road to all manner of speculation.

Looking again at the map of Britain in the age following the Roman withdrawal, we find that although Northumbria seems to be almost empty in comparison with midland and southern England, there is one small area in its south-eastern corner where the black symbols of Anglo-Saxon burials are numerous enough to catch the eye. They provide good evidence of settlement in the pagan Saxon period in the East Riding of Yorkshire and more especially on the Yorkshire Wolds, yet this evidence is difficult to interpret. Many of the burials were excavated by those who were ill-qualified to perform such work and who had no understanding of the problems involved. No precise record was made of the circumstances in which material was found and very often the material itself has since been lost. Burial urns made convenient cockshys for the 'navvies' who found them when they were building the Yorkshire railways in the nineteenth century. Yet a little still remains, and by comparison with similar material from other parts of England and from north-western Germany, we may advance to conjecture which, if it falls far short of certainty, may yet be a little more than speculation.

Detailed study of the chronology of Anglo-Saxon pottery, in relation to the settlement of England as a whole, has seemed to suggest that in some places the earliest settlers did not come as hostile invaders intent on conquest, but as mercenary soldiers in the pay of Rome, at a time when Britain was still a valued part of the empire. Such an interpretation is in keeping with the opinion of Gildas, the nearest we can get to a contemporary writer, at least insofar as he claims that the Saxons first came to Britain at the invitation of those who needed their military aid against other enemies. Whereas Gildas placed the invitation in the fifth century, some archaeologists now think that the Saxon mercenaries may have come in the fourth. When this thesis is applied to Northumbria our attention is drawn to two places; Sancton which lies on the Wolds in close and significant relation to the Roman roads, and York itself. Both sites have yielded pottery which is claimed to be among the earliest of its kind and to belong to times falling before, rather than after, the withdrawal of the Romans.

Whether the invitation was made under Roman rule, or whether it was sent by those in power afterwards, current opinion about the earliest phase of the Anglo-Saxon settlement in Britain as a whole does seem to lend support to the view that the English first entered Northumbria in the guise of Germanic auxiliary troops, who fought in the service of the Britons and were given lands on which to settle. Let us, however, remember that this is conjecture rather than established historical fact, and that even if generally true, there remain wide limits of date within which the episode might have fallen. One thing at least seems certain. Whatever the nature and timing of the English entry into Northumbria, in numbers it was very much less than in the more southerly parts of the country. Leaping over some two centuries, to an age when contemporary historical records once again begin to be available, we find that the East Riding of Yorkshire, with York itself, is the nucleus of an English kingdom which we now call Deira. Bede, following his usual practice, did not use the geographical expression, but wrote always of the *Deiri*, the Deirans. According to the weightiest Celtic scholarship, we must now reject an earlier view that this name derives from a Celtic word signifying 'water', and so meaning 'the land of the waters', a meaning which was in any case singularly inappropriate to the dry chalk of the Yorkshire Wolds; but even if the precise etymology remains unknown, there is general agreement that the name is Celtic rather than Anglo-Saxon in origin. Why was it that a kingdom governed by Anglo-Saxon kings came to have a Celtic name? This question, like so many others relevant to the age, is more easily asked than answered, but we may surely suppose that the kingdom of Deira came into being in circumstances very different from those which gave birth to the kingdoms called after the East Angles or South Saxons. Not that Deira is unique in this respect. The kingdom of Lindsey, its southern neighbour across the Humber estuary, preserved part of the Roman name of Lincoln; and its northern neighbour, the kingdom of Bernicia, the other constituent half of what became the kingdom of Northumbria, likewise has a name of Celtic origin, though again philologists have not been able to agree upon its etymology.

How did it come about that our hypothetical group of mercenaries, settled on the Wolds and close to York, if not within the city itself, were able to turn the tables on their paymasters and themselves achieve the mastery? Neither side has told us how or when this happened, but history is so full of parallel situations that we surely do no violence to historical probability by envisaging a rebellion, a military take-over in the jargon of modern politics. And if we turn again to Gildas, we find him telling of precisely this, a Saxon rebellion against British masters, not specifically in Northumbria, but throughout Britain as a whole. He lived near enough to the event to be trusted in his general outline, even if there remains room for argument about the details of date and consequences. So it seems likely that the beginnings of English hegemony north of Humber lay in an army revolt leading to the control of York and the East Riding. We cannot say when this happened. There was an English king ruling in Deira when Augustine reached Canterbury in 597 and he may have had predecessors, but if so their names have not been preserved.

What of the other English kingdom north of Humber, the kingdom of Bernicia? The Yorkshire Wolds, though catching the winter snows driving in from the North Sea, present a genial face for much of the year, smoothly rounded, well drained, as good for the sheep they once nurtured as for the malting barley they now grow. Durham, dropping abruptly to the sea in many places, was always more heavily wooded inland, and the coastal plain of much of Northumberland had less to offer those who were not aware of the value of coal. If Widsith, our imagined bard, had followed that

north-easterly road from Hadrian's Wall, that men now call the
Devil's Causeway, to the Breamish, and then followed the water
of Till to its junction with Tweed—the country crossed by the
Earl of Surrey on his journey to the meeting with James IV of
Scotland at Flodden Field—he would have found himself again in
softer, richer lands, plentiful in rivers falling to the sheltered
Tweed valley, the crimson lands of the Merse that bring wealth to
those who own them, whether monastic orders or feudal earls.

Here lay the heart of Bernicia, its origin very different from that
of Deira. South of Tweedmouth the age-long convulsions of the
earth's crust have left a small group of rocky islands lying a mile or
two offshore, one larger stretch of land which each rising tide
shears from the mainland, and long stretches of flat, and sometimes
treacherous, sandy shore dominated by one huge rock which
presents an abrupt face to the landward side. The Farne Islands,
Lindisfarne and Bamburgh offered an almost impregnable
foothold on the mainland and a safe retreat to the sea should an
enemy press too hard. Here were the perfect conditions, not for an
immigrant people in immediate need of spacious farmlands, but
for a small warband, a group of Saxon pirates who could live
mainly from the sea. Good historical evidence records that on the
rock at Bamburgh, Ida, from whom later kings of Northumbria
were descended, began to reign in the year 547 and continued so
for twelve years to follow. There are no cemeteries here
comparable with those of Lincolnshire or East Anglia where the
dead can be counted in their hundreds. Where the soil covering is
deep, excavations at Bamburgh have yielded signs of continuing
occupation from long pre-Roman to late medieval times, but no
sign at all of any sudden large intrusion of an Anglo-Saxon
population. Ida's kingdom seems to have taken its origin from two
or three shiploads of men who for half a century or more could
only hold with difficulty what they had boldly won.

Meanwhile, what of those others against whom the mercenaries
of Deira rebelled, those who confined the Bernician pirates to their
rocky fortress? We who look back over the centuries can easily see
not only the issue that was at stake, but also the outcome. What we
call Northumbria had been under Roman military rule for more
than three hundred years. Who was to take their place when the

Romans left Britain around the year 400? That was the simple issue. The outcome was equally simple—the English who were militarily dominant during Bede's lifetime. The problem does not lie at the beginning or at the end, but in the middle span of something more than two hundred years. English supremacy was not inevitable. Supremacy might have gone to the native British; and had that been so the lands between Humber and Forth would have entered the Middle Ages as North Wales. It is possible, though unlikely, that the Picts might have triumphed, but their strength lay too far to the north, and in the outcome they never won any power south of the Forth. Towards the year 600 there was a much greater possibility that the Scots might have proved the victors, as their strength spread eastwards from Argyll and the western islands across the narrow waist of land from Clyde to Forth. And had that been so, the boundary between England and Scotland would have lain across the Humber Marches; but the Scots suffered a disastrous defeat in the year 603 at the hands of an English king. It was not until almost 875, after the destruction of the kingdom of Northumbria, that the Scots again began to move south, winning the Lowlands from the English and pushing their frontier down to the Tweed.

Taking the long view we can see clearly enough what the eventual outcome was. Our difficulty lies in trying to discover how it was that the native population—we may think of them either as British or as Welsh—lost their lands to the English. They have left no contemporary records, we do not know where they lived, we have not even found their cemeteries. The black Germanic symbols on the Ordnance Survey map of the Dark Ages are scanty enough, but we need to look closely indeed before we can find any of the blue symbols used for Celtic remains. There is a group of cemeteries in Lothian on the south side of the Firth of Forth, although it is by no means certain that they all belong to the fifth or sixth centuries, but for the rest, as the eye ranges from Mersey to Solway to Clyde, the map seems virtually empty. We should, however, be gravely misled if we interpreted this seeming emptiness as an indication that the English settlers in Yorkshire and at Bamburgh were facing an unpopulated countryside. Undoubtedly there were fewer inhabitants then than there are now; but there are several signs that the intruders did not achieve eventual mastery without a long and hard military struggle.

A possible explanation of the seeming contrast indicated by an archaeological map may be that the native population was predominantly Christian and therefore followed Christian burial customs. Many of the Germanic burials on the wolds left superficial signs above the ground, whether as primary or secondary interments in barrows, and where this was not so 'navvies' and builders, or farmers at the plough, took some notice when they turned up cremation urns or objects of metal, and even though much of this was later destroyed or lost, at least some survived. A Christian burial ground would make less impact if it were discovered in similar fashion. But perhaps more important than this, a burial ground once consecrated to Christian use, and associated with a centre of Christian worship, might continue in unbroken use for centuries into medieval and even modern times without ever being exposed to accidental or intentional excavation; and even when this did happen it would not have been easy to date the burials which they contained. Nevertheless, it remains true that we know very little indeed about the homes, weapons, personal and domestic belongings of those who found their country coming under pagan attack from the east. Moreover, save for a small number of memorial stones with inscriptions in Latin, there are no contemporary sources from either the British or the English sides describing the conflict between them. How then may we expect to know anything at all about what happened in Northumbria between 400 and 600?

As we approach this latter date it is possible to discern enough of the country's political geography to allow us to see that, where once there had been Roman military government, several independent native principalities had come into being. Their precise number is uncertain, their boundaries ill-defined. One of them, the kingdom of Elmet, lay mainly between Wharfe and Aire in the West Riding of Yorkshire, and travellers along the Great North Road may still see the name on signposts. Larger in area, and of much greater historical importance, was the kingdom of Strathclyde whose capital lay on that rock at Dumbarton of which Bede wrote. Save only for one brief spell, when the English

1   The Road to the North: Dere Street near Piercebridge

Above: 2   Beneath York Minster: a fallen Roman column and a late Saxon tombstone *Below:* 3   Old Yeavering: a crop of oats displaying the royal township

captured Dumbarton, the kingdom retained its independence for centuries, and its last recorded king, Owen the Bald, was on the losing side in a battle fought close by the banks of Tweed in, or about, the year 1018, long after the English kingdom of Northumbria had been destroyed. Other British kingdoms lay in between these northern and southern limits. One of them, seemingly the most important, was called Rheged, and although we cannot define its lands with any exactness, they seem to have embraced both sides of the Firth of Solway and to have included Carlisle.

The evidence is adequate both in amount and in quality to persuade us that in Northumbria (using the term solely in its geographical sense) the Roman withdrawal was followed on both sides of the Hadrianic frontier, which lost all its importance as a boundary, by the emergence of several native dynasties of British race, strong enough to keep themselves secure against any possible threat from either Picts or Scots in the north, and to resist, at least for a time, the new threat from the English in the east. The detailed history of this resurgence, a British heroic age as perhaps we may think of it, is lost beyond all possibility of recovery. Beginning with the hypothesis that a rebellion of mercenaries put the East Riding of Yorkshire under English control, and that a piratical warband established themselves on the rock at Bamburgh, can we learn anything about the way in which the British eventually lost control of the whole of Northumbria, save for Strathclyde? Historians who try to answer this question face in a particularly acute form the problem of evaluating historical evidence. We have nothing which even remotely approaches contemporary evidence, comparable, for example, with the letters written by Cromwell during the Civil War, or, to take an example nearer to Bede's age, the letters written by Gregory the Great to Augustine in Canterbury. Yet there is a body of material which purports to relate to events occurring in Northumbria during the fifth and sixth centuries. Some of this evidence apparently tells of a movement of people from an area near the Firth of Forth to north-west Wales and Anglesey, the purpose of the move being to expel settlers from Ireland who had won footholds in those parts. Some of it tells of fierce conflict between a number of British kings and the leaders of the warband settled at Bamburgh. At one stage, we are told, these intruders were kept under close siege in Lindisfarne, and at another, that the British kings fell out with each other, the most successful of them being murdered by an envious rival. So far as we can guess these wars between the British and the English were taking place in the 570s and the 580s, and if the evidence is to be trusted, we must then suppose that towards the end of the sixth century the English had made relatively slight progress towards the inland parts of Northumbria which were still mostly under British control.

Over and above the short notes which yield these few details there is a much larger body of material taking the form of Welsh medieval poetry and having as one of its themes the struggle between the British and the English. No one can deny the vigorous splendour of this battle poetry, apparent even to those who can only approach it through an English translation. One poet tells of the staring English dead after the English Flame-bearer had been defeated by Owein, Lord of Rheged:

> The host of broad England sleeps
> With the light shining in their eyes,
> And those who would not flee
> Were bolder than they had need.
> Owein punished them soundly
> Like a pack of wolves after sheep.
>
> (*Tr. Bromwich*)

It was not only victory that was celebrated, for another poem, called *Gododdin*, tells of a band of men who set out from Edinburgh to meet annihilation at the hands of the English near Catterick:

From the retinue of Mynyddog they hastened forth; in a shining array they fed together round the wine-vessel. My heart has become full of grief for the feast of Mynyddog, I have lost too many of my true kinsmen. Out of three hundred wearing golden torques who hastened to Catraeth, alas, none escaped but for one man.

(*Tr. Jackson*)

The manuscripts from which these two passages ultimately derive date from *c.* 1275 and *c.* 1350 respectively. A historian who makes a demanding approach to his evidence would be unlikely to devote much time to examining material about the Norman Conquest which dated from the seventeenth or eighteenth century. A like gap separates the earliest manuscripts of the poems attributed to the Welsh bards, Taliesin and Aneirin, from the English conquest of Northumbria, yet we cannot quite so easily dismiss these poems from the body of credible evidence. We ought to recognise the strength of Welsh medieval tradition, more familiarly centred upon Arthur, about a prolonged conflict with the English invaders. We ought also to pay heed to the detailed and cogent arguments advanced by eminent Celtic scholars in support of their belief that contemporary British poets did write of these wars whose disastrous outcome led to the destruction of British rule in Northumbria. That the conquest was achieved we know. That the process was bloody seems likely. Yet nations commonly glorify their past in defeat as much as in victory, and history so deeply embedded in romance is hard to identify, despite the most patient and skilful unwrapping of the accumulated layers of poetic imaginings. Arthur's myriad battlefields were scattered far and wide over Britain, and some of them were placed in Northumbria. Romantics said that Merlin met his threefold end—beaten to death by shepherds, he fell over a cliff into waters wherein he was pierced by a stake as he drowned—in the waters of Tweed at Drumelzier; but the brown, peaty waters of Tweed seldom run clear. It is not from Bede that we learn the tale of Merlin's death, nor of Arthur sleeping beneath the Eildons.

CHAPTER TWO

A King must secure his Kingdom

'THE PART OF a dragon is to be in his mound, wise in years, exultant in his trappings. A fish must bring forth its own kind in water. It is for a king to be in the hall bestowing rings.' For those who compiled the sententious sayings that we sometimes call gnomic verses, the king rewarding his followers with treasure seemed as much a part of the natural order of things as for the wild boar to live in the wood, for the salmon to be in his pool, for the devil to be in the fen and for the felon to be hanged. They supposed, too, that a king would be eager for glory, that retainers worthy of the name would not fail to urge a young prince to battle and that a king's first duty was to keep his kingdom secure. The royal hall, the rewarding of faithful followers and the fighting of battles have much to do with Anglo-Saxon kings, in the eleventh century no less than the seventh, in Wessex no less than in Northumbria. Alfred, greatest among them, was too practical a man to content himself with wise saws in telling of the needs of a king, if he is to give wise guidance and firm rule to the kingdom entrusted to his care. He must have men who pray and men who fight and men who labour, and for these—his tools of statecraft—he must have sustenance, land for them to live on, gifts and weapons, food, ale and clothing and whatever else those three orders might require. But beyond all he needed wisdom; 'because no man can bring forth any craft without wisdom, for whatever is done in folly can never be counted as a craft'.

Alfred wrote these, his own, views on the needs of a king in his English version of the *Consolation of Philosophy* written by Boethius in the sixth century while he was in prison and awaiting barbarous execution for crimes which he had not committed. Boethius who transmitted much that was noblest in Greek philosophy to western Europe, was one of the many who passed on Plato's ideas about the happiness of that world in which kings might be philosophers and philosophers be kings. Bede, too, knew of the phrase and used it in a context which seems remote from Plato's *Republic*—a letter to the king of the Picts whose emissaries had come to Jarrow. Bede had certainly never read the *Republic*, nor even Boethius whose great book only reached York after Bede's death. An approach to the rulers of what was, at least in origin, a barbaric kingdom, through the writings of Plato, Boethius and even Alfred the Great, may seem no less irrelevant than incongruous; yet if Bede could echo Plato to a Pictish king in the early years of the eighth century, a York scholar could, as we shall see, apply the words of Boethius to the affairs of a Northumbrian king two generations later.

The merit of this approach is that it brings us face to face with a problem that is central to our theme—how far, if at all, we can discern the kings of Northumbria behind the characters presented to us in our historical sources. Looking back to what is now so distant a point of time, some may think it a matter of no great importance that almost all that we can now learn about King Oswald of Northumbria was written nearly a hundred years after his death. Surely, they will say, Bede was a great historian, a man who examined his evidence with care, a man too intellectually honest to be capable of misrepresentation; and they will be right, but only within the limitations of their questions. The honesty of a historian may be judged by the accuracy with which he records his facts—whether or not it was correct to say that Edwin was killed on 12 October in the year of the Lord 633, in his forty-eighth year—but it may also be judged by the extent to which he remains true to his own aims and beliefs. We may be able, if we are lucky, to check the former by reference to another witness, but we cannot hope to check the latter without knowing what those aims and beliefs were. All historians select what seems relevant to their topic, and the selection of one part involves the rejection of another.

The notion that more than seven hundred years of history could be told in substantially less than 100,000 words without the most rigorous selection would surely have seemed laughable to Bede, nor did he attempt to do other than make his purpose abundantly clear to those who would read, or listen to, his *History*. He wrote expressly of the good that had been done by good men in the hope and belief that others might be inspired by their example, and conversely that the example of those who had done ill might be shunned. If we were to look more closely into his idea of what constituted the good we would find it to lie in all things which tended to the unity of faith within the catholic church. This conception will seem neither narrow nor bigoted to those who remember how recently Christianity had come to England, how much of Europe was still pagan, and how strong was Bede's faith.

Kings in Northumbria, as in other parts of England, had played their part for good or ill, but it is difficult for us to see them, at least in the seventh century, in any other light than that in which Bede placed them. These early kings left no letters, no law codes, no judgements, no household accounts. We have none of their personal belongings and, save in one instance, we know nothing of their appearance. If we make bold inferences from their recorded deeds, we may forget that most of what they did was not recorded at all. Perhaps, we may conclude, what has been recorded may tell us more about Bede's ideas of what a king should be, or should not be, than about what he actually was; and such a conclusion might lead us on to wonder about the influences which shaped Bede's ideas of what constituted the quality of goodness particular to a king. Yet it may be useful to gather a few facts which seem to be well established and which may be able to speak for themselves.

Northumbria's dual origin is reflected in the survival of two royal families until the middle of the seventh century, with the Bernician family playing the dominant part. The origin of the Deiran family is unknown, its earliest recorded king, Ælle, being no more than a name, remembered only for the puns which pleased a Whitby monk, though whether they similarly pleased Gregory the Great is another matter. His son, Edwin, first Christian ruler in Northumbria, was the only member of the dynasty to achieve distinction as a king. After a reign of about seventeen years (precision is impossible because we know neither the day nor the month of his accession), he was killed in battle on 12 October 633. It may be that our record of his family is incomplete, but so far as we know he had two sons by his first marriage to a daughter of a Mercian king. The first was killed in the same battle as his father and the second was murdered some years later by Penda. There was one grandson, but he died in childhood exiled in Gaul. Edwin's only son by his second marriage, to the daughter of a Kentish king, likewise died in childhood in Gaul. After the extinction of the direct line, a cousin (Osric) became king. He reverted to paganism and was killed within a year. His son (Oswine) ruled for seven years in Deira and was then murdered (651) after being betrayed by the man whom he believed to be his most faithful friend. A nephew of Edwin, called Hereric, was poisoned while in exile and he is the last male member of the family whom we can trace. In summary, of these eight males three were killed in battle, two were murdered, one was poisoned and two died in childhood as exiles in a foreign land.

The facts do indeed speak for themselves—with startling clarity. Divorced from all other evidence they seem to show the first half of this seventh century (*c.* 616–51) as an age characterised by war, murder, treachery, apostasy and infant mortality. The women were rather more fortunate than the men. Of the two daughters of the poisoned Hereric, one married an East Anglian king, and later became a nun at Chelles in northern France, and the other was Hilda, renowned abbess of Whitby. Of Edwin's three daughters by his Kentish wife two died in infancy. The third was Eanflæd. After marrying a Northumbrian king in the Bernician line she went to Whitby which she came to rule jointly with her daughter Ælfflæd.

The much longer history and more numerous branches of the Bernician dynasty would make detailed examination excessively tedious, but we may look at the fates of those who became kings. Beginning with Ida, seven pagan kings ruled from 547 to *c.* 593, but they are no more than names. We do not know how any of them died, nor are we even sure that they all belonged to the same family. Æthelfrith, the last of the pagans, was killed in battle, as his brother had been before him, though he was never king. During the reign of Edwin, whose fate we have already noted, the Bernician family found refuge in the far north, returning to Northumbria after Edwin's death. Four members of this Bernician family reigned during the years 633 to 685. The first of them, Eanfrith, like his Deiran counterpart, turned apostate and was killed within a year. Oswald was killed in battle against Penda of

Mercia, his body dismembered and his head put on a stake on the battlefield. Oswy died of illness. Ecgfrith was killed in battle against the Picts, his brother having been killed previously in battle against the Mercians. The next in succession, Aldfrith (685–704), died of natural causes, to be followed by his son who succeeded at the age of eight and was killed eleven years later.

The facts again speak for themselves. Hindsight allows us to see that the normal expectation of a Northumbrian king in the seventh century was to be killed in battle. Only by success in war could he fulfil a king's duty to keep fast hold of his kingdom, and the success which initiated his reign was usually followed by the failure which cost him his life. Fate rarely allowed him to enjoy the blessings of prosperity in his old age, to receive wealth, treasures and the brimming cup of mead among his kinsmen. He was the man whom the spear must slay, whom war must kill. Regarded thus baldly the fates of Northumbrian kings seem totally lacking in the hallmark of any golden quality, telling rather of an age of violence, with short reigns opening in triumph and ending in disaster. The impression, though stamped on only one side of the coin, may well be fair and true. The history of other Anglo-Saxon kingdoms in this age—Mercia or Wessex—has left much the same sort of record in their annals. Kings succeed to their kingdoms, fight battles and are killed. These other kingdoms had no historian to stamp the other side of the coin. Yet even if Northumbrian kings were warriors in a barbarous age, we ought to ask what they achieved by their warfare.

Their main achievement was the same as that of other warrior kings in warlike ages—the enlargement of their kingdom and its defence against the attacks of their enemies. We may guess, even if we cannot prove, that the lamentations of the Welsh poet over the disaster near Catterick, relate to the last occasion on which the British of the north, from Edinburgh and thereabouts, collaborated with their countrymen from further south and west, from Yorkshire, Lancashire and North Wales, against the encroaching English, and that the failure of their attempt marked a loss of power from which they were never able to recover. That this disaster for the British occurred during the reign of Æthelfrith seems a likely inference from Bede's remark that he had conquered more British territory than any other English king; that in some parts of the newly-won land the British were exterminated and their lands occupied by the English; and that in other parts the British were made to pay tribute. In such tribute Æthelfrith would find the means of rewarding his followers, of fulfilling the duty of a king to be in his hall bestowing precious rings.

The first battlefield to be named by Bede was called in his time *Degsastan* which might have been expected to grow into a modern name 'Daystone'. The place was of great renown when Bede wrote about it over a century later—*locus celeberrimus* as if to suggest that it had become the subject of some heroic tale or battle poem, as the battle of Maldon was to do in much later times—but despite the efforts of many ingenious and learned men, we can only repeat the words of a scholar who wrote in 1722; 'this place, so famous in the time of Bede, is today unknown'. Yet if we cannot locate the site, we know that the battle was fought in 603, that the Northumbrians were led by Æthelfrith and his brother Theodbald, that their opponents were not the British, but the Scots, and that despite the death of Theodbald and the destruction of his part of the army, the Northumbrians won a complete and decisive victory. Bede leaves us in no doubt about his view of the importance of the battle. From that day to this, he writes, no king of the Scots living in Britain ever dared to wage war against the English people. We can see the rightness of Bede's judgement from our more distant point of view. Æthelfrith's victory destroyed any prospect of the Scots becoming dominant over the Lowlands in that age and prepared the way for English supremacy to extend to Edinburgh and the Firth of Forth.

This success achieved in the north, Æthelfrith turned towards Northumbria's southern half. He annexed Deira and won a victory over the Welsh at Chester shortly before 615, a victory whose territorial consequences are hard to assess. To suppose that Chester was occupied, and that English rule was thereby extended to the Irish Sea, would be to go beyond the evidence—whose curious nature will attract our attention in due course—and also to mistake the nature of warfare in seventh-century England. We are not concerned with armies of occupation, but with raiding warbands gathered for an occasion and seeking out their enemies, often at a great distance, before being killed in battle, sold into slavery or returning home with the spoils of war. Yet we may believe that, in the decades before and after 600, what had begun as a pirate band at Bamburgh was turning into the strongest military power in northern Britain. Æthelfrith's victory at Chester was followed swiftly by his death in a battle fought near the river Idle, close by the Roman road from Doncaster to Lincoln. His opponent was Edwin whose host in exile, Rædwald of East Anglia, brought him powerful military aid, overwhelming Æthelfrith before he had time to summon the full strength of his army. The Welsh remembered him as Æthelfrith the Twister. To Bede he was a man of the greatest courage, a man most eager for glory; words which send our thoughts at once to the maxims of later poets. 'A king is eager for glory . . . majesty must keep company with glory, the bold with the brave.' There were many others who, in this age of the great migrations, won a kingdom for themselves, but Bede turned to the Book of Genesis for his counterpart: 'Benjamin shall ravin as a wolf—in the morning he shall devour the prey and at night he shall divide the spoil.' No one could ever pretend that Æthelfrith was other than a pagan warrior, a man who thought that Welsh monks who prayed for his defeat had best have their prayers answered promptly and that with the sword; and Bede, regarding the monks as heretics, seems not to have disagreed with his attitude.

Edwin was in his forty-eighth year when he died, his forty-second when he became a Christian, his thirty-first when he began to reign after at least ten years of exile. The figures are an important reminder that most of Edwin's life, longish by the measure of the times in which he lived, was spent as a pagan. The Welsh poets who loved him no more than they had loved Æthelfrith, remembered Edwin as one of 'the three chief pests of Anglesey nurtured by itself', an allusion to a tradition that during his exile he had been nurtured at the court of a Welsh king, as foster brother to that Cadwallon whom Bede loved as little as the Welsh loved Edwin. At another time, and in circumstances of which we know nothing, he was at the court of a Mercian king, for so we can best explain how it came about that he had children by the daughter of a Mercian ruler. She was called Cwenburg but we know nothing of her life. The tale of his visit to Rædwald at the East Anglian court is familiar; there he will have seen the treasures later buried at Sutton Hoo where, as now seems most probable, Rædwald himself was the king commemorated with such splendour. Since his second wife was the daughter of a Kentish king, Frankish by her mother's blood, it seems likely that he had also visited Kent. We are not told why it was that a West Saxon king sought to have him assassinated, but the incident speaks of offence given at some previous time, and Edwin sought vengeance with an expedition to far-distant Wessex where he slew five West Saxon kings. To these exploits we may add the conquest of the British kingdom of Elmet, seemingly in vengeance for the poisoning of a kinsman, Hilda's father, who had taken refuge there; and the conquest of the Mevanian Islands, usually said to be Anglesey and the Isle of Man. Given these facts and a loose rein to the imagination, we would have no difficulty in seeing a bold and far-travelled king, a hard unforgiving man whose path it were wiser not to cross, one who may either have been embittered by the hardships of exile or enriched by the breadth of his experience; one whose might was no less than Æthelfrith's, whose majesty was greater; a king who inspired fear and was perhaps not always to be trusted.

Given these facts, and these alone, imagination would not have found place for communings with a celestial night-time visitor at Rædwald's court, of deep talk about the truth of Christian teaching with his councillors assembled in the hall, of the woman who might cross the island from sea to sea with her new-born babe and take no harm, of the bronze drinking-cups which were hung for the use of travellers by springs along the highways. Yet Bede's comment on these same cups tells us something of Edwin's character that persuades us of its truth. 'No one dared to lay hands on them except for their proper purpose because they feared the king greatly nor did they wish to, because they loved him.' The phrase is neatly turned, but it is the fear which lies first, the love which comes second. Men may indeed have feared this warrior who rode in majesty accompanied by his standard bearers and retainers, with something of the panoply of a Roman emperor about him, such as befitted his claim to pre-eminence among all his fellow kings in Britain—Bretwalda, as men called him later; ruler of the English and likewise of the British, as Bede describes him, not merely king of Northumbria. This was a formidable man and the achievement of Paulinus may seem all the greater when at last he accepted Christianity.

If it be true that Edwin turned against his foster brother Cadwallon, conquered Anglesey and drove him into exile in Ireland, then so much the greater would be Cadwallon's triumph when, with Penda's aid, he killed Edwin and destroyed his army in a battle fought in Hatfield Chase, in the southern Marches, on 12 October 633. If it be true that Edwin proved false to those who have given him a home in his days of misfortune, so much the more might Cadwallon think himself justified in the savagery of his onslaught against the countryside of Northumbria after Edwin's death. Bede castigates him for the bestial cruelty of his assault in which he spared neither women nor innocent children, putting all to death by the sword, as if he meant to wipe out the whole of the English race. So skilfully has Bede drawn us towards Edwin by his narrative art, that it almost takes a Welshman to remember that Æthelfrith had once slaughtered a great host of innocent Welsh monks and that Edwin himself, 'one of the three pests of Anglesey' as they said, had given ill reward to the Welsh king who was his foster father. If not Bede's father, then certainly Bede's grandfather will have lived through the days when Cadwallon ravaged Northumbria for a whole year, even as far north as Glendale where the burning of the township at Yeavering tells of his presence; an occasion vividly alive to the imagination of those who, beneath the September moon, may have seen the valley of Tweed aflame with burning straw on harvested fields.

Æthelfrith fell to Rædwald and Edwin; Edwin to Cadwallon and Penda; but within a year of his triumphant vengeance Cadwallon fell to Oswald in the battle at Heavenfield, hard by Hadrian's Wall and close enough to Hexham for the monks to make their annual pilgrimage to the site. The death of Cadwallon removed the most formidable, though not quite the last, of Northumbria's Welsh enemies. As the seventh century advances, though warfare remains and kings must still be warriors eager for glory, the pattern changes. The British attempt to defend their lands had failed. The struggle now was less between English and British or Welsh, than between rival English kings seeking to extend their dominion outside the boundaries of their own kingdoms. For twenty years after Cadwallon's death two successive Northumbrian kings, Oswald and Oswy, both ranked among the Bretwaldas, were greatly tested by Penda their southern rival. Northumbria was repeatedly attacked from the south and in 642 Oswald 'was killed in a great battle by the same heathen people and the same heathen Mercian king as his predecessor Edwin in a place called in the English tongue *Maserfelth*, on 5 August in the thirty-eighth year of his age'—the place, as we now think, was Oswestry—the Christian saint killed and his body mutilated by the barbarian pagan. Men remembered the occasion in later years when they said that the battlefield had lain all white with the bones of saints.

So it is represented; but the conflict was between Mercia and Northumbria; it was about military supremacy, about the capture of the enemy's treasure, not about paganism and Christianity. The great conflict in the Marchlands, something more than a mere provincial struggle between Northumbria and Mercia, came to a head in 655 in a battle fought near one of the many rivers which run into the Humber, a river now known to us only by the name which Bede used—*Winwæd*. Of all the battles recorded by Bede this is the one which he describes at greatest length, perhaps because it was an occasion on which, against all but impossible odds, a Christian triumphed over a pagan. Following repeated attacks by Penda against Northumbria, King Oswy sought to buy peace by promising Penda 'an incalculable and incredible store of royal treasure and gifts'. The nature of this treasure must be left to the imagination, aided now by Sutton Hoo, and also by knowledge of other great treasures amassed by successful warrior kings in the migration period among the Huns, the Merovingians, the Franks and others. The pre-eminence won and maintained by Edwin, Oswald and Oswy will have carried with it very great material gain—the stuff with which kings could give followers rich rewards. The slight material remains from the royal township at Yeavering included only a single gold coin; but Bede's reference to Oswy's treasure surely entitles us to believe that the kings who built and used the massive timber halls at Yeavering (Plate 3), and others at Milfield, now no more than patterns in crops photographed from the air, were well able to meet the highest expectations of those who believed that a king's duty was to be in his hall bestowing precious rings.

Penda, as Bede tells us, refused the bribe and assembled a mighty army, thirty legions, of men experienced in war. Oswy had already lost two elder brothers killed in war. One of his sons, Ecgfrith who later succeeded him, was a hostage at the Mercian court; his nephew (Oswald's son), who, in Bede's words, 'ought to have helped them, was on the side of his foes and was leading the enemies of his own uncle and of his native land', though in the event the turncoat withdrew in the hour of battle 'and awaited the outcome in a place of safety'. Penda was supported by the king of East Anglia and in all probability by an army from Wales. It was said that he had thirty times as many men as Oswy. Nevertheless, it was to Oswy that the victory went, aided by heavy rains which caused the river to overflow its banks, so that many more were drowned in flight than had been killed in the battle itself. The heathen Penda was killed. The Christian Oswy was strengthened in the possession of his kingdom north of Humber and in his supremacy over the other English kingdoms south of Humber. Oswy reigned for another fifteen years after his great victory. Dying of sickness at the age of fifty-eight, he was the first Northumbrian king of whom we know for certain that he was not killed in battle or in some other violent way.

But the tale of the warrior kings is not yet quite complete. Most of the battles, whether in victory or defeat, had been fought along the southern Marches—Chester, Idle, Hatfield Chase, Oswestry, *Winwæd*—but the northern frontier was not always peaceful. Between Bamburgh, stronghold of pirate kings, and Spurn Head at the mouth of Humber there lie more than one hundred and sixty miles of coastline, but from Bamburgh to the Firth of Forth there are fewer than fifty. Save for *Degsastan* whose site we do not know, there are no accounts of any battles fought between Bamburgh and the Firth of Forth, and we do not know how this part of the country came into English hands. There are several strongly fortified hill-top sites, yielding hints of occupation after the

Romans had left, where men could have held out against attack. Such were Ruberslaw, dominant in the shire of Roxburgh, and Dalmahoy and Traprain Law closer to Edinburgh; but there are no records to tell of any attack, save only for two words in Irish annals, which seem to say that Edinburgh was besieged in 638, and it may be that the besiegers were English. Northumbria's opponents in the south were English and Welsh, sometimes acting in alliance, but in the north they were neighbours not only to the British of Strathclyde, but also to Picts and, less closely, to Scots. Oswald and Oswy are both said to have held dominion over the Picts and Scots, but there were none to send detailed information to Bede about the history of these northern parts, and we do not know when this dominion was acquired or how far it extended.

The last of the Northumbrian Bretwaldas was Ecgfrith, aptly named after the sword's edge by which he mainly lived and duly died. At the beginning of his reign the Picts were in rebellion against Northumbrian domination, and they paid the price by filling two rivers with their corpses, so that the victors were able to pass over dryshod in pursuit of the vanquished. In 674 Ecgfrith was on the southern frontier triumphing over Wulfhere, king of Mercia, who had brought the other southern English kings together in coalition. In 678 he was again battling with the Mercians, this time in defeat, and thereafter no Northumbrian king ever tried to extend his authority south of the Humber Marches. In 684 he sent an expedition to Ireland under the leadership of one of his generals 'who wretchedly devastated a harmless race that had always been most friendly to the English, and his hostile bands spared neither churches nor monasteries' and he quickly suffered the penalty of his guilt at the avenging hand of God. Stern words these from Bede who wrote them in the monastery whose first endowments had been given by this same king and whose very name was carved on the dedication stone of Bede's own church at Jarrow. In the next year—the year in which that same church was dedicated to St Paul—Ecgfrith, against the advice of his friends, and especially of Cuthbert, led an army beyond Forth and Tay deep into the Pictish kingdom. The enemy making pretence of flight—as did the Normans at Hastings— lured him into narrow passes amid the mountains and there, at

Dunnichen Moss in Forfar, he was killed and most of his army with him; the end of a reign which in its military aspect seems not greatly different from that of the ravening wolf Æthelfrith: 'in the morning he shall devour the prey and at night he shall divide the spoil'. For although Ecgfrith gave land to the church and lived among Christians, his wife preferred a monastery to marriage, and he kept Wilfrid in prison, chained hand and foot and in a cell by himself. Ecgfrith's virtues were still those of the warrior, even though he may have supposed himself to have secured means of buying a happy eternity by the endowment of monasteries.

· Bede saw in Ecgfrith's death not only the avenging hand of God, but also a turning point in Northumbrian history. He writes that from that time (685) the hopes and strength of the kingdom began to 'ebb and fall away', borrowing from Virgil a phrase which he had found in the works of some grammarian. The Picts recovered their independence, as did the Scots and some of the Britons. Northumbria had reached limits of expansion which were only surpassed for a very brief period after Bede's death. We may accept Bede's judgement that the kingdom was moving into an age of reduced military strength, but we must also try to recognise a change of rather a different kind, a change less immediately obvious. At the time of Ecgfrith's death Bede was aged about twelve, and his teachers were grown men. When he wrote his *History* Bede was near to sixty, and at some point, not to be defined exactly, there came a change from writing about kings as men long since dead, whom none had known personally, to writing about kings who were either more recently dead or still alive, kings who were still remembered by the living. In other words, we need to recognise a change from writing about the distant past to writing about contemporary history. Perhaps we define this boundary too sharply if we place it at the time of Ecgfrith's death, yet when Bede wrote his account of Ecgfrith's reign some forty-five years later, it seems unlikely that any of Ecgfrith's own contemporaries will still have been living. And so we may fairly ask whether Ecgfrith and his great predecessors were intended, in Bede's eyes, to serve as examples to those who were ruling in later times, whether the kings of more distant times were different in themselves from those of more recent times, or whether any apparent difference is to be explained by the difficulties which face historians who write about contemporaries.

Save for the battles which they fought, we know very little about these warrior kings of the seventh century. We can ask a great many questions to which we get no answers. What laws, if any, governed the succession? Was there any organised court with officers of state, any means of local government? What taxes were due to the king? Did he reward individuals with bullion or land or both? How did he raise his army? How was justice administered and did any of these kings issue a code of laws? Could any of them read or write? Can we say of any one of them that he was wise or foolish, gentle or savage, kind or cruel, civilised or barbaric? The string of questions could be lengthened, but answers are not to be found. Yet there is surely something to be learnt from the manner in which they are presented to us, chiefly, but not solely, by Bede, even though that something may tell us little about the kings as they were. The case of Ecgfrith is instructive. Eddius, biographer of Wilfrid, compares Ecgfrith the king and Wilfrid the bishop with Joash king of Judaea, and Jehoiada the great high priest. When the priest was alive the king pleased God and triumphed over his enemies, but when the priest was dead the king displeased God and diminished his kingdom. So also with Ecgfrith—when he lived in peace with the bishop he won glorious victories, but when the king quarrelled with the bishop his triumphs came to an end. Wulfhere, the Mercian king, attacked Ecgfrith, but Wulfhere 'was not guided by God', while Ecgfrith 'trusted God, like Barak and Deborah, to guard his land and defend the churches of God'. So on this occasion Ecgfrith might triumph, but not so after his armies had ravaged Ireland. For this sin, Bede tells us, Ecgfrith paid with his life. 'And although those who curse cannot possess the kingdom of God, yet it was believed that those who were rightly cursed for their wickedness swiftly suffered the penalty of their guilt at God's avenging hand.' Death at the hands of the Picts was the inevitable consequence of attacking the innocent Irish.

The same attitude colours the account of Penda and Oswy. Before the great battle at the *Winwæd* Oswy 'looked to the help of divine mercy as a means of deliverance from barbarian wickedness. Binding himself by an oath he said: "If the heathen will not accept our gifts, let us offer them to Him who will, to the Lord our God." And so he vowed that should he be victorious, he would offer his own daughter to be dedicated to God in holy virginity and that at the same time he would give twelve estates as endowment for building monasteries.' We have seen the outcome of the battle. The vow was kept and after the destruction of the heathen ruler, the neighbouring kingdoms were brought 'to a state of grace in the Christian faith'. As Gibbon might have remarked, God had proved more amenable to bribery than Penda. So also with Oswald who triumphed through the cross at Heavenfield. The very name of the place, *Caelestis Campus*, given to it 'in former days as a sign of future events' was a sure omen that a heavenly victory would be won there. So also with Æthelfrith's victory over the Welsh at Chester, preceded by the slaughter of the monks. This episode is presented to us by Bede as the fulfilment of a prophecy made by Augustine after he had failed to secure the co-operation of the British clergy, a prophecy fulfilled several years later. Bede writes: 'The man of the Lord, Augustine, is said to have prophesied with threats that if they would not receive peace with their brothers, they would have to receive war from their enemies, and if they would not preach the way of life to the English people, they would suffer the vengeance of death at their hands. By the workings of divine judgement all things came to pass exactly as he had foretold.'

Today there may be those who want to know the outcome of Æthelfrith's expedition towards Chester and Wales. Searching through their treasury of clichés, they may say that Æthelfrith drove a wedge between the British of Cumbria and the British of Wales, thus bringing the vanguard of English supremacy to the very shores of the Irish Sea. Not so Bede. The British had been doubly at fault—they never preached Christianity to the English and they had refused to accept the authority of Rome in the observance of the passion and resurrection. They were rightly chastised, as Augustine had foretold, by a pagan Englishman behaving in the manner of an avenging Old Testament warrior. Even when Bede wrote this account and described the slaughter of the monks of Bangor, the church in Wales, alone among the churches of Britain, still denied Rome's authority on the Easter problem. This pagan English king, scourge of a heretical Welsh church, was succeeded by Edwin whose power on earth had increased as a sign that he would become a believer and would have a share in the Heavenly kingdom. We are forcibly reminded that Bede wrote his *History* so that men might be inspired to imitate the good and to shun the evil. These seventh century kings were warrior kings, warlords in an age when men lived by the sword. Their successors were intended to see them as instruments of divine providence, as revealing the hand of God at work in the past. Only once do we catch a glimpse of something different.

During Oswy's reign a member of Edwin's family called Oswine reigned in Deira. 'He was both handsome in appearance and tall of stature. Pleasant in speech and of courteous manner, he was generous to all, to nobles and common people alike. And so it came about that all men loved him for the royal dignity displayed in his character, his appearance and his noble deeds, and from almost every kingdom men of even the noblest birth flocked to serve him. Among all his other gifts of virtue and modesty with which he was, if I may say so, greatly blessed, the greatest is said to have been his humility, as one example will be enough to show.' The example tells how Oswy gave Bishop Aidan a valuable horse, so that he could ride instead of walk as was his custom, but Aidan gave the horse to a beggar. The king, hurt at the seeming rejection of his gift, suffered the bishop's rebuke: 'Surely this son of a mare is not dearer to you than that son of God?' and later repented in all humility. Afterwards when the bishop was questioned by a priest about the sadness which seemed to be afflicting him, he replied—'I know that the king will not live long, for never till now have I seen a humble king. And so I think he will be quickly snatched from this life, for this nation is not worthy to have such a ruler.' The prophecy was fulfilled. Oswy attacked Oswine who disbanded his own small army when he saw a great host approaching. He took refuge with a man whom he believed to be his most faithful friend, but was betrayed, and Oswy caused him to be most foully murdered. In the event Oswy died of sickness but one wonders what Bede's comment might have been had he been killed in battle the next year. This courteous, handsome, humble king assorts ill with the war lords. He was too good for this world.

There were certainly lessons to be learnt from reading about the kings of the past, but what about the kings of the present, Bede's contemporaries? He refers to five—Aldfrith, Osred, Cenred, Osric, Ceolwulf. Their reigns span the fifty years from 685 to 735 when Bede himself died; but who save scholars, has heard of any of them? They are not commemorated among the saints, they do not figure in stained-glass windows, no churches are dedicated to them. Were they obscure men of no importance, men who had no claim to be set beside the great warriors of the past? Osred succeeded at the age of eight, was murdered at nineteen and was remembered as an evil man who raped nuns and destroyed monasteries; but it is not Bede who says so. Cenred and Osric were both suspected of being concerned in Osred's murder, though again it is not Bede who tells us this. Ceolwulf is the king to whom Bede dedicated his *History*. We know, but not from Bede, that he was taken prisoner soon after his accession, then restored to his kingdom, finally to become a tonsured monk in Lindisfarne where he lived for many years. What Bede tells us is that: 'both the beginning and the course of his reign have been filled with so many and such serious commotions and setbacks that it is as yet impossible to know what to say about them or to guess what the outcome will be'. In short, Bede tells us next to nothing about contemporary kings, and the few hints that we can gather from elsewhere speak rather of a present view markedly free from that enchantment which proverbially colours the more distant past. Are we to infer that a contemporary account of Edwin or Oswald might have been similarly free from that gilded quality which their historian has bestowed upon them?

There yet remains one of these five, a man who impressed himself not only upon Bede, but upon several others who have left some record of him. This was Aldfrith, successor to the battling Ecgfrith. Illegitimate by birth and no more than half-brother to kings (some said that his mother was an Irish princess), he spent his early years in search of learning among the Irish. We know that he was in Iona the year before he became king. His wife, of the West

Saxon royal family, later became a nun at Barking and is believed to have been the foundress of that community which is today Wimborne Minster in Dorset. While in Wessex he met and established a close friendship with Aldhelm, most learned of all West Saxon scholars in the convoluted ways of Irish scholarship. His education seemed to fit him better for the priesthood than as successor to the mighty Ecgfrith in the government of what was still, despite Ecgfrith's defeat by the Picts, the most powerful of the Anglo-Saxon kingdoms. His reputation as a scholar stood high among the Irish, Eddius comments on his wisdom, Bede on the range of his learning and Alcuin calls him both *rex* and *magister*. Adamnan, abbot and scholar himself, came from Iona to visit him, bringing with him a copy of his book *On the Holy Places*, taken down at the dictation of a Gaulish bishop shipwrecked on his voyage back from Palestine. Aldfrith himself gave Bede's monastery a large estate in return for a book *On Cosmography*.

Aldfrith's friendship with Aldhelm remained, and from Wessex Aldhelm sent the king a collection of learned works. They included a weighty treatise on the mystical significance of the number seven in the scriptures, and another on the metric art. It would be pleasant to think that the learned king greeted with some merriment the passage in which Aldhelm tried to express in Latin the sounds appropriate to a wide variety of earth's creatures, an early exercise in onomatopoeia. Here Aldfrith could read (and let not today's reader turn to either his Latin or his English dictionary) that bees say *ambiz* or *bombiz*, that asses either *onk* or *rude*, that cranes *grudd*, *gruunt* or *gruggle*, and that when a wine jar is poured it says *bilibit*. We still feel at home with Aldhelm when he writes of horses—*equi hinniunt*. With this parcel, surely to Aldfrith's great delight, and certainly still to ours, there was a collection of one hundred riddles, all composed by Aldhelm himself. Aldfrith reigned nearly twenty years (685–705), a man very different from his predecessor, a man perhaps not so very far removed from the Platonic notion of the philosopher king. We can hardly doubt that his patronage of learning had much to do with Northumbria's greatest scholarly achievements. Imagination, seeing him more concerned with his books than with sharing out treasures of gold in his hall, may have remarked too little the fact that one of

Northumbria's first and greatest scholars was not a monk but a king.

The narrative of Bede's *History* ends in 731, and as he surveys the state of Britain in that year he does so in a spirit of thankfulness for all that had been achieved since the distant times of Julius Caesar's invasion, for the long and gradual changes which had turned a pagan country into a Christian society. The times were peaceful and prosperous, the English were living in friendship with both the Picts and the Scots. Only the British continued in obstinate hostility to the catholic church, breaking that unity of doctrine which was otherwise complete, and which in Bede's sight transcended all other kinds of unity. And they were paying for their obstinacy by continuing to be in part subject to the English. We may think that Bede was justified in this spirit of hopefulness as he looked back over more than seven centuries of history, yet he leaves us in no doubt at all of the uneasiness with which he regarded the present. There were the troubles of Ceolwulf's reign; the reign was barely two years old, but the king had been forcibly seized, and Acca, bishop of Hexham, a man greatly beloved of Bede, had been expelled from his see. Of the latter incident we know nothing more and of the former we may suspect that the king was involved in some dynastic dispute.

Two generations, some sixty years, were to pass before the whirlwind came out of the north and began the destruction of the Northumbria which Bede had known. What is to be said of the kingdom and its rulers in these later years? Are we to suppose that it fell into rapid decay as the centre of military and political power passed beyond the southern Marches to Mercia itself? Historians have often thought so, depicting a scene in which treachery, violence, murder were the normal face of political life. They point to the many kings who reigned, to the few that escaped violent death, and indeed it is easy to bring out the record of conspiracy and rebellion. But we must be wary lest our vision of the scene be too easily coloured by the nature of the sources we must use. As Bede tells the narrative of the seventh century the scene is enriched by many incidents embroidered with much splendour, the tale is not the less colourful for being moral, even though it may sometimes seem less real for being remote. After Bede there is no narrative. Instead we must depend mainly on brief annals which tell baldly of events, annals which, by their brevity, compress the record within a smaller physical space and so too easily persuade us that nothing else happened but the killing of kings. We see the seventh-century kings as Christian warriors of heroic stature, and forget that it is Bede's achievement to have made them so, yet they too were killed in battle, expelled from their kingdoms, murdered and poisoned.

These several fates would certainly be prominent if we were to compile a bare list of kings who ruled after 735, specifying no more than the manner of their death. We can read in the annals of the time how Catterick was burnt by one tyrannical king who, by the judgement of God, himself perished miserably in the same year, how another king had three ealdormen treacherously killed, how the sons of a third king were deceived by false promises and miserably killed. Anyone who chooses to contrast the violence of this age with the achievements of Edwin and his successors, can easily do so, but he must then gild over the violence of the previous age. Then, as now, those who recorded the news gave prominence to the sensational. The burning of York was noted, but not the building of the new cathedral church. No annalist thought to write: 'In this year a very splendid cross was erected at Bewcastle'; or: 'In this year the library at York acquired a copy of Virgil's Aeneid'; or: 'In this year the mildness of the seasons enabled the scribes of Jarrow to meet the growing demand from overseas for the works of the venerable Bede.' Yet such things were happening while kings were being murdered, and even if we allow ourselves to think only of kings, to the exclusion of scholars, scribes and sculptors, the colours of the age are not all sombre.

There was a king called Alhred who reigned for nine years (765–74), rather longer than the sainted Oswald. The annals tell us nothing about him save that he was eventually driven out of his kingdom to find refuge with the Picts—seemingly an uneventful reign with a violent ending, but other more scattered sources hint at something different. Among other ecclesiastical events of the reign we know that a bishop Aluberht was consecrated in Northumbria for work as a missionary bishop among the

Germans. The king is not said to have been directly concerned, but when we read in a continental source that this same king summoned a synod which resulted in the sending of another Northumbrian, Willehad, to work as a missionary among the Frisians, we can hardly doubt the king's active interest in what may be counted among the greatest of the Anglo-Saxon achievements. Willehad eventually became bishop of Bremen where he built a cathedral which was dedicated in 789. There now survives only a very small fraction of the correspondence which passed back and forth over the North Sea in the eighth century, but among this correspondence there is a letter written by this same obscure King Alhred to another Anglo-Saxon renowned among the missionaries, Lul, who was educated at Malmesbury and eventually became bishop of Mainz. The king, with his queen, writes as one who is following the work of the missionaries with the greatest interest. He asks that he and his wife, together with many of their friends and kinsmen (whose names he enclosed) may be recorded in their book of remembrance and be commended to the protection of God in prayer. For his part he has done as much for those whose names have been sent to him by Lul. 'In all the monasteries subject to our authority they are commended with the everlasting memorial of writing and offered daily to God with the help of prayers.' He concludes his letter by asking Lul to help his ambassadors at the court of Charlemagne, and finally he mentions the presents which he is sending to Lul himself—twelve cloaks, a gold ring and a substantial gift to be used as an endowment. If the Northumbrian annals show us only a king who was driven out of his kingdom, these other sources show us an educated man who was concerned that his kingdom should play a vigorous part in the great English missionary movement to the Germans and that he himself should be in touch with Charlemagne's court.

We can only imagine what picture of Alhred might have been drawn for us by such a historian as Bede, and we may similarly wonder about another of these later Northumbrian kings, Ælfwold, who reigned for ten years (778–88). We are told that he was a pious and just king, a most glorious king, but yet there are no recorded incidents to reveal his piety, his justice or his glory. Nevertheless one event of high importance occurred during his reign—the arrival of two legates sent from Rome by Pope Hadrian to examine the whole state of the church in England. No such legation had been sent to England since the days of Augustine almost two hundred years before. When news of their arrival in Northumbria reached the king who was then living in the remote north of his kingdom, he 'forthwith with all joy fixed a day for a council' and he later subscribed the decrees which issued from that council. One of them, to which we shall return later, was concerned with the ordination of kings. An occasion such as this might have filled several chapters of a *History* such as Bede's. Two years after their arrival Ælfwold was murdered near the Roman Wall and 'the body of the excellent king' was brought to Hexham with a great company of chanting monks and clergy to be honourably buried in St Andrew's church. On the site of his murder the faithful built a new church and dedicated it to God, St Cuthbert and St Oswald.

It is easy, and not wholly wrong, to generalise about Northumbria's seventh-century kings by saying that their first duty was to enlarge and defend their kingdom by winning battles. The rewards of the hall followed naturally. No such generalities can be applied to the kings of the eighth century. Their kingdom was neither greatly enlarged nor greatly diminished, but neither was life less violent. It may be facile to say that as these kingdoms reached stability and boundaries became more readily recognised, the vigour which had once had its outlet in raiding expeditions was more apt to explode in internal strife; yet there does seem to be ground for thinking that dynastic feuds became an increasing source of weakness in Northumbrian kingship. We are attracted by the scholarship of Aldfrith, as we might have been by the qualities of Alhred and Ælfwold had those qualities been more fully exemplified in the accounts of their doings. We may well think that they were men whose characters were more marked by Christian virtues than those of the earlier warrior-saints who were only warriors in life and only saints in death.

The success of a Germanic warband, the old Tacitean *comitatus*, depended on loyalty to the chief, an attitude which brought death with honour or life with victory. No doubt there had always been traitors, but some may have found it more difficult to be loyal to a king whose chief interest lay in the work of the missionaries across the sea, rather than in raising an army to destroy the supremacy of Mercia under the mighty Offa. These later kings may have been less formidable men, but some at least were more civilised, readier to believe that it might be a king's duty to learn, or even to teach. There could not be many, such as Alfred the Great, whose military prowess was matched by the power of their intellect. Compilers of maxims might proclaim a king's duty to be in his hall, rewarding the faithful followers who had urged him on to battle, but when kings were able to read for themselves they found different maxims elsewhere. What were their thoughts when they read the answer to the question put by Peter: 'Behold we have forsaken all and followed thee; what shall we have therefore?' This was the text upon which Bede wrote his commemorative sermon on Benedict Biscop, a nobleman who had abandoned all in sure expectation of the hundredfold reward, the inheritance of everlasting life. What did kings think when they were enjoined not to lay up treasure for themselves upon earth? And if they followed this injunction, what did their disappointed retainers think? And suppose that a king were actually to forgive his enemies? We know the fate of one such king, not a Northumbrian, but a ruler among the East Saxons. He was murdered. 'It was two brothers who committed this crime. When they were asked why they did it, they could give no other answer except that they had been angry and become the king's enemies because he was too often accustomed to spare his own enemies and would gently forgive them the wrongs they had done as soon as they asked him. Such was the king's crime for which he was killed—that he devoutly observed the teaching of the gospels.'

There are signs that attitudes towards earthly kingship were markedly affected by Christian teaching during the eighth century. We can point to several instances of where a king abdicated in the hope of gaining entry into a celestial kingdom, not only in Northumbria, but also in Essex, Mercia and Wessex. Bede writes with evident approval of Cenred, king of Mercia, who went to Rome where he became a monk and so remained till his death. With him went Offa, of the East Saxon royal family, leaving, as Bede puts it, wife, lands, kinsmen and homeland for

Christ and for the Gospel so that he might receive 'a hundredfold in this life, and in the world to come life everlasting'. Late in the seventh century Ine of Wessex went to Rome after a long reign. He was buried in St Peter's, and Crispus, archbishop of Milan, composed an elaborate epitaph for his tomb. Bede remarks that at this time many Englishmen, nobles and commons, laymen and clergy, men and women, were eager to do the same. In Northumbria Ceolwulf, the king to whom Bede dedicated his *History*, abdicated in 737 and entered the monastery at Lindisfarne where he remained a monk for nearly thirty years. Eadbert, whose reign recalls a little of the military might of earlier kings, abdicated and entered a monastery at York where his brother was archbishop. The example set by kings was followed by several members of the nobility. We know too little of the age to be sure of men's motives—whether they were seeking earnestly for the kingdom of God or running away from secular responsibilities—but the movement was certainly open to all manner of abuse, as Bede well knew, and we may see in it one cause of increasing weakness in Northumbria's government. It would be long before men could learn how to reconcile firm rule with Christian precept rather than with Germanic maxim. Success in battle had won the treasure to reward the retainers who helped their lord to further success in battle. There must have been many disappointed retainers who watched the treasure go instead to the church, and perhaps this was one reason why so many of them set themselves up in spurious monasteries, in which they lived as bogus abbots or monks with their wives and families; thus not only escaping military duties but also securing their estates in hereditary right and perhaps some endowments as well. The sequel to Charlemagne's triumph over the Huns was recorded by a Northumbrian annalist, how he had carried away fifteen waggons of gold and silver and precious robes of silk, and had ordered all to be distributed to the churches and to the poor.

Bede foresaw that the flight to spurious monasteries would be a cause of military weakness. During most of the eighth century Northumbria had no need of warlords to fight against external enemies, but when the need came in the ninth there was none to meet it. Strong kings were lacking, but at the same time ideas about kingship were developing. The papal legates in their chapter on kingship decreed that the king must be lawfully chosen by the priests and elders of the people. Since a bastard could not become a priest, neither could he become 'the Lord's anointed and king of the whole kingdom', as the scholarly Aldfrith of illegitimate birth had been. It is hard to tell whether these Italian legates were writing only from a biblical and Mediterranean background, or whether there were those who did in fact regard a Northumbrian king at this date as being the Lord's anointed. Eardwulf was consecrated and enthroned in York cathedral in the presence of the archbishop and three bishops in 796, an occasion likely to have been of some splendour in the setting of the new church. Relations with Charlemagne's court were close at this time, and men will have known that some years previously Charlemagne had sent his two sons to Rome to receive papal unction. It was to Eardwulf that Alcuin wrote a long letter of exhortation to the observance of those Christian virtues which befitted a king. He must consider the sins for which his predecessors had lost life and kingdom—perjury, adultery, avarice, fraud, injustice—and the virtues which would enable him to establish himself in his kingdom and to preserve his nation from the wrath of God which had already been manifested in the sack of Lindisfarne. 'Never would so much blood of nobles and rulers be shed in this nation, and never would pagans thus devastate the holy places, nor so much injustice and arrogance prevail among the people, if the manifest vengeance of God did not threaten the inhabitants of the land.' Three years earlier Alcuin had reminded another king that upon the goodness of himself there depended the prosperity of the nation, the victories of his armies, the temperateness of the seasons, the abundance of the earth, the blessing of sons and the health of the people. Almost the last recorded incident in Northumbrian history before the Danish attack on York, tells of a campaign led by Eardwulf against the Mercians. The king's head was not staked upon the battlefield as Oswald's had been, for the campaign was brought to an end by negotiation leading to a treaty confirmed with an oath upon the Gospels. Thus, writes the Northumbrian annalist, the words of the poet were fulfilled—

Stars clearer shine when Notus' blast
Hath ceased the rainy storms to breed.
When Lucifer hath night defaced,
The day's bright horses then succeed.

(*Tr. H. F. Stewart*)

The poet was Boethius, the speaker Wisdom.

CHAPTER THREE

The Nature of Things

IT IS A curious circumstance that despite their awareness of unseen powers which might affect the fates of men, and despite, too, the rich abundance of their language, the Anglo-Saxons failed to adorn their world, and ours, with even the imagined exploits of their own gods and goddesses. They knew about the evil spirits and the giants who were the progeny of Cain; about the dragons which lived on mist-shrouded heaths or, in fiery flight, foretold horrors to come; and they knew about the demons who multiplied amid the poisonous vapours of fenland to torment Christian hermits. The grey wolf haunts their battlefields while his companion, the black raven, plucks at the eyes of the dead. Yet we look in vain for anything to compare with the teasing ways of those who passed their time on Olympus idly making sport with men. We find no Hercules, no Minotaur, no Aeolus loosing his winds from their gloomy cavern at Juno's bidding to scatter the ships of Aeneas. Yet we can hardly give adequate explanation by saying that the Anglo-Saxons were barbarians and not Greeks. The descendants of those once so destructive Vikings bequeathed a mythology whose richness has brought fame to musician and scholar alike in ages more receptive to the *Twilight of the Gods* than to the *Sermon on the Mount*.

The fabricators of genealogies made Wodan the progenitor of several Anglo-Saxon royal families, but for the rest he remains enshrined only in a few place names or caged with three of his fellow deities in the middling days of the week, keeping company with Sun and Moon at the beginning and with Saturn at the end. Now and again we can catch an uncertain glimpse of a cosmos peopled by deities not yet reduced to the status of common weekdays. The month of March, so men read in books, was known to the Anglo-Saxons as Hreda, the goddess to whom men made sacrifices at that season, the season as we may surmise of the spring equinox. She has vanished without trace. Eostre, from whom the month of April was named, has proved more tenacious of life since she now claims for her own the season of Crucifixion and Resurrection wherever the Christian religion is practised by those who speak the English language. We are told that November was called the month of blood, for in this month the animals which were going to be killed because there was not enough fodder to keep them alive through the winter, were first dedicated to the gods.

The skulls of goats or sheep buried beside what may have been a heathen temple at Old Yeavering in the foothills of the Cheviots, and the head of the goat from which Gateshead takes its name, are other slight reminders of hungry deities. Yet for all our efforts the Anglo-Saxon cosmos remains an empty place. There is no serpent encircling the earth, no wolves seek to devour the moon, no god waits patiently by the rainbow till the time shall come for him to sound his horn. The old gods were destroyed. It may be that some were bad sailors who did not care for the crossing of the sea only to succumb before the anathemas of churchmen. Or it may be, as Kipling remarked, that England is no place for gods. Weland, their smith, survived longer than most. Perhaps the Anglo-Saxons were too heavily engaged with Vikings and Normans, but whatever may be the reason, we know, alas, nothing of the exploits of their gods and goddesses on earth or their delights elsewhere, whether supposedly real or wittingly imagined.

What then did men believe about the world in which they lived? Of the many who have left not so much as a name behind them, we shall scarcely be mistaken in supposing that for those who survived the perils of birth to die a probably painful death perhaps twenty or thirty years later, there would be little opportunity and less inclination for philosophical speculation about the nature of the world in which they struggled to maintain even that brief span of existence. Life was hard, perhaps scarcely tolerable without a promise of better things to come. All men knew, and doubtless wished that it were not so, that the season was occasionally hot but much more often cold. They saw, without needing to wonder why, that the sun rose and set at different points on their horizon and they knew that the translucent skies of the northern summer nights would be followed by the long and bitter hours of winter darkness. There was a kindly abbot who used to rise secretly in the night and after disguising himself in another's clothing so that he might not be recognised, would go outside the locked gates of his monastery and give alms to the wretched poor who were huddled in the warm ashes and other monastic debris, seeking comfort for their frozen limbs. Now and again winter would strike with even more harshness than his normal wont. Such a year was 764 when deep snow, hardened by cruel frost, lay on the land from the beginning of winter until the middle of spring. Trees and plants perished and many sea creatures were found dead. Even within the protection of a stoutly-built monastery the fingers of the scribes were so stiff with the cold that they were unable to make copies of the works for which missionaries in Germany were waiting.

Most men had seen occasions when a dark shadow took from them the light of the sun by day or of the moon by night, and such portents could not but be harbingers of impending disaster. An eclipse of the sun at the beginning of May in the year 664 was long remembered, for on the selfsame day of its occurrence there died both the king of Kent and the archbishop of Canterbury. As the year advanced there came a vicious onslaught of plague which first depopulated large parts of southern Britain, afterwards spreading to Northumbria and thence across the sea to Ireland, killing great numbers of men wherever it struck. People in Essex deserted their Christian faith and began to rebuild the ruined pagan temples, hoping that the old abandoned gods might give them better protection. Some of the monks, hearing that their bishop, Cedd, had died of this same plague in his monastery at Lastingham in Yorkshire, went north to be beside his body. They all died except for one small boy—small wonder that men remembered the plague of 664.

Annalists have recorded for us something of the fear by which men were moved as they watched these strange events whose causes only a few understood. On 14 August 733, we read, the sun was eclipsed about the third hour of the day, 'so that its whole orb seemed to be covered with a black and terrifying shield'. And in

4   Old Melrose: where Cuthbert became a monk and Dryhthelm
swam in the ice

Above: 5 The Inner Farne: where Cuthbert died in his hermitage
Below: 6 Holy Island: Cuthbert's monastery may have lain on the
Heugh, between the Norman priory and the sea

the next year 'the moon was suffused with a blood-red hue for about a whole hour around cockcrow on 31 January. Then blackness followed and finally its own light was restored.' In 756 there was an even greater marvel. When the moon was at the full on 24 November it was 'covered with a blood-red colour; and then the darkness gradually diminished and it returned to its former light. For, most remarkably, a bright star, following and crossing the moon, preceded it when it was illuminated at the same distance as it had followed it before it was obscured.' In the same year a Northumbrian king led his army to victory at Dumbarton but almost the whole of that army was destroyed on the homeward journey, and the king himself later gave up his throne and became a monk. With the brilliance of the night-sky not dimmed by the sodium lamps of modern cities, men were more aware of these nocturnal portents—the *aurora borealis* for example: 'there were seen in the air fiery flashes such as mortals of that age had never seen before; and they were seen almost the whole of the night of 1 January.' And, sure enough, these portents were followed by the death in the same year (745) of three bishops and an abbot. There were meteors and comets too. Read the words of Bede himself: 'In the year of our Lord 729 two comets appeared around the sun, striking great terror into all beholders. One of them preceded the sun as it rose in the east in the morning and the other followed it as it set in the west in the evening, as if to herald dire disaster in both east and west; or surely one preceded the day and the other the night to show that calamities threatened mankind at both times. They bore a torch of fire towards the north, as if for starting a blaze. They appeared in the month of January and remained for nearly two weeks. At this time a terrible plague of Saracens wasted Gaul with cruel bloodshed.' These twin comets foretelling the Saracen attack on Gaul, after they had overrun Spain, remind us of that other comet which foretold the approach of Norman William in 1066. They remind us too of the 'horrible lightnings and dragons in the air and fiery flashes' which foretold the attack on Lindisfarne by the Vikings in 793. The credulous neither of this age nor of that will allow themselves to be disturbed by knowing that portent and sequel were united with the benefit of hindsight. Indeed it was no great matter whether or not a particular eclipse was visible in England. All that concerned an annalist was that disaster should follow celestial warnings.

'Comets are stars, their long hair ablaze with flames; appearing suddenly they are harbingers of revolution in affairs of state or pestilence or wars or winds or surging tides.' The words are Bede's. Are we then to suppose that this man, reckoned among the great scholars of the Middle Ages, believed that the world in which he lived was ruled in its daily course by the whimsical appearances of hairy stars and fiery dragons, little, if at all, more reliable than the fantastical prognostications of today's tabloid astrologers? Were these the beliefs of the man who, no doubt to his own dismay, was set beside Isidore of Seville in Dante's Paradise? Despite the necessary preoccupations of most men with the inescapable demands of the seasonal round and the hardness of the common task upon which their scant livelihood depended, there were a few—the intellectual élite as the neo-barbarians would call them—who asked for something more than food, shelter and clothing. If we had been able to join this small band in the schoolroom at Jarrow, with Bede as our teacher, what would we have learnt about the earth which so reluctantly yielded these necessities of life?

We would have been there, I think, not as boys concerned with the elements of reading, writing and arithmetic, but probably as men, and perhaps not all of us young, who would have already passed beyond the elementary stages of education, and we would have brought to our task a rather detailed knowledge of what we nowadays regard as one book—the Bible. We would have known large parts of this book by heart, especially the Psalms and the four Gospels. The story of creation and all the other riches of the Book of Genesis would have been very familiar. We would have read the chronicles of the kings and the writings of the prophets, or at least we would have listened while others had read aloud. From Ecclesiastes we would have learnt that to everything there is a season and a time to every purpose under heaven, and among the many familiar texts would have been a line from the Book of Wisdom—*sed omnia in mensura et numero et pondere disposuisti* (but thou has ordered all things in measure and number and weight). In other words we would have been taught that despite all the seeming changes and chances of a capricious fate the world had been created by God and was a place ruled in an orderly fashion, a place in which effects were produced by causes which could be ascertained by those who took the trouble to discover them. God was not the president of the immortals sporting with men, giving play to all the whims and fancies of a random chaos. All this must have been difficult to learn for those whose lives seemed to be governed by pain and hunger, fire and sword, plague and famine.

The class in cosmology at Jarrow, and in those many other European centres of learning at which Bede's scientific treatises were studied for centuries after his death, were taught, as we might expect, that the earth created by God and inhabited by man lay at the centre of the universe and that round it there moved sun, moon and stars. They were also taught, and here many, and perhaps most, readers of today will be surprised, that the earth was called an orb because that was literally just what it was—a round ball. Doubtless there were many who were smilingly incredulous, preferring to trust the evidence of their own eyes which told them that despite the ups and downs of hills and valleys the earth was unquestionably flat, saying with the fenland farmer: 'It may be round where you are, but it's certainly flat where I am.' This was why Bede was at pains to explain exactly what he meant. It was not to be supposed, he wrote, that the earth was a flat circle shaped liked a shield. It was a circle evenly rounded on all sides, like a ball used for playing games. In other words the earth was a globe.

The arguments used by Bede to support this claim were drawn from the apparent behaviour of the sun and the stars. He knew that there was great seasonal variation in the times of daylight in different parts of the earth. When it was winter in the north and the sun was taking a more southerly course, those who lived in the south saw sunrise sooner and sunset later than those who lived in the north. But when summer came to the north the position was exactly reversed and the northerners received the sun sooner and lost it later. This variation, he explained, was due to the intervention of the earth's globe. This same circumstance explained why many of the brightest stars which shone in the heavens above the southern regions were never visible in the north. In particular he instanced the star *Canopus*. Not only was this star invisible to the people who lived in Britain, but even those who lived as far south as Italy were unable to see it; conversely many of the northern stars were invisible in southern parts. The reason for this was not because the light of the more distant stars gradually weakened to the point of extinction as one moved away from them, but simply because the circular mass of the earth got in the way and obstructed man's view. For those who found it difficult to envisage what he meant about the stars being obscured by the earth's sphere, he suggested that they should imagine a very lofty mountain with people living round it on all sides. From such an illustration they would very easily see how the central mass of the mountain would prevent the people who lived on one side from seeing those who lived on the other.

When we recall that there still survive more than one hundred and thirty manuscripts of the work in which Bede expounded these views about the roundness of the earth, and that this work was very widely read not only in Britain, but also in France, Spain, Germany, Switzerland and Italy as well as other countries of western Europe, the persistence of the modern belief that the educated men of medieval Europe supposed themselves to be inhabitants of a flat earth seems surprising. We may perhaps wonder that Bede who lived so close to the.sea, and knew so much about its behaviour, did not use the argument from the gradual disappearance of a ship below the horizon; but we need to remember that most shipping from Tyne and Wear is likely to have been coastal, and that in any case the ships of his age did not have the lofty superstructure that is needed for this kind of observation.

Bede taught that the globe of the earth was divided into five distinct zones or circles. Isidore of Seville, discussing the same scheme, had used a passage from the *Georgics* of Virgil and, despite his cautious attitude towards the works of pagan poets, Bede too thought the illustration apt:

Five zones comprise the heavens; whereof one is ever glowing with the flashing sun, ever scorched by his flames. Round this at the world's end, two stretch darkling to right and left, set fast in

ice and black storms. Between these and the middle zone, two
by grace of the gods have been vouchsafed to feeble mortals.

(*Tr. H. Rushton Fairclough*)

Virgil's fiery zone was equated by Bede with the equinoctial
zone where the sun was ever present and by its great heat rendered
the zone unfit for human habitation. At the two extremes were the
northern and southern zones which were so far distant from the
sun that they remained everlastingly frozen. As illustration of
these, Bede was able to add evidence of a kind which may have
been known at least by hearsay to some of those who were among
his pupils: 'witness the frozen sea which lies one day's sailing from
the island of Thyle towards the north.' The land of the midnight
sun and the limits of the Arctic ice-fields were not unknown to the
sailors of his age.

So far Bede's world seems familiar enough—a circular earth,
the equinoctial or, as we should say, equatorial belt, the northern
and southern polar zones. Between the two frozen zones of far
north and deep south, there lay two temperate zones. Both were
habitable. Bede and his fellow countrymen lived in the more
northerly of the two temperate zones, but although the southern
temperate zone was believed fit for human habitation, so far as
Bede had been able to discover nobody did in fact live there. I have
not found any passage in Bede's writings which shows awareness
of the schoolboy's question about why those who live underneath
the earth do not fall off; nor have I found any hint of the idea of
gravity. Yet I would have expected those who asked why the
bottom did not fall out of the Ark (see p. 97) to have put the
problem posed by the roundness of the earth. It may be that this
was why Bede seems cautious about admitting the possibility that
there might be men living under the earth, for in all his writing on
this theme the contrast is between 'above' and 'below', rather than
'on this side' and 'on the other side'.

It is part of Bede's greatness as a teacher that while he does not
hesitate to handle the most difficult problems, he never fails to be
aware of the difficulties of understanding which some of his pupils
will have had. In particular he probably kept in mind those who
were not in his own monastery where matters could be explained

by word of mouth and a simple diagram, but who lived in distant places and had to depend on the written word of a textbook with no one to expound the difficult passages. After concluding his exposition of the five terrestrial zones with a passage from Pliny, he writes: 'People who warm themselves in the bitterest winter cold beside a hearth which has been built in the shape of an oblong provide a very simple example of these zones.' The scene is instantly alive, whether the fireplace is one lying along the centre of a rectangular hall with openings in the roof to allow smoke to escape, or whether it has been built by travellers outside to give light and warmth in the darkness of a cold night. The equinoctial zone is where the fire itself is burning. All that lies within it, or immediately adjacent to it, is too hot to touch. Everything that is too far away from it is frozen stiff with cold. 'But between the two, on both sides of the fire, are the temperate zones and these are good for making yourself warm on whichever side of the fire you may have chosen to place yourself.' All that Bede need now ask of his pupils was to imagine the fire moving round like the sun, so making five lines—one very hot in the middle, two frozen hard at the edges and two temperate in between.

Observation of sun, moon and stars, access to the works of some earlier writers, especially to parts of Pliny's *Natural History*, and the comments of travellers who had gone as far south as Jerusalem, and as far north as the polar seas, produced what may well seem to us a remarkably well-informed account of the earth, especially when we recall that, so far as we know, the limits of Bede's own travels were south to York and perhaps north to Lindisfarne. He could talk with men who knew about the northern ice-fields and he could read about a tall column which stood north of the Holy Places in Jerusalem and which cast no shadow at the season of the summer solstice, when the sun in the centre of the heavens blazed directly down upon Jerusalem at the centre of the earth. As we shall see, there were other matters of importance about which Bede drew rational conclusions upon direct observation, and yet from our modern standpoint we can see how easily the class in cosmology could move from the rational to the fanciful.

Facing the seemingly random ways of ordinary life, men of

learning found a means of escape from total confusion in the discipline of numbers. 'Take away number from everything and everything perishes', Isidore had said, and it was perhaps the dependence upon the unfailingly regular behaviour of number that led men away from the rational and towards the schematised. They learnt, rightly enough, that there were four seasons in the year—winter which was cold and damp, spring which was damp and warm, summer which was warm and dry, autumn which was dry and cold. The pattern was complete and pleasing, as each succeeding season took one of its qualities from the one that had gone before and gave the other to the one that followed after, but this was not the end. In addition to the four seasons there were four elements—water, cold and damp like winter; air, damp and warm like spring; fire, warm and dry like summer; and earth, dry and cold like autumn. But according to some men of learning, man himself was said to be a microcosm, and so he had four humours—blood, damp and warm, like spring and air; red bile, warm and dry, like summer and fire; black bile, dry and cold, like autumn and earth; phlegm, cold and damp, like winter and water. And so the great scheme of fours was complete, with man's own nature depending on the predominance of one or other of his four humours. Those in whom blood prevailed were cheerful, glad, tender-hearted, much given to laughing and talking; red bile made men thin (though much given to eating), as well as bold, irascible and nimble; black bile made men solemn, well-ordered in their ways and cunning; a prevalence of phlegm made men slow, sleepy and forgetful. Bede, of course, was by no means the first, or the last, to use this scheme which lent itself to diagrammatic representation. The four rivers of paradise, the four beasts before the throne of God, not to say the four Gospels, offered ample embellishments.

The pupils of the school at Jarrow would acquire a varied assortment of information about other aspects of the earth upon which they lived. As for the four elements, two of them, water and earth, were named in the story of creation as they had read it in the Book of Genesis. Of the other two, they were taught that fire had lain hidden from the first in the iron and stone which were found in the earth, and that air was mixed with earth itself. Hot springs showed that there was a burning fire placed in the centre of the earth and when the rivers of hot water ran over metal deep in the earth, they broke out at the earth's surface, not merely hot, but sometimes boiling. In the account of Britain with which Bede opened his *Ecclesiastical History* he commented on these hot springs, remarking that they supplied hot baths 'suitable for all ages and both sexes, in separate places and adapted to the needs of each'. As for the air, if you took some earth, mixed it with water and then exposed it to the sun you would see vapours rising from it.

Physicists of today might not quarrel with the view taught at Jarrow that 'the colliding of matter of all kinds produces fire' (as when a boy produces sparks by striking two stones together), but anyone hoping to discover a seventh-century atomic physics would find instead that the application of the dictum was to the production of lightning by the collision of clouds; while the ensuing thunder was caused by winds escaping from the clouds punctured as it were by the lightning. And we move from the ludicrous back to the scientific when we read that the thunder and lightning occurred simultaneously, but that the light travelled more quickly to the eye than did the sound to the ear. There were no volcanoes in Britain, but men had read about the eruptions of Etna and they were told that these were caused by water leaking from the Mediterranean into the earth itself. Then as now Britain experienced earth tremors, some of them great enough to be recorded by annalists. They were said to be caused by winds rushing violently through caves. Moving from earth to universe, we return to the schematised with a vision of seven heavens—the number itself is laden with mystical significance. First came air, aether, Olympus and fiery space, and beyond these lay the firmament, the heaven of the angels and the heaven of the Trinity.

The five zones of earth, the four elements and the seven heavens were no doubt all topics upon which much time was spent in the monastic schools of western Europe. Yet their interest was largely theoretical and there were other matters touching day and night, sun and moon, time and tide, which were of immediate practical importance; as we can readily understand if we divest ourselves of every modern means by which we tell the time, the day of the week, the date of the month and the number of the year. Remove all watches, clocks, radio time-signals and almanacks. Remove also the more elaborate sundials horizontally set with benefit of compass and detailed knowledge of the earth's movements round the sun, as well as its gyrations upon its own axis.

So far as we know, the only means of telling the time which would certainly be available at Jarrow consisted of a very simple dial cut on a semicircular block of stone. This stone would be set vertically in a south-facing wall, usually no doubt the wall of a church, as in the south wall of the church at Escomb in the county of Durham, a church which is believed to date from the seventh or the eighth century. Another example may be seen on the south face of the sculptured cross at Bewcastle (Plate 9), this too probably dating from the same period. In its simplest form such a stone was marked with three incised lines set at angles of forty-five degrees and radiating from the midpoint of the horizontal diameter to the circumference. At the midpoint of the horizontal a gnomon was placed, but we do not know exactly how it was shaped since on surviving dials only the holes remain. The dial marked in this way was intended to show the hours of daylight divided into four equal portions, notionally of three hours each. Sometimes these four divisions were bisected by shorter radiating lines which did not reach as far as the circumference, and in this case each smaller division would notionally be of one and a half hours. Dials of this kind—*horologium* in Latin—are the only devices for telling the time which have survived from Bede's world. The use of an hour-glass seems improbable, since men lacked skill in making glass, let alone the fine aperture for the sands of time. Some of the monks from Jarrow who were in Rome in 701 saw in a church there wax candles on which were inscriptions recording the number of years which had elapsed since the Crucifixion, but I am not aware of any evidence from Bede's Northumbria of the use of candles for measuring the smaller intervals of time such as Alfred the Great is said to have devised. Nor have I found any reference in Bede's writings to the use of a water clock, though his remarks about the tides point to some means of measuring short intervals of time with some accuracy.

It is obvious that the crude sundial would not be a very effective means of telling the time. The day, if strictly defined, meant the period within which the sun completed its supposed circuit of the earth, but in common speech, Bede tells us, the day was the period when the sun was visible above the earth. Herein lay an essentially physical problem since the sun was above the earth so much longer in June than it was in December. But there was also a theological problem. Jesus himself had said: 'Are there not twelve hours in the day?' The variation in the length of the daylight hours in Jerusalem was not so marked as to give rise to the problem which faced those who lived in more northerly latitudes. If one day comprised the hours of daylight and Jesus had said that there were twelve hours in the day, then it followed for those who lived in Northumbria that each hour of a summer day would be longer, almost an hour and a half, and each hour of a winter day would be shorter, a bare three-quarters. Alternatively if each hour of the day was to be of the same length, there would need to be more of them in the summer—as many as eighteen, and fewer in the winter —little more than six.

The conflict between the physical reality of the northern world and the theological arguments deriving from Mediterranean lands was a very real one and there was no obvious solution. The difficulty continues to be reflected in Anglo-Saxon calendars of later times, when it was common practice to make an artificial division between the hours of night and day for each month of the year. This division is not found in the only Northumbrian calendar to have survived from Bede's age—Willibrord's—but a glance at a northern calendar of ninth-century date shows that in November sixteen hours were assigned to the night and eight to the day, while the daytime hours of December were reckoned at only six, though taking an average through this month as a whole, the sun was certainly above the horizon for more than six hours daily. With this latitude in measuring time we need not be surprised at the varying length of the *punctus*, the term used for a subdivision of the hour. At one point, Bede tells us that one hour contained four *puncti* and at another, when lunar calculations were involved, that there were five *puncti* in one hour.

When we consider practical difficulties of this kind, and the primitive sundials of the age, let alone the seasons of the year when the skies might be overcast by day and by night for weeks on end, we may well wonder how great were the errors in reckoning time, not merely as to the hour of the day, but perhaps even as to the day of the week. There are, here and there, a few hints that theories about time and seasons did not always correspond with realities. Bede's abbot, Ceolfrith, wrote a long, and to the modern reader rather tedious, letter to a king of the Picts. The topic was the right method of calculating the date of Easter. Discussing the date of the spring equinox, he says: 'Now the equinox, according to the opinion of all eastern nations, and especially of the Egyptians who took the palm from all other learned men in calculations, usually falls on 21 March, as we ourselves can also prove by examining a sundial.' Ceolfrith seems to be saying here that observation of the shadow cast by the gnomon on the Jarrow sundial had confirmed the date given by the Egyptians and other authorities. But the remarkable point about this passage is that at the date when the letter was written, shortly after 700, the spring equinox was on 17 March. Are we to suppose that the sundial was so inaccurate that it could be four days wrong? And if so was there room for error of this magnitude in the church calendar as a whole? Or was it simply that the abbot preferred to accept the testimony of ancient and outdated authority to the evidence of the shadow cast by the gnomon at Jarrow? When Bede wrote his first school treatise *On Times* he stated that the two solstices and the two equinoxes were to be dated to the 8th of the kalends of January (winter solstice), April (spring equinox), July (summer solstice) and October (autumn equinox). In the modern calendar these dates correspond with 25 December, 25 March, 24 June and 24 September. Some twenty years later when he wrote his greatly enlarged work on the same theme, he repeated these dates which rested on ancient written authority, but then went on to show that not only the spring equinox, but also the other three seasons, must be placed somewhat earlier than the 8th of the kalends in their respective months. Evidently some attempts were being made to take direct observations even though the results seem not to have been very accurate.

Perhaps such observations seemed of greater practical importance to Northumbrians than they may have done to Egyptians, for Britain, so Bede told his readers (some of whom lived in Italy and Spain), 'lies almost under the North Pole', and because of this there were seasons of the year when those who were keeping watch at midnight found it hard to say whether it was the evening twilight that was still lingering or whether it was the dawn that was breaking. Cuthbert watching his sheep on the Lammermuirs might well have found it so on a fine night late in June. Although we are not to suppose that Bede himself had ever seen the land of the midnight sun, he had learnt about it from travellers of his own times and he was able to put his knowledge to good use in his comments on a passage in the Second Book of Kings. Hezekiah the king was ill and seemed like to die. In answer to his prayer the Lord sent Isaiah to him with a promise that he would be healed, and when Hezekiah asked for a sign, Isaiah replied: 'Shall the shadow go forward ten degrees or shall it go back ten degrees?' Hezekiah asked that it might go back ten degrees for this seemed the more difficult thing. Bede explained to his readers that by the shadow moving ten degrees Isaiah was referring to the lines 'which we make on our sundials to mark the twelve hours of the day'. He then remarks that Hezekiah sees that it would be a greater marvel if the sun were to go, so to say, into reverse, than if it were merely to move forward towards the east, as if for the dawning of the next day without any intervening night. 'For those who live in the island of Thule which lies beyond Britain, or in the uttermost parts of Scythia' frequently observe during the summer that the sun which has set in other parts of the world, remains visible to them and can be seen throughout the whole of the night as it moves round above the horizon from the west back towards the east.

Northumbrians, Alcuin most eminent among them, who went to the Frankish court late in the eighth century, would have met there an Irish scholar called Dicuil and from him they would have learnt more about northern latitudes. He was able to deny the opinion held by some classical geographers that the sea round Thule, by which he seems to have meant Iceland, was frozen solid, and that there was perpetual daylight there from the spring to the autumn equinoxes and then perpetual darkness from autumn until the following spring; though he had been told that one day's sail to the north of the island the sea was frozen over. Seemingly before he left Ireland he had talked with some priests who had lived on Thule from 1 February to 1 August and they had told him that, for some days on either side of the summer solstice, the sun seemed to hide itself as if behind a small hill. There was no darkness, but light enough to allow a man to 'do whatever he might wish, as though the sun were there, even to remove lice from his shirt'. Dicuil also knew about various groups of islands north of Britain, including the Faroes. Some of them had been inhabited by Irish anchorites, but at the time when he was writing, he believed that the anchorites had left because of the activities of Norwegian pirates.

The apparent oddities of the sun's behaviour in polar regions and the long northern days seem to have made less impact upon the minds and feelings of men than the long hours of darkness. 'Night (*nox*) is so called because it is noxious (*noceat*) to the perceptions and occupations of mankind.' The play upon words had its appeal for the bookmen of the age, even though they did not have the dictionaries which might have led them to suspect a distant relationship between 'pernicious' and 'nocturnal'. Night was the time when thieves and robbers found opportunity for doing harm to others. Night was the time given to mortals for the refreshment of the human body, lest it fail by unceasing labour, and humanity so perish. Night was the time when the earth's shadow was cast upwards into the heavens, sharpening to a point in the likeness of a pyramid, and occasionally that shadow fell across the moon, though no other star suffered a similar eclipse. The point needed to be explained in the schoolroom: 'In the making of a shadow three things must meet together at one time—a light, a solid body and a darkened place. Where the light is equal to the solid, it will cast an equal shadow; where the light is smaller than the body, the shadow will increase to infinity; and where the light is larger than the body, the shadow will diminish to the point of vanishing.' We can easily see the diagram on the blackboards of today's nursery schools, but what did the pupils of Jarrow school use for blackboards?

Above all else, night was the season of moonshine, a source of inspiration alike for poets and old wives' tales, an indispensable aid in the making of calendars and a helpful companion for travellers on land or sea.

> Compelled by fates that likewise rule the sea,
> I roll out month-long periods of time
> In sure-returning cycles. As the light
> Of glorious beauty slowly leaves my face,
> So does the ocean, flowing from the shore,
> Lose its increase of waters in the deep.
>
> (*Tr. Pitman*)

The riddle is Aldhelm's, one of the collection which he sent to the scholarly Aldfrith, king of Northumbria, with whom he had been intimate as a student at Malmesbury. The subject was a favourite one with the riddlers, though not all had the poetry of Aldhelm who was the greatest Anglo-Saxon master of this art. The reference to the ebbing tide would certainly have won Bede's approval, for this was a topic of which he was master, but not so the foolish imaginings of those who used the position of the new moon's horns as a basis for long-range weather forecasts. They said that if both horns lay downwards when the moon was new, a month of storm would follow, but if one of the horns was upright the month that followed would be calm. How could anyone believe, Bede asked, that the shape of the moon whose position was fixed in the aether could possibly be changed by the winds or clouds which lay so far beneath it? Was it really credible that the moon should take fright at some approaching storm and struggle to lift up one of its horns higher than the law of nature permitted? Yet for all Bede's ridicule, the superstition, and others like it, have survived.

To other questions he gave lucid answers. How can I tell what the age of the moon will be on any particular day? This was an easy one to answer, at least Bede thought it so, but, with evident disapproval, he supplied a table which would do all the work for those who lacked the skill or would not take the trouble to make their own calculations. Others wanted to know how many hours of moonshine there would be on any particular night. This too could be answered by rule, derived in this case from Pliny, but another question was more difficult. The class in cosmology was rightly taught that the sun was much higher in the sky than the moon. Why is it then (someone had asked) that when we go outside at certain times of the month, we can see the moon way up in the sky and at the same time we can see the sun low down near the ground? Why should the moon seem to be so much higher than the sun? Bede's answer was ingenious and seemingly based on his own observation. He bids us imagine a very large and lofty church which has been illuminated in honour of some saint's festival. Among the various lamps there are two of very splendid workmanship hanging by chains from the ceiling. As we enter the church at one end, the lamp which is nearest will seem to be the higher of the two, although it does in fact hang down closer to the floor than the more distant one. As we move along the body of the church we shall see that the relative position of the two lamps will change, and we shall eventually realise that the more distant lamp, which had at first seemed to be the lower of the two, is in fact the higher. As Bede fully understood, an observation of this kind could only have been made in a large building, but what we know of the original size of the larger churches at both Wearmouth and Jarrow suggests that they would both have been spacious enough for this purpose, and the same is likely to have been the case at Hexham, Ripon and York. The point could certainly be demonstrated in the surviving Anglo-Saxon church at Brixworth in Northamptonshire if there were lamps hanging in the right places.

The importance of the moon as an aid in the making of a calendar is self-evident, especially in the problem of finding the right date for the celebration of Easter, and there are some indications that even the pagan Saxons had acquired a considerable understanding of lunar cycles. Of course it was much easier to work from the shorter lunar cycle, of approximately 29.5 days, than from the much longer solar year of about 365.2 days. The difficulty, though it was one which Bede had completely mastered, arose in seeking to reconcile the solar and lunar years. The pagan Saxon calendar, we read, was based on lunar months of which three were allotted to each of the four seasons of the year, but because of the disparities of lunar and solar cycles, a series of

years based on twelve lunar months quickly passed out of phase
with the seasons, and for this reason it was necessary to insert an
additional month every so often, making a complete year of
thirteen months instead of the normal twelve. The pagan Saxons
seem to have advanced so far in their understanding of these
matters as to have learnt how often it was necessary to have an
embolismic year, as it was called, of thirteen months, if they were
not eventually to find themselves observing summer in the middle
of winter. The most accurate way of keeping a lunar calendar in
step with the solar seasons was to work on a cycle of nineteen
years, of which twelve had twelve months each and the other
seven had thirteen, though naturally the embolismic years had to
be scattered more or less evenly through the complete cycle of
nineteen.

Aldhelm knew that moon and sea were linked by natural law,
but unlike Bede and his pupils, he did not live where he could
watch the daily ebbing and flowing of the ocean tides. Many of the
riddles composed by Bede's abbot, Hwætbert, were on themes
which had often been used by others, but when he riddled on Land
and Sea, he did so as a man who had often stood upon the beach
watching the ever-changing embraces of friendly foes:

We do not want to be peaceful, nor do we wish to be parted.
War is for ever between us, yet with arms that are yielding;
Peace established below, and therefore the battle quiescent:
Each from the other one guiltless always plucking the harvest.

The abbot has caught that brief moment when the flood tide has
reached the full and the onslaught of the advancing waves yields to
the loving embrace of land and sea, before the ebb tide sets in and
preparation is made for the renewal of war. But he, like many
other Northumbrian monks, needed to know more about the sea
than its poetry. There was a good harbour at Whitby. Strong tides
gave deep water between shifting sandbanks in the Humber
estuary leading shipping on to York. There were harbours at
Wearmouth and Jarrow. Careless monks caught on their raft in a
westerly gale were swept down the Tyne past the Black Middens
and out to sea, to be saved by Cuthbert's prayers and the turning

tide which proved more effective than the modern aids which failed to prevent a newly-built ship striking on those same rocks in 1974. Today's tourist, or pilgrim of whom there are still many, can drive his car across the tarmac causeway to Holy Island, and still with feckless ignorance get caught in that swift but silent flood which will cover his car from wheelbase to rooftop in less than an hour, and may sweep it away into the unyielding embraces of the sand. For Northumbrian monks the regular ebbing and flowing of the tide was a matter of living or drowning, and perhaps it is not surprising that those who learnt about tides from Bede's writings came to be remarkably well informed.

The puny and insignificant tides of the Mediterranean encouraged neither the observation nor the study of lunar influences upon the sea. A priest Philippus who wrote a commentary on the Book of Job in the fifth century and who had evidently read something about tides, expressed the commonly held view that the movements of the tide occurred at one and the same point of time through the rivers of all districts and all countries. It was not in Bede's nature to accuse a respected Biblical commentator of talking nonsense, but he could, and did, ask his readers whether this could possibly be true and he continued; 'We who live by the far-flung shore of the British sea know that when this sea has begun to flow at one point it is at the same time beginning to ebb at another, and so it seems to some of us that the receding water runs back from one place towards another place, and that after leaving the shore which it has approached, it makes haste to revisit its former shores once more.' Here is an informative statement evidently based in part on personal observation and in part on talk with sailors. We may wonder just how men without clocks, or any means of rapid communication, established the point that the tide was flowing at one part of the coast while it was ebbing at another. Here, too, is an intelligible explanation of what happened to all the water when the tide ebbed, a problem which might have been difficult for Philippus to explain. Naturally Bede knew about the peculiar position of Lindisfarne: 'as the tide ebbs and flows the place is surrounded twice daily by the waves of the sea like an island and twice, when the shore is left dry, it again becomes attached to the mainland.' He also knew something, though not the full complexity, of the tides in the Solent. 'In this sea the two ocean tides which break upon Britain from the boundless northern ocean meet daily in conflict beyond the mouth of the river Hamble. . . . When their conflict is over they flow back into the ocean whence they came.' Bede's picture is of the tide flowing southwards along the eastern and western shores of Britain, curling round the cliffs of Dover and Land's End and meeting in the Solent. Yachtsmen might wish that it was all as simple as that.

It was, of course, upon the behaviour of the tides along the Northumbrian coast that Bede based his further teaching upon this subject. We must marvel greatly, he wrote, at the close companionship of the ocean with the course of the moon. 'For, as we have already explained, just as the moon regularly rises or sets at an interval of four *puncti* later each day than it had risen or set on the previous day, so also each tide, whether it be by day or by night, by morning or by evening, does not fail to rise or fall later each day by almost the same interval of time. A *punctus* is the fifth part of an hour, for five *puncti* make one hour.' In other words just as the rising and setting of the moon occur approximately forty-eight minutes later each day, so also do the top and bottom of the tides. Yet the companionship of moon and tide was closer than this. Not only did the sea follow the moon in ebb and flow, rise and set, it also followed the moon as it waxed or waned with increase or decrease of strength; when the moon was full or new, the tidal flow was strongest, but at other times it diminished. 'The tides which grow in strength we call *malinae*, those which diminish in strength we call *ledones*.' The distinction is the familiar one between springs and neaps, though we do not now understand the etymology of either *malina* or *ledo*. Just as the spring tides covered the beaches and filled the estuaries to a greater degree at the full, so also the ebb left a greater expanse of the shore uncovered. *Malinae* and *ledones* were regular in their occurrences, but sometimes when they were driven on or held back by the wind, they might arrive sooner or later and with greater or lesser vigour than was usual. At the spring and autumn equinoxes the tides would flow more strongly than at other seasons of the year; at the winter and summer solstices they were feebler.

Bede's treatment of the tides is remarkably full and accurate, witness to his own observations by the mud flats of Jarrow Slake, which gave their name to his monastery, and to the extent of Northumbrian seafaring. Here indeed was a matter of vital importance for all those who lived along the northern shores. Here was knowledge which even allowed the compilation of tolerably accurate tide-tables. Yet we may sense that Bede saw in this wonderful companionship of moon and sea something more than the making of a nautical almanack. Day by day, month by month, year by year, the moon rose and set, waxed and waned, in perfect harmony with the waters of the ocean—the waters which God had caused to be gathered together in one place and the lesser light which had been made to rule the night; the moon revered by men as 'the eye of the night, dispenser of dew, foreteller of storms'. For those who had eyes to see and patience to understand, the world which God had created was no random chaos, but a place of order whose seeming aberrations could not only be explained and understood, but even trusted.

CHAPTER FOUR

The Wide Expanses of the Sea

FISHERMEN CASTING THEIR nets for salmon at the mouth of
Tweed are no friends to the grey seals who come into the river
looking for their share, enchanting the artist with the ease and
power of their movements in turbulent waters, and beckoning the
romantic with the dark magic of their eyes. An idle spectator of
both seal and fishermen was once greatly startled by the firing of a
maroon to summon the crew of the Berwick lifeboat. The waters
of Tweed, in brown and peaty spate from the hills, and driven by a
violent and sudden blow from the west, had caught a sailor
unaware and broken the twin rudders of his catamaran. The
lifeboat itself had almost vanished from sight before it caught up
with the disabled boat rapidly drifting towards the eastern
horizon. It was easy to make the change in time and place, from
Tweed south to Tyne, from the age of radar to Bede; and to see in
all its detail an incident of which he had learnt from one of the
monks of his own monastery.

Near the mouth of Tyne, on its south bank and perhaps close to
South Shields, there lay a monastery which had once been filled
with monks but which now, changed like all else by time, as Bede
writes, housed a company of virgins. On one occasion some of the
monks had gone up river with rafts to bring back a load of wood
for use in the monastery. On their return downstream they had
reached a point opposite their landing-place when a sudden wind
sprang up from the west and carried them swiftly down towards
the river mouth. When their brethren saw their plight they tried to
launch boats but they could not prevail against wind and current,
and could only watch from the rocks as the rafts were carried so far
out to sea that they looked like five very small birds riding on the
waves. The prayers of Cuthbert, standing amid mocking pagan
yokels on the opposite bank, achieved what the modern world
entrusts to the lifeboat, and with a change of wind the rafts came
safely back to shore.

There was a monastery on the north bank of Tyne, near the mouth, as well as others at South Shields and Jarrow on the south bank. There was yet another at Gateshead further up river, but still within the tidal range. Today's visitor to Jarrow and Wearmouth will find the churches of both monasteries set against a backcloth of ships, gantries, warehouses and all the other trappings of busy seaports. Further south on the Durham coast he will find the site of Hilda's monastery in a similar setting at Hartlepool. At Whitby, ruled so long by Hilda as abbess, he will look down on a busy fishing harbour. Turning back to the north and passing beneath Tyne, he can see Coquet Island, small and close inshore, once renowned for its companies of monks. Cuthbert came by boat from Lindisfarne to meet Ælfflæd on Coquet Island. She had slightly the longer journey, but we do not know whether she chose to travel from Whitby by sea or overland.

Still keeping for the most part in sight of the sea the traveller will soon have his view of the Farnes, the landward cliff of the Inner Farne white with bird droppings (Plate 5), of the castle on the rock at Bamburgh, and beyond that, with a necessary detour round an inlet of the sea alive with the call of seabirds, he will see the long low strip of Lindisfarne, cut off by a belt of silver blue if the tide is high and gold if it is low. Sometimes, though not often, all may be hidden in the mists driving in from the north-east. Across Tweed and into Berwickshire, where the cliffs rise high and sheer, peopled by guillemots in the breeding season, he may make his way to Coldingham, wondering whether it was only the bolder, or perhaps the more wayward, among the nuns who braved the windy and dangerous heights of St Abb's Head, while their sisters lived more comfortably in some less exposed place not far from the sandy shore visited by Cuthbert in the night hours. Within a space of little more than a hundred miles along this eastern coast, the traveller could visit the sites of almost a dozen monasteries set on islands, close by the shore or on the banks of tidal rivers. And if he were greatly to extend his journey round the coasts of Scotland, the Western Isles, Ireland and Wales, he would be able to multiply this total several times.

It may be that such maritime sites were chosen because they were remote and more secure than inland sites, though there were a great many of these. It may also be that travel by sea was

sometimes found to be easier and safer than travel by land. For a
ship, as a royal pupil once learnt from his master, 'is a wandering
home, a lodging for all places, a traveller without footsteps'. But
one conclusion seems inescapable. When men who had abandoned
terrestrial warfare to become soldiers of Christ then chose such
exposed sites upon which to wage battle with spiritual weapons
only, they must have done so in the belief that seafarers were
peaceable men, not pirates. All that men had to dread from the sea
was the violence of its storms. Some of the greatness of
Northumbria rested upon this simple fact. In earlier centuries,
before Magnus Maximus had left for Gaul in search of a richer slice
of empire, high points on the Yorkshire coast—Scarborough,
Goldsborough, Huntcliffe, and some places on the Durham coast
too—had been topped with lofty look-out posts to give warning
of approaching raiders and to co-ordinate the activities of
defending Roman naval squadrons. They served the same purpose
as the more southerly Martello towers in the days when Napoleon
threatened England. Nowadays some eastern heights are dis-
figured by menacing metallic mobiles whose electronic eyes see
further into the distance.

We may think of Shakespeare's jewel set in its silver sea and
reflect that there have been very few periods in the history of that
jewel when it could lie undefended and without threat of attack.
Bede's age was such a one. Armies fought on land and coasts were
unprotected. How else could it have been that monasteries
accumulated rich treasures on exposed seacoasts and assumed them
to be safe from marauders, unless only peaceful sailors used the sea?
There was much bloodshed and much destruction when Britain
fell to the English, but thereafter we find no evidence of hostile
movements across the seas until long after Bede was dead and
Alcuin was almost an old man. The consternation, amounting
almost to disbelief, caused by news of the attack on Lindisfarne
shows how unexpected that attack was. Thereafter, there followed
in long succession, with brief intervals between, the invasions of
the sons of Ragnar Lothbrok, of Cnut and William the Norman.
Northumbria's greatness developed in a short breathing-space
between migratory movements such that among many travellers
one remarkable man could journey to Rome six times, bringing

back books and other treasures for Northumbrian churchmen and scholars.

A beachcomber by Guile Point, across the narrow channel from Lindisfarne, was once so lucky as to find, unbroken, a handsome glass demijohn, showing by its cork that it had held Greek wine. Cuthbert's monks (lucky, as we may think, to escape the plethora of plastic bottles) will perhaps have found the sea less generous with its flotsam and jetsam, though Cuthbert himself accepted with gratitude a twelve-foot baulk of timber which was exactly suited to the small building he was constructing for his daily needs, above a rock conveniently hollowed out by the regular finishing of the tide.

Familiar creatures of the sea and shore played their part in biblical exegesis, as well as witnessing to the sanctity of holy men. The long necks and curved beaks of cormorant and shag, to be seen today in their hundreds perched with outspread wings on the rocky ledges of the Farnes, found their way into the decorated pages of Gospel books. Men read in the Book of Genesis how God had blessed his creation, saying: 'Increase and multiply, and fill the waters of the sea, and let fowl multiply in the earth.' Augustine had expounded the passage by commenting on the cloudy and moist air in which birds fly, and on the peculiarity of Mount Olympus which was so lofty that it was above the clouds and the rains. Such was the rarity of its atmosphere that men who traced marks in the dust on top of the mountain found them still there undisturbed a year later. Bede rejected this airy nonsense, preferring to take his illustration from the works of God lying nearer at hand, in the waters and along the shores of the Northumbrian coast. When God had said: 'Increase and multiply, and fill the waters of the sea', he was referring, Bede wrote, to two kinds of living creatures, fishes and birds, for just as no fish could live without water, so there were many kinds of birds which were more at home amid the waters than on the land, even though they sometimes came out on to the land to feed, to rest and to breed their young. And when God said, 'let fowl multiply in the earth', he was referring both to the birds which feed on land and to the birds which feed from the waters. For there were some birds, Bede explained, that were so dependent on the waters that they spent much of the year hidden in their depths, like fishes, but even these birds sometimes came to the land, especially for breeding and feeding their young. Anyone who cares to watch from the shore, unaided by binoculars or spectacles, as the tern and the more distant gannets dive for their daily food, can easily understand how men of an earlier age explained the absence of some birds at certain seasons by supposing that they were resting beneath the waters from which they fed. Even in 1767 that celebrated observer of nature, the Reverend Gilbert White, was prepared to give some countenance to the opinion, 'strange as it is', of a Swede who wrote 'as familiarly of the swallow's going under water in the beginning of September as he would of his poultry going to roost a little before sunset'.

It is the gentle Cuthbert, more than any other of the northern holy men, whom we find associated with the creatures of sea and shore. When he was a monk at Melrose he had occasion to go by sea to the land of the Picts. His voyage may have taken him from near Tweedmouth to the Firth of Forth or beyond, but he and his companions became storm-bound at one point and were unable to continue their journey. The providential discovery on the shore of two pieces of dolphin's flesh, cut as with a knife and washed clean, saved them from starvation. No doubt many other travellers were glad of a stranded dolphin or seal, even though the meat may not always have been so well prepared. There was an occasion when Cuthbert was walking along by the river Teviot. He turned to the boy who was keeping him company and asked: 'Do you think anyone has got dinner for you today?' The boy answered that he did not know of any kinsmen who lived in those parts and would not expect any such kindness from strangers. As they continued their journey an eagle came circling from the sky to settle on the river bank. Running off towards it, the boy found that it had a large fish. He took it from the eagle and brought it back to Cuthbert who rebuked him gently, saying: 'Why didn't you give our fisherman his share to eat since he was hungry?' The fisherman got his share—no less than half the fish—but unhappily we are not likely nowadays to see the White-tailed Eagle catching salmon in the Teviot.

We may recall the birds, two ravens it was said, who began to pull pieces for their nests from the roof of the shelter which Cuthbert had built near the landing-place close by his island hermitage. When they ignored the gentle motion of his hands, he turned upon them more sternly, much perhaps, as the abbot turned upon the unfortunate jackdaw of Rheims. Like that celebrated jackdaw, they came back in penitence with outspread wings, drooping heads and humble croaking. Forgiveness won, they returned each with a piece of lard which Cuthbert was able to use to grease his boots for a whole year. Perhaps most enchanting of all is the tale of Cuthbert's visit to Coldingham, a mixed house of monks and nuns, but ruled as was the custom by an abbess. Cuthbert spent some days in the monastery, but while there he kept to his habit of walking by night on the seashore. A suspicious monk, anxious to know more of Cuthbert's nightly wanderings, followed him, only to observe him going into the sea—and the Berwickshire sea is very cold—up to his loin cloth, even being soaked as far as the armpits by the tumultuous waves. Coming out of the water he knelt to pray, 'and immediately there followed in his footsteps two little sea animals, humbly prostrating themselves on the earth; and, licking his feet, they rolled upon them, wiping them with their skins and warming them with their breath. After this service and ministry had been fulfilled and his blessing had been received they departed to their haunts in the waves of the sea.' The terrified monk lay hidden among the rocks and paid for his curiosity by being brought near to death, until relieved with confession and pardon.

It is scarcely surprising that the handsome eiders, and their rather dowdy wives, who still breed prolifically on the Farnes, are affectionately known as Cuthbert's birds. And strangers who find on the beaches the stems of crinoid fossils do well to call them Cuthbert's beads. Deeper waters housed stranger creatures. 'Canst thou draw out leviathan with a hook?' Jehovah had asked of Job. 'Canst thou fill his skin with barbed irons? Or his head with fish spears?' Those who had read about the saintly Columba knew the story of a monk who ignored his advice to take a circuitous rather than a direct route from Iona to Tiree. Half way across, a whale of enormous size rose up like a mountain and threatened the travellers with gaping tooth-filled jaws. With difficulty they escaped.

Another traveller, forewarned by Columba of the monster's presence, blessed both the sea and the creature, who thereupon plunged into the depths. A monk seeking a desert place amid the sea, was blown northwards with his companions by southerly winds for fourteen days and nights. Suddenly 'they were met by loathsome and exceedingly dangerous small creatures covering the sea, such as had never been seen before that time; and these struck with terrible impact the bottom and sides, the stern and prow, with so strong a thrust that they were thought able to pierce and penetrate the skin covering of the ship'. We might think that the ship had been attacked by walruses were it not that the travellers strain our belief by reporting that the creatures were about the size of frogs, 'very injurious by reason of their stings'. A monster of great size and appetite lived in Loch Ness. Columba once deprived him of a meal—and perhaps that is why, as so many people fondly suppose, he is still there.

Misty lands, clouding man's vision and inspiring his imagination, were good breeding-places for monsters. What other tales of sea-monsters were current in Northumbria we cannot tell for sure. Alcuin's pupils at York may have known about the great swimming-match between Beowulf and Breca, who were together in the sea for five nights until they were driven apart by stormy waves, the bitter cold and the darkness. Each swam with drawn sword in hand. Beowulf, protected by his armour, was able to save himself from one monster who dragged him to the sea bottom, and when all was over the corpses of nine monsters of the sea were strewn along the beaches, while the surging ocean carried Beowulf to the land of the Finns. Visitors to the British Museum may see there a small, highly-decorated bone casket, known as the Franks Casket after the man who gave it to the Museum, or the Auzon Casket from the French family who once owned it (Plate 16). The bone of which it is made came from a foolish whale who was so careless as to let himself get stranded on a stony shore. An inscription carved upon it in runes tells how sad he felt when he realised his mistake. He would have been glad of the sympathy of another and more circumspect whale upon whose broad back, bare of sand and with only a tree or two growing here and there, Brendan's fellow-voyagers celebrated their Easter mass, and then lit a fire at which to cook their dinner. After some preliminary heaving, sufficient to allow the travellers to take to their boat, the whale made off to sea, the fire still burning on its back. The tale of Brendan's voyage, though set in the sixth century, may not have been written down before the ninth, but the island whale who swims away is the subject of several stories. The theme lent itself readily to Christian allegory, witness the charming Old English poem which tells how sailors fasten their high-prowed ship with cables to land which is not land. They set up their camp, light fires and rejoice in the kindly weather, until the land, which is no land, suddenly plunges to the bottom of the ocean. Even so are men ensnared by the deceitful ways of the devil. But the poem about the Anglo-Saxon whale called Fastitocolon (Brendan's whale was called Jasconius), is first found in the Exeter Book and we do not know when or where it was originally composed.

> Upheaved, swiftly I run, but leave not my home when I bear things,
> Tenuous, vagrant I am, conveying abundance of burdens;
> Snow does not cover, nor hail strike, nor does frost overcome me,
> Less from above am I pressed, than by what lies hidden within me.

The laden ships which weigh upon the waters of the sea in this Jarrow riddle are almost as elusive as the monsters which press them apart from within. The shifting sands of Lindisfarne do not bring up their food nor have today's frogmen yet found a Northumbrian ship. The slake by Bede's monastery was once known as Ecgfrith's Harbour; this was the king who had ships enough to send a military expedition across the sea to Ireland. A predecessor, Edwin, could have used a makeshift means to ferry his men across the straits to Anglesey, but the conquest of the Isle of Man would have needed stouter vessels. Yet when we ask about these ships—where they were built, of what materials, how long they were and how propelled—we do not find easy answers. As a young man, Ceolfrith, Bede's teacher, once visited Botolph, a popular saint in the later Middle Ages and claimed by his

Cambridge church as the patron saint of travellers. Botolph's monastery lay in East Anglia, perhaps at Iken where the river Alde, sticky with mud at low tide, floods over the marshes at high. A little way upstream lies Snape where many visitors have enjoyed another tale of the sea, *Peter Grimes*. Snape, now so full of music, was the scene of the excavation in 1862 of an Anglo-Saxon ship-burial. The care taken by the excavators to record what they found tells us that the buried ship was clinker-built of eight or nine strakes aside, about fifty feet in length and with a blunt stern. The burial deposit itself had been robbed at an earlier date and all that now survives is a glass claw-beaker and a gold ring set with a late-antique onyx intaglio personifying *Bonus Eventus*—and we may rejoice that the lord of the ring has secured its safekeeping in the British Museum. The ship from Snape is now known only from the excavators' plans. Two other ships are from the more famous site at Sutton Hoo, above the left bank of the Suffolk Deben. One of these two had been all but totally destroyed before skilled archaeologists could reach it, but enough remained to show a boat about twenty-five feet in length. The other was impressive indeed.

Virtually all its timbers had perished, but it had left its ghost clearly imprinted on the sand in which it had been buried so that the outlines of strakes, cross-timbers, clench nails could all be traced in detail. All that was missing were the upper parts of stem and stern posts. Here was a great open boat, some ninety feet long and with a maximum beam of about fourteen feet. This is more than twice as long as the nave of the church in Canterbury in whose northern chamber the first six archbishops were buried, more than twice as long as the smaller of the churches in which Bede worshipped at Jarrow and which today survives as the chancel of St Paul's. Those who have visited the museum housing the Viking ships from Gokstad, Oseberg and Ladby will have been impressed by their size, even allowing that a ship looks much bigger on land than it does in water. Yet the Sutton Hoo ship was larger than any of these. It was clinker-built, with nine strakes on either side of the keel plank. It had twenty benches and could be driven by forty oars. The excavators found no trace of any mast, or any means of support for one, yet seafaring men think that a ship with these lines could have carried a square loose-footed sail which would have helped it along at a brisk pace in winds well aft of the beam. Steering was not by the familiar modern rudder, but by an oar attached to the starboard side close to the stern. Both stem and stern posts are likely to have swept upwards to a considerable height and may perhaps have been carved in the manner known from Viking ships. The Sutton Hoo ship had seen much service when it was dragged up the bank to the royal burial ground above the Deben and we may surmise that it was built shortly after 600. With so little comparable material, it is difficult to know how to regard this ship, but since it was considered fit for the burial of a king, and a wealthy one at that, perhaps we ought to think of it as being built for a king rather than for less eminent seafarers. To the ship from Snape and the two from Sutton Hoo, we can add the remains of an oak ship found in 1970 in Graveney Marshes in Kent. It had been some forty-five feet in length and had probably served as a cargo boat carrying goods across the Channel in the days of Alfred the Great, but by this date the ship-building skills of the Vikings had become widely known in the west.

From the Graveney boat we can move back beyond Snape and Sutton Hoo to the Museum of Antiquities in Schloss Gottorp, Schleswig, where there is now to be seen the only survivor of three boats found in a peat bog at Nydam in 1863. This ship, some seventy-three feet long, was built of oak strakes with a maximum beam of less than eleven feet. Amidships it was broad and shallow, but narrowed almost to a v-shape at bow and stern. Provision was made for fourteen oars on each side. Buoyant and fast, it will have been less stable than the Sutton Hoo ship and is not likely to have been equipped with a sail. The Nydam ship may be representative of the type in use in the Germanic areas of the North Sea *c.* A.D. 400, a time when Roman Britain was hard pressed by her eventual conquerors.

The interment of the larger Sutton Hoo ship took place, we now think, at about the same time as Paulinus escorted the widow and children of King Edwin, lately killed in battle, back from Northumbria to her native Kent. They made the journey by sea. When one of these children, Eanflæd, returned to Northumbria to become queen in her turn, she again made the journey by sea. The travellers were caught in a storm and after the anchor had dragged, waves began to break over the ship and all seemed lost, until a priest on board remembered that Aidan had given him some holy oil and with this he was able to calm the angry seas. The alternative to facing the dangers of wind and weather in the North Sea was a long journey by land across the borders of several kingdoms which might well have been at war with one another; and even if they were not, there would always be danger from marauding bands. Given a measure of good luck and the good sense to choose the right season of the year, the sea voyage may well have been not only safer but also quicker.

It has been thought that the larger Sutton Hoo ship could have been driven by rowers, watch and watch, at a speed of up to five knots over quite long periods, and this without allowing for the use of a sail. But perhaps we should think rather of a series of shorter hops, since Northumbrian sailors knew enough about the tides to make them work for them. There is only one occasion about which we have some precise details of a voyage from Northumbria to Gaul. The occasion was when Bede's abbot, Ceolfrith, set off to Rome in 716 hoping to end his days there (see below, pp. 186–7). The journey from the monastery at Wearmouth began on Thursday 4 June, but the first stage consisted only of the crossing of the Wear itself. Thereafter, it seems that the abbot, an old and ailing man of seventy-four, went on horseback to some point near the Humber. On Saturday, 4 July, a full calendar month after he had set out, he embarked on a ship which was bound for Gaul. It called at three separate provinces on the way—perhaps East Anglia, Essex and Kent—before it eventually reached Gaul on Wednesday 12 August. The port is not named, but Quentavic, now silted up at the mouth of the Canche and near the modern Étaples, was a common port of entry into Gaul for travellers from England. Nearly six weeks from Humber to the north coast of France was slow going, but it may be that Ceolfrith was a passenger on a coastal trading vessel which stopped to load and unload on the way.

Whether the ships on which Paulinus and Ceolfrith travelled were rowed or sailed, there is no doubt that ships with mast and sail could have been seen in northern waters at this date. A priest who later became abbot of Lindisfarne, told Bede of an occasion when he had gone with two others from Lindisfarne to visit Cuthbert's successor in the hermitage on the Inner Farne. The distance was not great. A cormorant in his familiar flight—low, fast and straight as an arrow—would make nothing of it. 'Suddenly, while we were in the midst of the sea (on the homeward journey), the calm weather which had accompanied us was broken, and so fierce a wintry tempest arose that we could make no progress by sailing or rowing and expected nothing but death. After we had struggled for a long time in vain against wind and sea, we looked back to see if perhaps we could, by any effort, at least return to the island we had left. But we found that we were shut in by the storm on every hand.' The stormbound voyagers were rescued by the prayers of those on Lindisfarne who had come out to watch their progress in the boiling seas. They came safely to land and then, we read, they carried the 'little vessel up from the sea'. No doubt there were a great many journeys between Lindisfarne and the Farne Islands and no doubt a sail was used when the wind was favourable.

Columba and his companions on Iona were faced not only by the short, though often turbulent, passage to Mull, but also by the wider strait between Mull and the Scottish mainland. Travellers to more distant islands, and to Ireland itself, faced heavy gales and dangerous overfalls caused by strong Atlantic tides forced through narrow passages. Not surprisingly, we read much about boats in the story of Columba's life. Sometimes they were very small. Once, while journeying on the Scottish mainland, the saint roused his companions from sleep, telling them to fetch their boat which they had left in a house across the stream and put it in a hut closer at hand—the saint knew that the more distant house was going to be burnt. This sounds like a small coracle, such as could easily be carried and put to good use when river or loch gave opportunity, perhaps no larger than those which may still be seen on the Severn. On another occasion, when he was in Iona, the saint told two of the brothers to cross to Mull and look for a thief who had come secretly from Coll, intent on cattle thieving. They would find him hidden during the day among sandhills underneath the boat which he had covered with grass. Somewhat larger than these was the boat which Columba used when he was visiting the land of the

Picts. As he was about to embark on Loch Ness, hostile magicians raised adverse winds, but despite the storm Columba entered the boat and while the sailors hesitated, he bade them hoist the sail and the boat moved off against the wind at great speed.

On other occasions we read in the same source of ships 'under full sail' crossing from Ireland or exploring the northern isles. Columba was blessed with great skill in raising favourable winds. One incident seems to speak of preparations for the building of a substantial ship of wood. Iona itself could not provide the wood that was needed so 'dressed timbers of pine and oak for a long ship' were first dragged overland and then sailors assembled a flotilla 'of boats and curachs to tow the timbers through the sea to Iona'. The contrary winds which had blown for several days, suddenly changed so that 'with full sails throughout the long and devious route, that whole sea-transport' came safely to the island of Iona. On a similar occasion, some years later, when oak timbers were being brought across the sea to repair the monastery a favourable wind sprang up so that the sailors could leave their oars and raise 'the yards cross-wise, and the sails, stretching tight the ropes'. The setting of these stories belongs to the sixth century, though they were not written down till the seventh. From later, though not very much later, times we find it always assumed that Beowulf's voyages were made under sail. Especially vivid is the poet's setting of his homeward voyage:

> Forth went the ship
> To plough the deep, and left the Danish land.
> A spread of canvas by the mast was set,
> Her sail held by its sheet; the timbers thundered;
> No adverse wind across the waves delayed
> The galley in her course; the bark drove on,
> The well-wrought vessel skimmed with foamy neck
> Forth o'er the sea, across the ocean currents,
> Till they could sight the headlands of the Geats,
> The well-known cliffs.
>
>   (*Tr. Waterhouse*)

Although we have had to range rather widely to gather even a

7 St Paul's Church, Jarrow: chancel and tower

8 Detail of South Wall of Chancel of St Paul's Church, Jarrow

9 The Bewcastle Cross: south and east faces

meagre amount of information about the ships of this age, there is a great deal of evidence that men went from Northumbria to Ireland, Germany, France, Italy and elsewhere, and since at least some part of their journeys had to be made by sea, I think we are justified in imagining a considerable amount of shipping and a large variety of ships ranging from small coracles to large vessels of oak. There was the boat which Brendan and his companions used; wood was used for the ribs and the frame, but its covering was made of tanned oxhide stretched over oak bark; the seams were covered with grease on the outside and a supply of fat and of spare skins was kept in the boat for future repairs. Yet the vessel was large enough to require a mast, a sail and equipment for steering.

It was in a boat made in this fashion, though smaller and with no sail, that three Irishmen reached Cornwall in the days of King Alfred; and they were lucky to do so, since they set off haphazardly without any oars. Visitors to the western coasts of Ireland will have seen such lightly-built craft—sometimes apparently walking upside down as three or four fishermen carry them on their heads—though with canvas, and perhaps now plastic, instead of hide covering. At the other end were the coastal trading vessels. In the eighth century kings were granting bishops the right to take tolls on ships entering the port of London, as Mercian charters attest. Evidently their cargoes were valuable. We have no comparable Northumbrian documents, but this need not prevent us from thinking it likely that similar ships were making their way up the Humber and Ouse to York. Bede, practical man that he was, knew about the virtues of pitch, or bitumen as he calls it. He borrowed Isidore's definition of it as 'an exceedingly hot and powerful glue', but he added his own comment: 'its virtue is that wood which has been smeared with it cannot be consumed by worms nor by the heat of the sun nor by the blowing of the winds nor can it be dissolved by immersion in waters.' This was the comment of a man who had watched the shipwrights of Tyne and Wear.

Bede had once faced an awkward question about Noah and his Ark in the schoolroom. After considering the sensible shape of its roof, so well suited to throwing off the rains, he posed the question again for the benefit of those who might read his commentary on

Genesis. 'How was it possible for eight men to serve daily food and drink to so great a multitude of birds, animals, beasts and reptiles, especially when Scripture says nothing of any command by God about taking drink into the Ark? How did it come about that the dung and urine of so many living creatures did not make the place intolerable to those same creatures by their stench, and how was it that the bottom of the Ark did not go rotten, even though its timbers had been thoroughly covered with pitch?' The problem was a very real one, especially to men who may have known about the difficulty of carrying livestock on slow boats, and Bede, certainly familiar with stables and cow byres, was not the man to evade it. Yet the truth of the Bible was not open to question and therefore the answer could only be found in the miraculous powers of God.

Why, we may ask, did men cross the seas in this age? We can often say why particular men, and women, travelled abroad. They went as pilgrims or as men seeking knowledge or as missionaries wanting to bring Christianity to pagans descended from a common ancestry, but the question is difficult to answer in its more general aspects. The convenience of historical partition leads us to suppose that with the coming of Christianity to England the age of migration was past, but men may still have been leaving their low-lying sea-swamped homes along the Frisian coast in search of better land in England in the seventh century. We know that there was a settlement of Frisian merchants in York in the eighth century, but we do not know the nature of the goods in which they traded. If Bede's travellers from Thule were merchants they might have been trading in Scandinavian furs, but they may also have been hermits in search of remote uninhabited islands. Had they been sea-captains able to tell tales about northern lands, such as were told in later years to Alfred, we would probably have read more about them in Bede's writings. He was greatly interested in geography, but he certainly knew much less about Scandinavia than Alfred. The great Scandinavian trading centres—Birka in Sweden, Kaupang in Norway, Hedeby in Jutland—did not become established until after the Northumbrian monasteries had had their first taste of Viking savagery. We lack direct evidence for trading between Northumbria and Scandinavia in early times, even though we may suspect some contacts.

Looking south to Germany and the Low Countries, we can often point to particular items reaching Northumbria—blankets made of goat's hair, casks of wine, a silk robe for Bede's relics, a load of tin for a belfry roof—but these were sent as gifts between churchmen and may not safely be used as evidence of regular trade in such commodities. Alcuin sent oil, needed for liturgical purposes, and asked that it might be distributed to places where bishops needed it, remarking that it was then scarcely to be found anywhere in Britain. It may be that German wine reached Northumbria as a cargo, perhaps by way of London, Ipswich or York. Pottery, claimed to be from the Rhineland, has been found at Whitby which has also yielded coins in sufficiently large numbers as to suggest some kind of commercial activity based upon the harbour, but in general coined money seems to have been much rarer in Northumbria in this age than it was in southern England. Whether or not some villagers used coal from exposed surface seams, or gathered from beaches, there is no evidence that it became a commodity of trade in these days. The Keelmen of Tyne, celebrated in song, are first heard of in the cartulary of Tynemouth priory in the fourteenth century, though the name which they used for their boats may be found in *Beowulf*.

Many, indeed most, Northumbrian travellers are unknown to us either by name or from the details of their journeys, but some upon whom Northumbria's greatness rested were remembered in writing. Among them was Wilfrid, who was familiar with the seas round Lindisfarne where he lived in his boyhood as the servant of a nobleman suffering from paralysis. When he was about eighteen he was moved, like many others in this age, to visit the church of St Peter, chief of the Apostles, in Rome itself. He went to Kent, though whether by land or sea we do not know, and after delaying there for a year until trustworthy companions could be found to accompany him on the long journey, he crossed to Gaul and made his way south to Lyons and so eventually to Rome where he visited many of the shrines of the saint. He made the long journey to Rome a second time when he was in middle age and a third time when he was an old man of seventy. The cross-channel route is likely to have been from one of the Kentish ports, perhaps Richborough, Dover or Sandwich, to Quentavic, although we know that some travellers made the longer crossing from Southampton to the mouth of the Seine. Once in Gaul we may guess that travellers directed their steps towards the Rhone valley, perhaps along a westerly line which would take them through Paris, Sens and Autun, or a more easterly line through Rheims. Once in the Rhone valley they would pass through a succession of ancient and still prosperous Roman towns—Lyons, Vienne, Orange, Avignon and Arles. Sometimes the remainder of the journey, from Arles to Ostia, was completed by sea. We know enough about the journeys from Rome to England by Augustine and Theodore, and from England to Rome by Wilfrid and his contemporary Benedict Biscop, to be sure that in the seventh and eighth centuries men preferred to travel along the Rhone valley rather than to venture upon the crossing of the Alps by the Great St Bernard pass, though this was the way some archbishops of Canterbury went to Rome in the eleventh century. How long such a journey would take we cannot tell. Theodore, newly-elected archbishop of Canterbury, left Rome on 27 May 668, and reached Canterbury a year later to the very day, but we know that he was delayed on the way, and he may well have set out from Rome with the expectation of reaching England before the onset of winter.

The crossing from Kent to the mouth of the Canche, though somewhat longer than the modern Folkestone–Boulogne crossing, was nevertheless regarded as the *via rectissima*, the most direct route, for an English traveller going south. Roman roads gave easy approach to the sea from both sides, and a mile or two south of the Canche, where now lies St Josse-sur-Mer, there was in Alcuin's days a small monastic cell which Charlemagne had given to Alcuin so that he could be hospitable to travellers. But this was certainly not the only route to the continent. We are told that when Wilfrid was about to set off for Rome in 678 report reached him that his enemies in Gaul, supposing that he would be following the *via rectissima*, were preparing to waylay him. Indeed men said that a luckless bishop of Lichfield, making the journey at this same time, was mistaken for Wilfrid and that after being captured and robbed of all his money he was 'left naked and in the utmost straits of misery'. Whether or not the story was true, the fate is one which is likely to have befallen many travellers. Of the route taken by

Wilfrid on his second journey to Rome we know only that the ships (for there were more than one) sailed eastwards before a gentle west wind and came safely to Frisia. We can only conjecture that the voyage was from London to the Rhine mouth. On the north bank of the Rhine at Dorestad, not far from Utrecht, there lay the principal trading centre of Frisia. Some years later in 716 when Boniface the great West Saxon missionary went to Frisia, he travelled, as we learn from his biographer, by sea from London to Dorestad. We seem justified in supposing that a considerable amount of shipping will have passed back and forth in this age between Thames and Rhine. Boniface chose to make the short sea crossing on his second journey in 718 but we know that a kinsman who later became bishop of Eichstätt in Bavaria made a channel crossing from Southampton to Rouen.

We do not know how Wilfrid crossed the sea on his third journey to Rome, but there is picturesque detail of an earlier voyage when he had gone to Gaul to be consecrated bishop at Compiègne. It was well for him that he went with the support of armed men, for on the return voyage from Gaul, against contrary winds, the ship was caught in a storm half-way across the Channel. The priests on board sang psalms and hymns, giving time to the oarsmen, but the violence of the south-easterly wind drove the ship ashore on the Sussex coast where it was left high and dry by the falling tide. This was a part of the country as yet pagan and Wilfrid's biographer made the most of the stirring scene which followed. We see a huge host of pagans intent upon seizing the ship and killing or capturing the stranded seafarers. In front of the pagans their priest stands upon a high mound and by his magical arts calls down curses upon the men of God, but one of the Christians hurls a stone from his sling and pierces the wizard's forehead so that he falls dead upon the sand—even as the young David had once disposed of Goliath. The pagans, undeterred, make ready for battle. So also do Wilfrid's men who resolve that they will win either death with honour or life with victory. Three times they throw back the pagan onslaught—even as Gideon with his three hundred had once slain 120,000 Midianites. As the pagans make ready for their fourth attack, the tide turns—'before its usual hour'—the ship is refloated and a south-west wind brings it safely to port at Sandwich. Eddius was not the man to lose such an opportunity of glorifying his beloved Wilfrid. If the hosts of Midian were in fact somewhat smaller, so no doubt was the number of Wilfrid's companions (said to be one hundred and twenty, equal to the number of years lived by Moses) and of the hostile South Saxons who attacked him. Yet there may be truth in the story of the shipwreck and the mischance had important consequences, for in later years, when Wilfrid was exiled from Northumbria, he returned to Sussex and converted its people to Christianity.

Another storm at sea had remarkable consequences of a very different kind. A Gaulish bishop, Arculf by name but of unknown see, was returning from a journey to the Near East which he made about the years 679 to 682. His ship was caught in a storm and, like some of those from Philip of Spain's Armada, was driven far to the north along Britain's western coasts. We know nothing of the eventual fate of the ship, but presumably it was wrecked somewhere in the western isles since Arculf eventually found his way to Iona whose abbot at the time was Adamnan, the ninth abbot of St Columba's monastery and himself a man of scholarly interests. During Arculf's sojourn at Iona, Adamnan questioned him closely about all that he had seen in his travels and embodied the answers in a book *On the Holy Places*. Shortly afterwards Adamnan visited Northumbria and took with him a copy of his book which he gave to King Aldfrith, himself a scholar of high repute among both English and Irish; and from the king the book came into the hands of Bede who quoted from it in his *History* and used it for a short work which he himself wrote on the topic. Pilgrims had been visiting the Holy Lands for some centuries before Arculf's visit, and of course Bede had been able to learn something of those lands from other works he had read, but we can easily imagine the joy with which he will have seized upon this new book, coming to his monastery by such an unexpected route and taken down from the lips of a man who had visited the holy places as recently as the time of Bede's own boyhood.

Arculf's travels to the Near East which took him to Alexandria, Damascus and Constantinople, as well as the cities of the Holy Land itself, fell in an age when Byzantine power had been greatly curtailed at the expense of Moslem expansion. Jerusalem and Alexandria had been captured and in Bede's own lifetime occurred the conquest of Spain and incursion into France where, as Bede himself recorded towards the end of his *History*, the continuing Moslem expansion was eventually checked. Arculf had spent nine months in Jerusalem and he was able to give Adamnan a great deal of information on places of the first importance to Christian men. He gave Adamnan a plan, drawn on a wax tablet, of four of the Jerusalem churches. Foremost among them was the church of the Holy Sepulchre which he had frequently visited and was able to describe in close detail, even to the colouring of the rock. Next was the church of the Holy Mary which does not now exist and whose exact site is uncertain; then the church of Golgotha, with its great bronze chandelier suspended above a large silver cross, where once the wooden cross itself had stood; and finally the basilica built by Constantine on the site where the crosses of the Lord and of the two thieves had been found two hundred and thirty-three years after the Crucifixion. This wax plan will have been too fragile to have survived for long, but it was evidently soon transferred to parchment for we can still see it in a ninth-century manuscript of Adamnan's work in Vienna.

Arculf also told Adamnan about some of the relics famous in Christendom, the chalice used at the Last Supper—'it has the measure of a Gaulish pint'—the lance and the shroud. Outside Jerusalem, he had been greatly impressed by the octagonal church of the Ascension, built upon the summit of Mount Olivet with its centre left open to the skies. Here pilgrims were shown the Lord's footprints. High up in the church were eight glazed windows through which the radiant brightness of eight lamps shone with wonderful clarity upon the surrounding countryside. All this seems a far cry from the Gaulish masons who built the church at Jarrow, yet men may have sought to emulate the glories about which they could read. Of Jerusalem itself we have a vivid picture as Arculf saw it when the city was thronged with a great concourse of people gathered from many nations for the fair which was held each year in September. Men could scarcely move through the streets for the camels, horses, oxen and asses laden with many different kinds of merchandise. The streets were fouled and stinking, but as soon as the fair was over there came a great downpour of rain flowing in torrents along the steeply sloping alleys and purging them of all filth. Some of this Bede put into his *History*, but there was much else that he could read about touching Bethlehem, Nazareth, the river Jordan and places further afield.

Those who visit Constantinople today can still see Justinian's famous building, the church of the Holy Wisdom (the dedication of the great new church built in York when Alcuin was there) in much the same condition as it was when Arculf saw it, saving only the mosaics which are mostly somewhat later. They are not, however, likely to be told two stories which Arculf heard from certain well-informed citizens about a man whose continuing steadfastness under torture had earned him the title of confessor. In the city of Diospolis (Lydda), Arculf was told, there was a statue of the confessor bound to a column and undergoing a flogging. On one occasion an unbeliever attacked the statue. His lance penetrated the column as easily as if it had been a mound of snow and then stuck so fast that it could not be withdrawn until suitable expressions of penitence had been uttered. Arculf himself, presumably on a subsequent visit to Diospolis, was able to place his own fingers in the holes left by the infidel. The second story told of a soldier who struck a bargain about his horse with the confessor's image before setting off for the wars. On his return he tried to escape from his bargain, but the confessor proved the better horse-dealer of the two. Though Arculf may not have known it, the confessor was roasted to death, slowly, and thereby became a saint: his name was George. These stories brought from Constantinople by a Gaulish bishop in the seventh century and carried by the ill chance of a storm and shipwreck to Iona and thence to Aldfrith, scholarly king of Northumbria, and to Bede, constitute, so far as I am aware, the earliest evidence we have for knowledge among the English of the man who later became England's patron saint. The widespread popularity of Adamnan's own book, and of Bede's shorter version, may have led to some small cult of the saint in Northumbria, for in a collection of miscellaneous liturgical forms compiled in the tenth century and now known as *The Durham Ritual* we find the blessed martyr George named in a collect for the 9th of the kalends of May, that is

23 April which is still St George's day. We cannot suppose it to have been more than an accident that the church of St Paul at Jarrow was dedicated on this same day of the year. The story of Arculf's travels would probably have been put into writing if he had returned safely to his own Gaulish homeland, but we, no doubt like Bede in his own day, may be thankful for the storm which led to a shipwreck in the western isles of Scotland and for the chance which took the bishop to an interested scholar at Iona.

We may also be thankful to an English nun of Heidenheim in southern Germany who wrote the most notable of Anglo-Saxon travel books. This book told of the adventures and misadventures of Willibald in Italy, Sicily, Cyprus and the lands of the Near East. He was fascinated by volcanoes, which Bede supposed to be caused by water leaking out of the Mediterranean, and he noted that pumice stone was used for smoothing vellum. But Willibald was a West Saxon. We are fortunate in having these two accounts of great pilgrimages successfully completed in this age, if only because they give substance to an attitude to life widely held by men and women, perhaps especially among the Irish: the notion that merit was to be won by abandoning one's home, one's kith and kin, one's native land, and going on a pilgrimage for the love of God—*peregrinatio pro amore Dei*. There were many to whom life itself was no more than a brief pilgrimage upon earth, prelude to eternity.

In the writings of this age the imagery of the sea is both vivid and frequent—the monastery is a haven of escape from the shipwreck of life, man ceaselessly tossed about by the waves of secular cares, man ever looking for a safe harbour for his ship dragging its anchor before the rising storms of the world. The embodiment of the true pilgrim's ideal is found in the three Irishmen who eventually reached Alfred's court after they had set out in secret from Ireland 'because they wished for the love of God to be in a foreign land, they cared not where'. Their spiritual descendants, of many races and differing beliefs, are still with us, but not all men travelled in quite so aimless or reckless a way. Many Northumbrians of Bede's time went to Ireland, often for the sake of the scholarship which they could find there. Hilda had wanted to go with her kinsfolk to the nunneries in Gaul. Benedict Biscop went to the Isles de Lérins in the Bay of Cannes, to learn about monasticism, and to Provence and Italy in search of books. Ceolfrith, like many others, wanted to go to Rome so that he might die beside the tomb of St Peter, but he got not further than Burgundy. It may have been no more than chance that took Wilfrid to Frisia, but his visit there marks the beginning of missionary activity in the Low Countries and the neighbouring parts of Germany, in which Northumbria played a leading part. We still possess the calendar which once belonged to Willibrord, most eminent of the Northumbrian missionaries, bishop of Utrecht and founder of the monastery of Echternach in Luxembourg, renowned centre of Anglo-Saxon studies. We know the names of some of the leaders of this missionary movement and of some also of the lesser men and women, but there were a great many others, priests, monks, nuns, messengers, who travelled back and forth across the North Sea and who continued to do so after an organised church had been established. Often their voyages would prosper, an easy run before a gentle western wind, often they would end in shipwreck and drowning, the fate which befell the first abbot of St Augustine's monastery in Canterbury. Such voyages, whether outward or homeward, could seldom be made without danger of a sudden storm. Not all voyagers could choose the summer season. Poets sang of the sea-weary spirits of men who had spent the winter on the ice-cold sea, hung round by icicles, stung by driving hail.

> The cry of the gannet was all my gladness,
> The call of the curlew, not the laughter of men,
> The mewing gull, not the sweetness of mead.
> There, storms echoed off the rocky cliffs; the icy-feathered tern
> Answered them; and often the eagle,
> Dewy-winged, screeched overhead.
>
> (*Tr. K. Crossley-Holland*)

Then, as now, men feared yet loved the wide expanses of the sea.

CHAPTER FIVE

First shalt Thou seek the Kingdom of God

'YOU ARE SITTING feasting with your ealdorman and thegns in winter time; the fire is burning on the hearth in the middle of the hall and all inside is warm, while outside the wintry storms of rain and snow are raging; and a sparrow flies swiftly through the hall. It enters in at one door and quickly flies out through the other. For a few moments it is inside, the storm and wintry tempest cannot touch it, but after the briefest moment of calm, it flits from your sight, out of the wintry storm and into it again. So this life of man appears but for a moment, what follows or indeed what went before, we know not at all. If this new doctrine brings us more certain information it seems right that we should accept it.'

This speech put into the mouth of a heathen priest forms part of the most famous of Bede's stories. After further debate, the priest himself rode off to destroy the idols and the temple which housed them, and on the Easter Day which followed, King Edwin and many others of his race were baptised at York in a church newly built of wood and dedicated to St Peter. The year was 627, thirty years after the arrival of Augustine at Canterbury. The story, told by Bede in a manner worthy to commemorate what was for him the greatest event in the history of his kingdom, suffers no loss of beauty by familiarity. Bede's account of the conversion has rather the quality of a great painting or symphony which reveal the depths of their meaning only by increasing familiarity to those who look or listen. This indeed is what it is, a work of art created by a historian, meant to be read aloud, and herein lies a warning.

Archaeologists, realists with muddy boots, turn to the story for its account of an Anglo-Saxon hall, seeing a rectangular structure with opposing doors in the long sides, a door in one end and a wall dividing the interior into two unequal portions, with a hearth for the fire in the larger, and they tell us of such halls excavated at Chalton in Hampshire, or nearer to Bede's homeland, at Old

Yeavering in the foothills of the Cheviots (Plate 3). Historians, wishing to show similar realism, may well ask how it was that a heathen of Germanic origin made such an excellent philosophical speech in Latin and how that speech came to be remembered until it was written down more than a hundred years after it was delivered. Naturally such an approach is to reduce criticism to absurdity, yet it helps to make the point that Bede, like all great historians, was an artist, and to remind us that the kind of truth which his account of the conversion brings to us is the kind of truth which we learn from Renoir or Mozart, rather than from computerised statistics. Expressed in another way we can only approach the conversion of the Northumbrians through the words of a man who was himself removed by more than a century from the events which he describes. Even at that distance of time, detail and episode are lost or transmuted, emphasis changed, tradition established. The flight of the sparrow expressed in vivid, simple terms a whole philosophy of life to be overthrown, like the images of the heathen temple, by those who accepted Christianity, and this for Bede was the truth that mattered most.

Two kings, Edwin and Oswald, and two bishops, Paulinus and Aidan, are prominent figures in this painting, but of the four, only one, and that the least beloved of historians, seems to appear momentarily as a living man rather than as a sanctified figure designed for a stained-glass window. A man who was baptised by Paulinus in the Trent remembered him as a tall man with a slight stoop. His hair was black, his face thin, his nose slender and aquiline. In his general appearance he was both venerable and awe-inspiring. The description was passed on to a Lincolnshire abbot from whom it reached Bede—a pity, we may reflect, that Hilda who was thirteen when Paulinus baptised her, did not record her own memories of the occasion. Paulinus spent twenty-five years with the other Roman missionaries in southern England before he came north as chaplain-bishop to Æthelberg of Kent who was to marry the still heathen Edwin, and had we known but a quarter of his doings in those years we would perhaps have been less ready to regard his return to Kent with his protégée as a flight from his responsibilities in Northumbria. Whitby tradition affords us a glimpse of Paulinus in Roman York, preaching to the heathen in a hall and then moving out into a public square where an archer despatched a crow croaking hoarsely in an unpropitious quarter of the heavens. The description seems appropriate to the old Roman headquarters building at the heart of the former legionary fortress with its hall and open courtyard, some of its remains still to be seen beneath York Minster (Plate 2).

Catterick was another Roman site where Paulinus preached and baptised, and away to the north of Hadrian's frontier, he visited a royal estate at Old Yeavering, staying there for thirty-six days. It was said that crowds flocked to him from every village in the district and that when he had instructed them, he baptised them in the river Glen. Some of the people who lived in those parts may already have been Christian. The mission of Paulinus in Northumbria covered seven years from 626 to 633, and when Edwin was killed in that year Paulinus escorted his widow and her children back to Kent and he himself became bishop in Rochester for a further eleven years. The Roman mission continued its activities in Northumbria under the leadership of a deacon called James who preached in York and often lived in a village near Catterick. James was still alive when Bede was born c. 673, and by that time is likely to have been well into his seventies or beyond. How much was achieved by Paulinus and how much survived the onslaught of Cadwallon, Christian king of Gwynedd, we cannot tell, but we must surely have respect, and perhaps much more, for this Italian who left the warmth and civilisation of his homeland to die after working for nearly forty-five years among the pagan barbarians of England.

Edwin had been baptised by an Italian in a wooden church built inside the military capital of what had once been a valued province of the Roman Empire. He was familiar with Roman buildings and on ceremonial occasions he was preceded by a standard bearer in Roman fashion. Oswald was baptised in exile among the Scots and when he returned to Northumbria after a victory won, as men later claimed, by the intercession of St Columba, he sent to Columba's foundation in Iona, remote and windswept—an island sheared from another island—for a bishop to restore Christianity to a kingdom whose rulers had lapsed to paganism in the year following Edwin's death. Aidan was sent and chose to dwell on another island, to become, in the eyes of a Northumbrian poet, a sacred land encircled by blue waters whose ebbing tide laid bare the shores and gave ready access to travellers. He and his companions founded a monastery on Lindisfarne, providing none but the simplest buildings of wood and thatch where monks could eat and sleep and worship. The Roman city and the island sanctuary nurtured different attitudes towards the forms of Christian worship. There were some like Wilfrid who loved the grandeur of Roman buildings such as he had seen in the ancient cities of Provence and in Italy itself. Others, like Cuthbert, felt the need to escape even from Lindisfarne to the complete isolation of an uninhabited islet among the Farnes. Today's traveller may gaze at the traffic-girt Colosseum through the windows of his bus from Leonardo da Vinci's airport near Tiber's mouth. He may, if he is so disposed, attend a bullfight in the great arena at Arles. Or he may go in a small fishing-boat from the harbour at Seahouses to be marooned for a brief hour or so on the island where Cuthbert's hermitage lay (Plate 5).

The long and savage history of sectarian strife (no whit abated in some parts of Britain even today) may lead us too easily into a distorted view of the conversion of Northumbria. There were indeed antagonisms. The Christian British had lost much of their land to the pagan invaders who killed their monks and destroyed their holy places. The first Christian king in Northumbria was killed in battle by the Christian king of a British kingdom. There were also, in Bede's time, theological antagonisms when the celebration of Easter on the wrong day was held to be a mortal heresy leading to eternal damnation. These antagonisms should be remembered, but they must not be allowed so to colour our view of the church in Northumbria as to present us with a sharp antithesis between Roman and Celtic, between English and Irish, between opposing sides representing in modern terms extremes of nationalist opinion. Cuthbert and Wilfrid were as different as men could be, the one seemingly so Celtic, the other so Roman, yet both were born of English parents, both knew Lindisfarne well. We too easily overlook the importance of other influences coming into England from Gaul.

Apart from political and theological antagonisms there were

very real differences in outlook, attitude and approach. Gregory the Great envisaged the new church of the English with a hierarchy of two archbishops, one in London and the other in York, each of the two metropolitan areas to be divided into twelve dioceses. A church so organised within the Roman Empire would have had bishops with their seats in the old imperial cities—Arles, Lyons, Paris and so forth—and something of this sort eventually happened in southern England with bishops becoming established in Canterbury, Rochester, London, Winchester and Dorchester, all former Roman towns. In northern England there were no towns of comparable size, and scarcely any small ones, only military centres which in one or two cases had grown into civilian towns. On Gregory's plan there might have been bishops at York, Catterick, Corbridge and Carlisle, but in the event York was the only northern Roman site to have its bishop in Anglo-Saxon times.

Ireland, whence sprang the Columban foundation on Iona, had never been within the Roman Empire. There were no towns in the Roman sense, only forts serving as royal centres for the small Irish kingdoms. Irish society was tribal in its organisation, still remembered as once nomadic. Irish bishops seem to have been territorial and tribal. By the time that Oswald received Aidan as missionary bishop from Iona the monastic element in the Irish church had become dominant, and we find its greatest strength consisting of confederations of monasteries which took no account of the boundaries between tribal kingdoms. It is to such a confederation that Bede refers when he describes Iona as holding pre-eminence over many monasteries which had been founded by Columba and his disciples, both in Britain and in Ireland. He writes of Iona: 'This island always has an abbot for its ruler who is a priest, to whose authority the whole province, including even bishops, have to be subject.' The bishop, though head of the ecclesiastical order, might yet live in a monastery and have to obey the abbot who exercised jurisdictional authority. Lindisfarne, as an offshoot from Iona, formed part of the Columban confederation or *parruchia* as it was called, and as such was subject to the authority of Iona. Within Lindisfarne itself, a bishop would be subject to the jurisdiction of the abbot, though the distinction came to be obscured because of the tenure of both offices by the same man.

About a hundred years after Aidan's arrival at Lindisfarne the situation had so changed that Bede found it necessary to explain to his readers the former peculiarities of the community.

Augustine and Paulinus, strangers in a land far distant from home, worked under the protection of kings, whether in Kent or Northumbria. Irish and Scottish monks were close to home even in Northumbria, where many of the people will have spoken a language not far removed from their own, and some of them indeed may already have been converted to Christianity. Their obedience was not to any king, but to their abbot, and ultimately to the abbot of Iona. They cared nothing for boundaries between kingdoms or bishoprics, but wandered where they chose, so much so that when the Roman form of diocesan organisation eventually prevailed, their erratic tendencies had to be restrained by ecclesiastical legislation. All they needed was a suitable site for their monasteries. Such a site was Lindisfarne, not unlike Iona. Another site was Melrose, not the place whose moonlit remains enchanted Walter Scott, but a more secluded spot where the Tweed swings in a sharp bend to form a delectable peninsula which looks today very much the same as it will have looked to Boisil or some predecessor who chose it for a monastery (Plate 4). And there were a great many others—Coldingham on the Berwickshire coast, Gateshead on the south bank of the Tyne, Whitby on the Yorkshire coast or Lastingham inland (this last lying, according to Bede, 'amid some steep and remote hills which seemed better fitted for the haunts of robbers and the dens of wild beasts than for human habitation'). Today's visitor to its ancient church, housing in its crypt some remains of Anglo-Saxon times, need fear neither robbers nor wild beasts, only his fellow tourists. From such places as these, Celtic monks preached Christianity to the people of Northumbria. James the Deacon was still there, giving instruction in the Roman chant to those who wished to learn.

We who live in an age seeming to offer more and more hurry and noise, less and less time simply to stand and stare, can all too easily romanticise the monasticism of other ages, seeing monks as escapists from the realities and hardships of daily life, finding comfort in the cosiness of an enclosed community. Indeed there almost certainly was some material gain in living as a member of such a community. The buildings inhabited by Wilfrid's monks at Hexham, or Bede's companions at Jarrow, were both solider and more elegant than those of farm or village. They offered better protection against rain, snow and the bitter easterly winds. They were less likely to catch fire, and there were many hands available to extinguish the fire if once it caught. Like the builders of the great parish churches and cathedrals of later times, men sought even then to express their devotion to God through objects made with all the skills at their command. At a more mundane level a community, which might number several hundred, was better able than a small family group to provide mason, carpenter, blacksmith and weaver, beekeeper, brewer and baker. One of the abbots of Wearmouth when Bede was still a boy was a man of great physical strength who enjoyed helping with the work in the bakehouse or the kitchen, the cow byre or the cornfield.

Monastic organisation left time over from producing the necessities of life; time for praising God, for reading and writing, for learning and teaching. All life in Bede's Northumbria was certainly hard, whether for farmer, sailor, soldier or monk. Those who lived in large groups may have been more exposed to the assaults of infectious disease; more than once we read of the almost total destruction of a monastic community from this cause. Bede as a young boy escaped such a disaster in the early years at Jarrow, and another young boy was the only survivor from a similar disaster at Lastingham. Bubonic plague, smallpox, tuberculosis —these and many other physical afflictions might be likely to claim more victims in places where men slept, ate, and shared a cup in common.

Disease apart, and this was indeed common to all men, the monastic life itself made heavy demands, with all the hours of day and night governed by strict rule. The imagery is always that of soldiers, cohorts of monks, protected by the Pauline armour, constantly at war. Yet the monks were not isolated from their fellow men. Often, when the Irish were concerned, the complaint was not that they hid themselves in the monasteries, but that they came out of them too often, preferring to roam about the countryside, vagrants expecting to be welcomed and housed by others. The monks themselves recognised a distinction between what they knew as the active and the contemplative forms of life. The active monk was expected to devote himself to righteous works, giving food to the hungry, drink to the thirsty, clothing to the old. He was to receive the destitute, visit the sick and bury the dead. He was to rescue the poor and helpless who had fallen into the hands of the strong. Men who lived such a life contributed much to the welfare of their neighbours, and in wider fields it was such men as these who travelled to Gaul and Italy, bringing back books for their libraries, and to Germany to preach Christianity to the heathen.

Contrasting with this active life was that of the contemplative, regarded as the higher way, but recognised as too difficult of achievement for all but the few. For Northumbrians the contemplative life was exemplified in the stories of hermits who withdrew to live as solitaries in the Egyptian deserts. Britain had no deserts to offer, but it had something almost as good, great expanses of fenland in East Anglia, where Guthlac made his home in the midst of 'a most dismal fen of immense size', and plenty of islands, many of them smaller than Lindisfarne. Today's visitors might be glad to pitch a solitary tent on St Herbert's Isle in Derwentwater, so called from the anchorite who lived there in a lonely state which would be hard to find today. He was a friend of St Cuthbert by whom he was visited each year. Cuthbert himself used to vary his way of living. We see him travelling about the Northumbrian countryside, preaching in the villages, healing the sick, visiting the community at Coldingham, going to see his foster mother, travelling to Carlisle where the town reeve took him on a tour of the old Roman walls and showed him a Roman well. Here is the monk and bishop living very much in the world, and taking a vigorous part in the affairs of the monastery at Lindisfarne when he was not travelling abroad. Yet he also felt himself drawn to a life of total solitude, where he could live wholly in the contemplation of God, freed from the distractions of office whether as abbot or bishop. On the Inner Farne, an island of some sixteen acres, about seven miles southwards across the sea from Lindisfarne, he built himself a 'city' (Plate 5). It was enclosed within an almost circular wall made of rough stone and turf, and so high that a man standing inside it could see nothing but the sky. Within this wall he made two buildings, one to live in and the other to pray in. And within this city on Wednesday 20 March 687, 'sitting there, he breathed his last and without a sigh went in the way of his fathers'—a victim, in all likelihood, of tuberculosis.

Bede, though no poet, composed a number of works in verse. One of them which he chose to insert in his *History* was a work in praise of virginity. Venantius Fortunatus, a bishop of Poitiers who died *c.* 600, also wrote a poem on virginity, and this same subject was celebrated by the great West Saxon scholar, Aldhelm, both in prose and in verse. The popularity of the theme is a reflection of a remarkable aspect of both English and Gaulish monasticism in this age—the notable part played by women. Bede tells us that towards the middle of the seventh century, when not many monasteries had yet been founded in England, both men and women used to go to Gaulish monasteries for instruction in the way of monastic life and for education, such as they could not get in England. It seems likely that it was through these contacts that there spread to England that kind of monasticism which consisted of foundations containing both men and women. Surprisingly perhaps, there is little evidence that the double house was in any way common in Ireland. Indeed we know of only one instance, and that not wholly certain, the house at Kildare, where both sexes are said to have worshipped in a common church with a high partition running down the middle.

Bede's hymn in praise of virginity was written to honour Audrey—we may use the modern equivalent of the Anglo-Saxon Æthelthryth whom we also remember, though perhaps unwittingly, when we use the word 'tawdry' which once referred to the trinkets sold at St Audrey's fair in Ely. Audrey was the daughter of an East Anglian king and some may be surprised to learn that one who was honoured by Bede's verses should have been twice married, first to an East Anglian princeling and then to a Northumbrian king. She withdrew from her second marriage, at first to Coldingham and then to her native East Anglia where she founded the monastery at Ely. It was Bede's belief that the first native Northumbrian woman to adopt the religious life was Heiu

who received the nun's habit from Aidan of Lindisfarne and who
founded a monastery at Hartlepool, probably in the 640s. Most
famous among the religious women of Northumbria was Hilda.
Related through her father to King Edwin, she was baptised by
Paulinus in her youth but did not become a nun until she was
thirty-three. She was abbess first of the double house at Hartlepool
and later of the more famous one at Whitby which she continued
to rule until her death in 680 at the age of sixty-six.

Theodore, an Asiatic Greek who became archbishop of
Canterbury in 669, was prepared, but only with some reluctance,
to accept what he evidently regarded as an unusual kind of
institution. Bede, on the other hand, had no doubts. He accepted
marriage as a worthy estate ordained by God for the propagation
of the human race and those who sought to prevent it deserved
condemnation, yet he believed that virginity was worthy of even
greater blessing. He is full of praise for such as Audrey and Hilda,
and even though we know little in detail about the organisation of
the double house, there can be no doubt at all that religious women
made a very great contribution to the age in which they lived, not
only in Northumbria and widely across England, but also among
the missionaries in Germany. Save only for one instance, the
double houses were of good repute. An Irish monk in the
monastery at Coldingham foretold that its buildings would soon
be reduced to ashes, and when questioned by the abbess he told her
of a heavenly visitor who had said to him:

"I have just visited every part of this monastery in turn: I have
examined their cells and their beds, and I have found no one
except you concerned with his soul's welfare; but all of them,
men and women alike, are sunk in slothful slumbers or else they
remain awake for purposes of sin. And the cells that were built
for praying and reading have become haunts of feasting,
drinking, gossip, and other delights; even the virgins who are
dedicated to God put aside all respect for their profession and,
whenever they have leisure, spend their time weaving elaborate
garments with which to adorn themselves as if they were brides,
so imperilling their virginity, or else to make friends with
strange men. So it is only right that a heavy vengeance from

heaven should be preparing for this place and for its inhabitants in the form of raging fire."

And in due course the vengeance foretold fell upon the monastery, though we may wonder if the Irish monk was being a little self-righteous, finding the vision a convenient way of improving his own reputation for sanctity, as well as explaining the destruction of a monastery by fire. Virginity may have been a desirable state in Bede's Northumbria, but priests were commonly married, and Bede did not condemn the mother and daughter who for a time ruled jointly over Whitby.

While we can, as we shall shortly see, recreate at least something of the physical appearance of, for example, Bede's monastery, it is more difficult for us to take the outsider's point of view, to see ourselves as farmer or villager with the monastery coming as a new and obtrusive element. What would be the attitude of a pagan Saxon to these men and women who wore strange clothes, who worshipped a new God and taught that those who continued to worship the old gods would surely be forever damned? What were the thoughts and feelings of the frozen wretches who huddled for warmth in the ashes thrown out from the monastic fires? To these and suchlike questions we can give no answers other than those suggested by the imagination. We do not know how strong was the hold of paganism among the English of Northumbria, nor can we be certain of the extent to which Christianity may have survived, or even prospered, among the native population since its first introduction during the Roman occupation. Yet, amid these uncertainties, it seems clear that the centres from which the Christian faith was propagated, the places in which men were trained for the priesthood and new generations taught, were these same monasteries. There is no trace of any division into separate parishes each with its church and priest. Bishop and diocese seem to play but a minor part. There was no archbishop at York till 735, and there seem to have been periods in the seventh century when there was not even a bishop there. There were occasional synodical councils, but no regular system of ecclesiastical government. It is difficult to discern anything resembling an organised church before *c*. 700, and even after that it seems slight enough. Moreover, even within the monasteries there was very little uniformity of observance. Had we been able to spend a while at Lindisfarne under Cuthbert, at Whitby under Hilda, at Jarrow under Benedict Biscop, at Hexham under Acca, we would have found great variety of practice. And perhaps it was from this very variety, this lack of stereotyped uniformity, that the age drew its exuberant, erratic brilliance.

As they varied in their observances, so also did the monasteries vary in their size. Some will have been small, short-lived communities of perhaps no more than half-a-dozen monks, and no doubt there will have been some monasteries whose very names have not been recorded. In other cases a name and little more has survived, through passing reference in Bede's *History*, but with nothing at all known about the men or women who lived there—such were Gateshead, Tynemouth and Coquet Island. Bede's own monastery, physically divided though spiritually one, came to number some 600 souls and although we lack any direct evidence and can do no better than guess, it seems unlikely that there will have been any villages in Northumbria as large as this. Perhaps only at York, Carlisle or Catterick would we have found lay communities of similar or larger size. A few among these many monasteries have left behind traces enough, either on the ground itself or in written record, to allow us to see a little of their material aspect and rather more of their spiritual, intellectual and artistic achievements. Among them are Lindisfarne and Whitby, the one of monks only, the other a double house of men and women, both of them originally Celtic foundations, and Whitby the scene of the famous synod which decided to follow the ways of Rome rather than those of Iona.

Today's visitor to Lindisfarne, or Holy Island as the maps rightly call it, will find the village dominated by the ruins of the Benedictine priory, founded as a cell of Durham sixteen years after Norman William's famous victory at Hastings, its soft pink sandstone now worked into curious patterns by the wasting salt-laden winds (Plate 6). Less than a mile away stands the castle built on a precipitous rock as protection to the small harbour, some thirty years before the execution of Mary Queen of Scots. Somewhere in this part of the island, perhaps on the ridge called the Heugh, above the lifeboat house, lay the monastery whose history began in 635 and ended about 875. None of the buildings of this monastery are now to be seen nor has any plan yet been recovered by excavation, but in the museum the visitor can see some of the small memorial stones carved with the names of those commemorated, as well as a rich collection of other stones variously carved with figure or pattern. For Holy Island's most precious treasures—Cuthbert's coffin, the saint's pectoral cross and the famous Lindisfarne Gospel book, the visitor must go to Durham and to the British Museum.

We know nothing at all about the appearance of the monastery in the time of Aidan its founder. His successor, Finan, built a church made entirely of oak, with no stone, and its roof thatched with reeds. What the original dedication was we do not know, but some ten years after Finan's death, and after the Synod of Whitby when the monks who preferred to keep to the Celtic ways had left, the church was rededicated to St Peter by Theodore, archbishop of Canterbury. Bede, troubled by the increasing wealth of the church in his own day, stresses the great simplicity of the life lived at Lindisfarne in the early days. Other than the church, there were very few buildings and those only of the simplest. The monks had no money but only cattle. They refused to accept gifts of land or other possessions, and when the king and his nobles came to visit them, they did so only to pray in the church and to share the ordinary daily fare. However simple life may have been in the past, times had changed before the end of the seventh century. Another bishop, the one associated with the making of the *Lindisfarne Gospels*, had the thatch removed from the church and covered the whole of it, walls as well as roof, with lead, and we may wonder where this valuable commodity came from. Moreover, the church had acquired the bones of a holy man who was to become the most famous of all English saints. Bones brought pilgrims and pilgrims brought money. It is hard to think of the *Lindisfarne Gospels* being produced in a monastery as humble and simple as Bede describes. Lindisfarne had played its part in the early days as a missionary base whence came monks to evangelise the Northumbrian countryside and to carry their missionary work further afield into the middle and southern parts of England. In later times the fame of Lindisfarne lay in its saint and his cult, unbroken from that day to this.

Whitby's Hilda was never a rival to Cuthbert in the long roll of Anglo-Saxon saints, but if her posthumous life was less active, she and those she gathered into her community probably made the greater contribution to the world of their own day. Like Lindisfarne, today's Whitby is dominated by the remains of the medieval abbey. When the rough places along its northern side were being smoothed into a foreground held to be suitable for a medieval background, a large area of the Anglo-Saxon monastery was uncovered—and removed. From what survives now, on plan or in photograph, we cannot determine with certainty the use of the individual buildings, and nothing recognisable as a church has been found. Yet some of the smaller objects recall for us a once vigorous and varied life. Spindle whorls, loom weights and even a piece of woollen cloth remind us of an earlier Gaulish monastic rule for nuns which required that all the clothing needed by them was to be made within the monastery. Fragments of glass cups, coloured glass beads, twisted glass rods of blue and amber, a piece of a moulded glass bracelet in ultramarine—these were numerous enough to suggest that at some time before the place was destroyed there were people there who knew about glass-making, though Bede tells us that the Anglo-Saxons of his days had to acquire the skill from foreign teachers. There were many objects for personal use—small brooches, buckles, pins, tweezers, combs, needles —some of bronze, some of bone. There were large quantities of cooking pots, drinking cups and bowls, as well as a surprising number of coins. And more interesting perhaps than all these, there were several *styli* of the kind used for writing on wax tablets, and a number of pieces of ornamental metalwork from the outer covers of books. The stylus tells us of a scriptorium, the book ornaments of a library, and happily the written records tell us something more of both.

The story of Cædmon has long been familiar. He was a man who seemingly worked on one of the Whitby estates and to whom, late in life, the gift of song came by heavenly inspiration. Some of the learned men in the monastery hearing of his new-found gift gave Cædmon a piece of scripture and asked him to turn it into verse. He did so and was then persuaded to enter the monastery. He seems not to have learnt to read himself, but rather listened attentively to what he was told and then turned all that he remembered into the verse of his native tongue. Hilda, herself greatly concerned with education for the priesthood and Christian teaching for the unlettered, will have been quick to see in Cædmon's gift a solution to a difficult problem—how best to convey the fundamental beliefs of Christianity to pagan people who could not read. No doubt monks went about the countryside preaching to those who cared to listen, but they had no parish church, no pulpit for a weekly sermon, not even spare copies of the Gospels. The scriptures were in Latin, there was no accepted English translation and men could not have read it even if there had been. But minstrelsy was deeply rooted in the past. Men were familiar with rhythmical alliterative verse telling their own tales in their own language. And so, under the direction of the Whitby scholars, Cædmon turned into English verse the story of Genesis and of the Exodus of Israel from Egypt—heroic themes that would have a strong appeal—as well as the fundamental parts of the New Testament—Incarnation, Passion, Resurrection, Ascension. Unhappily none of this poetry now survives, but we may surely think that it was of the greatest importance in spreading at least an elementary knowledge of the Christian faith among the people of Northumbria.

Generations of English schoolchildren have been taught that Cædmon was the first English poet, though his one surviving work, a short hymn in praise of Creation, scarcely justifies the claim. The significance of his story seems rather to lie in the use of native English verse as a means of evangelising the countryside. There could, however, be no effective teaching unless men were trained to fill both the lower and the higher orders of the church. While Hilda was abbess no fewer than five Whitby monks became bishops, and a sixth died after election but before consecration. Three of these six were designated for office outside Northumbria, and when we consider how few bishops there were in the whole of England at this time, the Whitby record is remarkable. There are two other counts on which Whitby deserves our attention. It was the site chosen for the famous debate on the Easter problem and other matters arising from differences between the Roman and Celtic churches, the debate in which St Peter, holding the keys of heaven, won the day; and it became the centre of a cult of Gregory the Great. Hilda, we may recall, had been baptised by Paulinus, and perhaps this was why she and her community were so greatly devoted to the memory of Gregory, himself responsible for sending Paulinus to England. The outcome of this devotion was the writing of a *Life* of the great pope, probably the first *Life* of him ever to be written and certainly the oldest now surviving. Crabbed in its style, ungrammatical in its form (though this may be the result of bad work by scribes and faulty manuscript transmission) it has nevertheless some claim to being the earliest surviving book known to have been written by an Englishman. In this book we read that when each individual teacher brings his own race to the Lord on the great day of Judgement, the people of England will be led by Gregory the Great.

Hilda founded the monastery at Whitby in 657. She died in 680 and although her foundation may have flourished for another hundred years we know next to nothing about its later history. Meanwhile other centres were coming to the fore—Ripon and Hexham, Wearmouth and Jarrow. A wandering monk, one who had set out on his pilgrimage from Iona as a young man and who died like Job, old and full of years, would have lived to see much that was newfangled, much that was startlingly different from the timber and thatch of Lindisfarne. Not least was the change from wood to stone, from the Scottish to the Roman way of building. When the English came to Northumbria they did not know how to make the mortar securing the stones of the many Roman buildings which they could see. If they had used stone for building, they could only have built the walls 'dry', as some Northumbrians still do, where walls stride across the fields and fells of sheep country. When Benedict Biscop was building his foundations at Wearmouth and Jarrow, he wanted their churches to be in the Roman not the Scottish style, in mortared stone not in wood, but in order to make them so he had to send to Gaul for men who knew how to make mortar—*cæmentarii* or makers of cement as Bede calls them (Plates 7 and 8).

Bede had certainly watched this new craft with close interest, for he describes in detail how stone was first burnt and reduced to ash by great heat. Afterwards water was added to the ash and the resulting mixture was able to bind fast individual stones built up course by course as a wall. The process is so familiar to us now that effort is needed to imagine the effect upon Bede of the recovery of this lost art. He himself was quick to see the spiritual lesson to be learnt—those who had passed through the furnace of this world's tribulations exchanged the darkness of their sinful nature for the shining whiteness of their virtue—though they had been crushed, they emerged from the burning stronger than they had been before. The object lesson was direct and visible to all who saw the making of mortar, and it is important for us that we should see this spiritual meaning. The tower of Babylon, Bede expounds, had been built of bricks whose material came from pits, sordid, earthy, evil, even as the builders themselves; but the temple of Solomon and the city of Jerusalem had been built of stone, with shining white marble from the island of Paros. Bricks were not used in Bede's Northumbria, but clean stone, even though it lacked the pure whiteness of Parian marble, represented spiritual purity, *candor innocentiæ*—the white heat that purifies, the burnt limestone that wins strength from the fire—and there was plenty of that limestone in Northumbria east of the hills. The new church built of stone at Whithorn in the far south-west of Scotland was called The White House, *Candida Casa*. No such whiteness was to be seen in the timbers and thatch of a church built *more Scottorum*.

The making of cement was not the only skill which caught Bede's attention. He writes in the commentary on the Song of Songs: 'We all know that turnery is both easier to see and more difficult to describe than other crafts. A man who works with a carpenter's axe or with a small knife or with a two-edged axe or with a mallet, not only needs to work much more laboriously, but also frequently needs to set a pattern before him and to look carefully about him with his eyes, lest he make a mistake. A man who works upon a lathe needs no external pattern, but he is able to keep control of the work which he is doing by that very metal tool which he is using.' We move easily from this passage to a sight of the stone baluster shafts, turned upon a lathe, which are still in place in the western porch of St Peter's church at Wearmouth. The

compass used for drawing (below, p. 195), the lathe used for
turnery and also the potter's wheel represent, with cement and
building in stone, something of the technology new to the age, and
they were useful in the object lessons which they might provide as
illustrations of theological truths.

Here then was one of the most dramatic changes witnessed by
our pilgrim from Iona—the rediscovery of mortar which enabled
men to build in stone on the grand scale. The same technique was
used by Wilfrid who had lived long in Gaul, whence Benedict
Biscop got his cement-makers, and had been to Italy. The churches
which he built at Ripon and Hexham were both of dressed stone,
with crypts, columns, side-aisles and spiral stairs leading up and
down. At least to his biographer, the church at Hexham seemed to
be the finest that had been built on this side of the Alps. We can
pardon some exaggeration and still see how different was this
church from the timber and thatch that Wilfrid had known as a
boy at Lindisfarne. If our pilgrim had been present at the dedication of the new church at Ripon (where a small community
of monks had once lived in the Scottish fashion) he would have
seen the altar vested in purple and gold cloth and upon it 'a marvel
of beauty hitherto unheard of', an illuminated copy of the four
Gospels all written in letters of gold on parchment that had been
dyed purple, to be kept in a case made wholly of gold and set with
precious gems. He would have found himself in the company of
kings, bishops and nobles, and when the preaching was over he
might have been able to share in a great feast which lasted for three
days and three nights—and perhaps he might have wondered
whether all this new-found wealth and splendour contained any
greater treasure than he had once known in Columba's Iona or
Aidan's Lindisfarne.

Returning in his old age to Wearmouth and Jarrow our pilgrim
would have found the stone churches there adorned both inside
and outside with sculpture, sometimes of figures, sometimes of
intertwined animals. The figures have weathered beyond
recognition, but the intertwined animals are still there in the porch
of St Peter's church at Wearmouth. Hanging on the walls he
would have seen paintings, brought from Italy, with scenes from
the Old and the New Testaments, the Virgin Mary and the

Twelve Apostles, and suspended from the ceiling, splendidly wrought iron lamps. The windows would be filled with coloured glass, not representing figures, but small pieces of various colours set in lead and probably giving a simple mosaic or linear pattern. This too was an unfamiliar skill for which craftsmen had been brought from Gaul. Moving about the monasteries, he would have seen roofs covered partly in lead and partly in limestone slates. Inside, he would have found floors of concrete, made of pebble and powdered brick, and on the walls of at least some of the rooms he would have found plaster, creamish in colour, some of it painted red.

Wearmouth and Jarrow may have lacked something of the grandeur of Wilfrid's Ripon and Hexham, yet all four may rightly be said to have been built 'in the Roman fashion'. They were more akin to the buildings Paulinus had seen in York than to those which Aidan had known in Iona or Lindisfarne. They reflect in their external appearance the increasing dominance of the Roman over the Celtic approach to Christianity. By the time Bede died, in 735, Northumbria had bishops in four different centres—York and Hexham, Lindisfarne and Whithorn. In York itself the wooden church built for the baptism of Edwin had later been enclosed within a larger stone church, but it seems not to have been built well, or else to have been neglected, for Wilfrid found that its roof ridge had collapsed and the inside had become fouled with the droppings of birds. He repaired the roof, covered it with lead, glazed the windows and whitewashed the walls. Our pilgrim coming from Iona could not have lived to see the changes made at York soon after the middle of the eighth century by Archbishop Ælbert. In St Peter's church where Edwin had been baptised, he dedicated a new altar to St Paul, enclosing it entirely with silver, precious stones and gold. Above it, there was a lofty chandelier and beside it a tall cross. Another altar in the same church he dedicated to the martyrs and to the cross, and for the priest serving at this altar he gave a large new ampulla of pure gold. In addition to this, the archbishop built a new church, its lofty roofs supported by massive columns and curved arches. Resplendent with light from its many windows, it had numerous side chapels and no fewer than thirty altars all with rich and varied furnishings.

Alcuin himself saw the building of the magnificent new church which was dedicated, like Justinian's in Byzantium, to the Holy Wisdom. It was a far cry from the primitive simplicity of Lindisfarne.

Those who sought the kingdom of God had certainly found great material wealth, all of it to be lost when the kingdom of Northumbria was destroyed. Yet Bede was already anxious about several aspects of the Northumbrian church before his death. Although he was able to find much that was good, he knew that bishops and clergy were too few in number. He had heard that there were many villages and hamlets, in inaccessible mountains and remote woodlands, where a bishop was never seen for many years at a time, though the people who lived there were expected to pay their dues to the church. There were many priests who knew no Latin, and Bede himself had often given such men copies of the Creed and the Lord's Prayer translated into their own English language. There was difficulty about finding estates adequate for the endowment of additional bishoprics. But what seems to have worried Bede most was the widespread abuse of monastic life.

Three aspects of Northumbrian monasticism were inherently dangerous. There was some tendency, more especially where Celtic influences were strong, for monasteries to be regarded as family possessions. As we have seen, after Hilda's death Whitby was ruled jointly by a mother and daughter. The abbess of a monastery at Watton in Yorkshire planned that her daughter should succeed to the office. At another Northumbrian monastery, in a succession of six abbots, brother succeeded brother on two separate occasions. At Wearmouth and Jarrow the founding abbot, Benedict Biscop, gave the strictest injunctions against electing his successor according to the claims of kin. The other dangers lay partly in the abuses that might arise in the double houses and partly in the system, not now fully understood, whereby those who lived in monasteries not only escaped military duties and some forms of taxation, but were also able to secure their monastic estates in hereditary right and so to bequeath them to their heirs in perpetuity. The result was the growth of numbers of spurious monasteries. Looking back over the previous thirty years Bede says that officers of government, members of the nobility, and even their servants, had exploited their opportunities by buying estates and setting themselves up with their wives and children, as monks and even abbots, although they knew nothing about monasticism and had no intention of leading anything approaching a monastic way of life.

The romantic view of the Northumbrian golden age must find room for these bogus abbots who escaped from military service, evaded their taxes and speculated in property. Yet Bede, when he wrote of such people, was ageing and sick, too sick to make the journey to York where a friend and former pupil was shortly to become the first archbishop. The evils of his own time, including the violent seizure of his own bishop, seemed, as is the constant way, to lend greater enchantment to times past. As with Bede, so with Alcuin, born at about the time of Bede's death. Oppressed with the evils of his own old age, sick and much buffeted by frequent journeys across the North Sea, he too looks back to a golden age; but it was the age of his own early manhood as pupil, and then master, in the school at York after Bede's death, the age when the church of the Holy Wisdom was abuilding, the age when the scholars of York were able to read books of which even Bede knew nothing.

CHAPTER SIX

Then they washed the Holy Bones

'THEN HE SAW that the end of his life was approaching and he prayed for his people as they fell and died there and he commended their souls and himself to God, crying out thus as he fell: "May God have mercy on our souls!" Then the heathen king ordered his head to be cut off and his right arm and had them set up as a trophy. After Oswald's death his brother Oswy succeeded to the kingdom of the Northumbrians and with a troop of his men he rode to the place where his brother's head stood fastened upon a stake, and he took the head and his right hand and brought them with all honour to the church at Lindisfarne. So it came about, as we have said before, that his right hand remains whole, with its flesh free of all corruption, even as the bishop said. The arm was laid honourably in a shrine fashioned of silver in St Peter's church in Bamburgh beside the seashore, and it lies there as incorrupt as when it was cut off.

'Afterwards the daughter of Oswald's brother became queen among the Mercians and she discovered his bones and brought them to the monastery at Bardney in Lindsey which she greatly loved; but in their human folly the monks refused to receive the saint and had a tent pitched over the holy bones lying inside the hearse. God then revealed that he was indeed a holy man, for throughout the whole night a heavenly light extended over the tent and reached upwards to the heavens, like a sunbeam of great splendour; and through all the countryside the people watched, marvelling greatly. Then the monks were much frightened and on the next morning they asked if they might receive with honour the saint whom they had before rejected. Then they washed the holy bones and carried them into the church in a shrine with all honour and laid them up. And through his holy merits many sick men were healed there of various diseases. The water with which they had washed the bones was poured away inside the church in one

10   A Group of Heads: a fragment from a Northumbrian cross

NOLITE IUDICARE SECUNDUM FACIEM
SED IUSTUM IUDICIUM IUDICATE
DICEBANT ERGO QUIDAM
ex hierosolymis
NONNE hic est quem quaerunt
INTERFICERE
ETECCE palam Loquitur
ETNIHIL ei dicunt
NUMQUID UERE COGNOUERUNT
PRINCIPES QUIA HIC ESTXPS
SED HUNC SCIMUS UNDESIT
XPS AUTEM CUM UENERIT
NEMO SCIT UNDE SIT
CLAMABAT ERGO DOCENS
INTEMPLO IHS ETDICENS
ET ME SCITIS ETUNDESIM SCITIS
ET AME IPSO NON UEHI
SED EST UERUS QUIMISITME
QUEM UOS NESCITIS

corner, and afterwards the earth which received that water brought healing to many. With the dust evil spirits were driven out of men who had previously been afflicted with madness.'

King Oswald was killed in battle against Penda of Mercia in August 642 in the thirty-eighth year of his life at a place which Bede called *Maserfelth* and which men of later times identified with Oswestry in Shropshire. Oswald's death in battle, fighting a pagan army led by a pagan king, was the foundation of a remarkable cult which led his devotees to claim him as the first English martyr. This account of his death, of his relics and of the miracles which they performed was written about 350 years later by Ælfric, prolific West Saxon writer of saints' lives and homilies, though he derived it mostly from Bede. Whether we read the account in the Latin of Bede or the Old English of Ælfric we find in it a story containing all the elements which went towards the making of a popular saint. Here was a young king who had been baptised in exile and whose victory at Heavenfield was won through the power of the cross, the first outward and visible symbol of the Christian faith ever to be erected in the kingdom of Bernicia, as Bede tells us. After his death his body was mutilated in pagan fashion, and his head left on the battlefield for carrion scavengers.

Whatever may be the reaction of men today—scorn, ridicule, revulsion or even reverence—we do well to recognise how great was the part played by the cult of saints, how great was the power of holy bones among those who lived in the age of Bede. Ridicule is easy. Was not Oswald's right arm at Peterborough, his left arm at Gloucester and his third arm at Durham, one head at Durham and another in Luxembourg, and yet the entire body at St Winnoc's in Flanders, presented by Edward the Confessor? But such ridicule would not have been understood by those who revered the bones of Oswald, Cuthbert or even Bede. These were the mortal remains of good men who, though long dead, still lived in an everlasting kingdom whence they might be able to bring help to those in need.

The cult of a saint depended first and foremost upon possession of his body and this might present difficulties when the saint had been killed in battle, particularly if his body had been dismembered, as in the case of Oswald. Edwin too was killed in battle, but his adversary, though a heretic, was a Christian, and so Edwin could not be claimed as a martyr. Even so, he was revered at Whitby whose monks told how his bones had been found. There was an English priest called Trimma who was told in a dream to go to Hatfield Chase where Edwin had been killed, to gather up his bones and take them to Whitby. The priest, a cautious man and timid, prevaricated with his heavenly visitor and finally decided to do nothing, recalling the teaching of Ecclesiasticus, that dreams have often caused many people to err. But the visitor came a second and a third time with sharp rebuke to Trimma who then thought it wise to do as he was bid. He made enquiries of a local farmer who directed him to a place where certain marks on the ground would show him exactly where he was to dig. He set forth eagerly, but was disappointed by his first excavation which revealed nothing. He tried a second time, digging with greater care, and this time he found what he was looking for and brought his treasure back to the monastery at Whitby where the bones were buried in St Peter's church, together with the bones of other kings. The monks and nuns of Whitby were satisfied that Trimma's excavations had recovered the bones of a king who had been killed many years before ever their monastery had been founded. Trimma added the detail, as if to persuade the doubters, that he had often seen the spirits of four of those who had been killed in the battle coming in splendid array to visit their own bodies. Even so, it was Bede's opinion that Edwin's head was in St Peter's church at York.

The saint who died in monastery or hermitage presented less of a problem, since the tomb of one who had been eminent for sanctity in life would not be quickly lost to sight and memory after his death, not before a cult could be established or at least encouraged. The decisive mark of sanctity was that the body should be found incorrupt several years after death. St Audrey, after leaving her second husband King Ecgfrith of Northumbria, and going to Coldingham, eventually died at her own foundation in Ely. She was buried in a wooden coffin amid the other nuns in the monastic cemetery, but sixteen years later the abbess decided that her bones should be taken up and placed in a new coffin in the church. When her tomb was opened her body was found to be as incorrupt as on the day on which she died. A doctor who had opened a tumour under her jaw shortly before her death, was called into the tent which had been erected over her remains and within which stood the whole congregation, the brothers on one side, the sisters on the other. He was astonished to see that the gaping wound had healed, leaving only the slightest traces of a scar.

Meanwhile some of the other monks had been sent off to find some suitable blocks of stone for a new coffin. They came back to Ely (by boat) bringing a white marble sarcophagus with a close-fitting lid which they had found among Roman remains at Cambridge. The body was washed, wrapped in new clothes, carried into the church and placed in the marble sarcophagus. St Audrey was more fortunate than Sebbi, a devout king of the East Saxons, whose stone sarcophagus was found to be too short for him by a handsbreadth. By chipping away at the stone, two inches were added to the length, but the body was still too long. The bishop and his monks debated whether they should look for a new coffin to fit the body or bend the body at the knees to fit the coffin. Fortunately for Sebbi while the problem was being discussed the accommodating coffin so changed its shape, that not only was there room for a pillow under the head, there were also four inches to spare at the feet.

If the story of Audrey's translation is somewhat macabre and that of Sebbi's coffin more than a little comical, the poet who told how Ultan the scribe was translated touches other emotions. In life Ultan's skill in shaping letters had been beyond compare, and many years after his death it was decided that his remains should be raised from their grave. The bones were washed and carried out into the sunlight in clean vestments. Suddenly two birds appeared and settled on the vestments, the feathers on their backs shining with variegated colours. Spreading their wings so that they lay over the dead man's skull, they sang joyfully all the day until the sunlight had dried the bones. Late in the day, after a bone from one of Ultan's hands had healed a monk who had been close to death, the assembled brethren carried all the bones into the church and placed them in a tomb which had been prepared for them. Whereupon 'the musical birds mingled with the lofty clouds and kept out of men's sight for ever more.'

It was a common practice for the bones of saints to be elevated some years after their death and put into a shrine. Another case was that of St Chad, abbot of the monastery at Lastingham and at one time bishop among the Northumbrians. At the time of his death he was bishop at Lichfield and his first burial place was the church of St Mary. Some years later he was translated to the new church of St Peter. The place where he was buried was covered over with a wooden shrine made in the shape of a house, and in its side there was an opening through which the devout could insert a hand and take out some of the dust which, being mixed with water, could heal both cattle and men. In Bede's own monastery the bones of two of the abbots, buried originally in separate parts of St Peter's church at Wearmouth, were taken up and placed together in one coffin, with a division down the middle lest they get confused. It seems likely that Bede's own bones were translated centuries before they went to Durham. Some thirty years after his death the abbot of Wearmouth wrote to an Anglo-Saxon missionary bishop in Germany thanking him for the silk robe which he had sent for Bede's relics, as if to suggest that the relics themselves might have been displayed.

We must not suppose that the honouring of the relics of saints or martyrs was in any way a peculiarity of Northumbrian civilisation. In many other lands, and in much earlier times, the burial places of holy men had been marked by the building of shrines which in some cases developed into cathedral churches. Those who read Adamnan's book *On the Holy Places* knew how the Lord's tomb itself had been enriched with marble and enclosed within a circular church, its triple walls divided by broad passages and supported by wondrous columns. Late in the second century the traditional burial place of St Peter, a grave lying within a great Roman cemetery, was marked by a simple shrine, a shrine which developed down the centuries into the St Peter's we know today. In Jerusalem, Rome and elsewhere in western Europe the memorial shrine precedes the church or cathedral which grew above it if the saint commemorated was himself of sufficient stature. In Northumbria the shrine develops within the church. In the cemeteries the graves of some Northumbrian monks and nuns were sometimes marked by small stones carved with a cross and bearing the name of the person commemorated, occasionally with a request for prayers. Sometimes the runic alphabet was used, sometimes the Roman. Several mutilated inscriptions from Whitby suggest that the practice of erecting inscribed stones to mark the graves of the dead was a fairly common one. In some cases it seems that tombs were becoming excessively elaborate, as we may infer from a remark made by Alcuin in a letter which he wrote to an abbess, widow of a Northumbrian king, though we do not know the whereabouts of her monastery. After many injunctions towards a Christian life, he turns upon those who waste their time in thinking about how best to adorn their tombs, condemning them roundly: 'Christ was buried in a cave, not in a temple. I say this because there are some people who build their own tombs while they are still alive.' Alcuin would not have commended the action of a bishop of Lindisfarne who is said to have had a great cross carved in readiness for erection over his tomb after his death. It is to Lindisfarne that we must now return for the most detailed account that we have of the death of a saint and the birth of a cult.

Cuthbert died in his hermitage on the Inner Farne in the year 687 after some weeks of severe illness. His own wish was for burial close by the oratory of his hermitage and it was only with reluctance that he agreed to have his body taken back to Lindisfarne, fearing that its presence might be a future cause of trouble to the monks. Where saints are concerned it is always wise to separate incident from prophetic speeches written by historians. To be thoughtful about the nuisance which one's own bones may cause to their owners is an endearing characteristic of sanctity. More convincing is the account of how the news of Cuthbert's death was conveyed seven miles across the sea by a monk who went on to the high ground and signalled with two torches. The message was seen by those expectantly watching for it and the body was brought back to Lindisfarne. First it was washed, the head wrapped in a cloth and an obley placed on the breast. Next it was robed in priest's vestments, with shoes in readiness for the meeting with Christ and then after being wrapped in a waxed shroud, it was finally buried in a stone sarcophagus in the church of St Peter on the right hand side of the altar.

Eleven years later in 698 it was decided to raise the bones from their tomb. 'And, on first opening the sepulchre, they found a thing marvellous to relate, namely that the whole body was as undecayed as when they had buried it eleven years before. The skin had not decayed nor grown old, nor the sinews become dry, making the body tautly stretched and stiff; but the limbs lay at rest with all the appearance of life and were still moveable at the joints.' Eye witnesses fell short of the extravagant claim made by a very much later writer that the body was still warm to the touch. The body was incorrupt, proof of sanctity established, miracles followed swiftly. A paralysed boy who passed the night wearing the shoes in which Cuthbert had been buried, was cured in the morning.

Cuthbert's body was then wrapped in a new garment and put, not into the original stone sarcophagus, but into a light wooden chest which stood on the floor of the sanctuary where it would be visible to all and there, so far as we know, it remained for nearly two centuries enriched no doubt by the gifts of pilgrims to the shrine. It survived the early Viking raids but when the monks were compelled to abandon Lindisfarne in 875 they took their saint with them and after seven years of wandering—an epic tale told by Symeon, historian of the church of Durham (see below, p. 224)—they settled first at Chester-le-Street, once the site of a Roman fort, and then in 995 at Durham where the relics were at first housed in a small wooden church. In 1104, after the building of the great new Norman cathedral, the coffin was opened and reburied with all solemnity behind the high altar at the east end, under the same roof as the bones of Bede in the Galilee chapel at the west. Cuthbert now possessed his own cathedral, most splendid of all that the Normans built in England, even surpassing St Audrey's at Ely and St Swithun's at Winchester. He rapidly became the patron saint of northern England, the guardian of the English Marches against the Scots—and the legends still grow. Today's visitor to Durham may be told how he shrouded the whole of his city in dense fog on the night when it was to have been shattered by bombs.

The shrine, ever more richly endowed, was destroyed at the orders of Henry VIII's Commissioners in 1542, but the original coffin—the light chest which had stood on the floor of the sanctuary in the church at Lindisfarne—was placed inside a new oak cover and reburied in the chancel. In 1827 it was opened once again and the contents other than the bones were removed to the library of the dean and chapter, once the monks' dormitory, where they may still be seen. Visitors will do well to look closely at the many fragments of wood, shrunken, dried and blackened with age, that survive in pieces large enough at least to let us imagine this light chest, this coffin reliquary, as it was when Cuthbert's body was placed inside it nearly 1,300 years ago. It is unique of its kind, the only substantial carved wooden object to have survived from the whole of Anglo-Saxon England. We may see it as a box, coffin-shaped, a little more than six feet long, with a double lid, and its outer surface covered with figures cut, not in relief, but by incision into the wood. On the outer lid was the figure of Christ, with the symbols of the evangelists at the four corners—Man and Lion, Calf and Eagle. Not many pilgrims, and perhaps even fewer today, will have known of the descent of these four creatures from the four beasts round the throne of heaven in the Revelation of St John the Divine, and from the four creatures in the vision of the prophet Ezekiel. According to Bede's exposition of these figures, the Man symbolised the incarnation, the Calf the humility of God who took upon him human flesh, the Lion represented the courage with which he underwent the pains of death and the Eagle stood for the glory of the resurrection. At the narrower end of the coffin the pilgrim would see the archangels Michael and Gabriel, and at the broader, a representation of the Virgin and Child. Moving to the long sides, he would see on the one hand the twelve apostles, set in two rows in the order in which they are invoked in the canon of the Roman mass, each individual identified by name, St Peter with his keys, St Paul with a beard; and on the other, five more archangels, of whom we can identify Raphael and Uriel. St Cuthbert would surely rest at peace with such protection.

Pagan Saxons were usually accompanied to their grave by some of their personal possessions—weapons or jewellery. It was not thought unseemly for this practice to continue with Christian saints, though not usually for common men, but the objects buried with them were only such as might be attached to their sanctity.

The dead Cuthbert wore beneath his priestly robes the pectoral cross of gold and garnet that he had worn during his life, a cherished possession which surely brought much distress to its owner when one of its arms broke and needed to be repaired and which was so deeply embedded among the robes in which he was wrapped that the monks opening his tomb in 1104 did not find it. On his breast there was laid a small square of oak incised with crosses, such as would have served as a small altar for the celebration of mass. No chalice was found, but one of the kind that Cuthbert might have used has been recovered from the grave of an unknown monk at Hexham, though it may date from later times. Also in the coffin were pieces of fabric, as well as a stole and a maniple, but as at other shrines visitors to this shrine often brought their own gifts, and these ecclesiastical vestments had been made by the ladies of the royal household in Winchester almost two and a half centuries after Cuthbert's death and presented to the shrine by King Æthelstan.

One of the possessions buried with Cuthbert may seem strange to modern eyes. This was a bone comb, not fashioned like a modern comb, but rectangular in shape with a circular hole in the central plate, with larger teeth on one side and smaller on the other. Harps and haloes have been associated by the frivolous with celestial activities, but not combs. Monks may have been bearded, even though they were also tonsured; yet in this age combs were greatly prized possessions and sometimes they were richly decorated, particularly those made of ivory. A comb, moreover, had a liturgical significance, since the combing of the hair formed part of the ritual in the consecration of a bishop, and it may have been thought that Cuthbert might need his comb for some sort of celestial consecration. There was also a belief, not the less to be commended for being ill founded, that by combing his hair a man tidied the brains which lay beneath it. Combs were often sent as gifts. Pope Boniface sent one, of ivory adorned with gold, to King Edwin's consort, as well as a silver mirror. Read what Alcuin writes to the archbishop of Mainz about 790:

I send you as many thanks as the number of teeth I have counted in your gift—a wonderful creature with two heads and sixty teeth, not as big as an elephant, but of beautiful ivory. I have not been frightened by the horror of the creature, but rather delighted by its appearance, though I was afraid that it might bite me with its gnashing teeth. Yet I smiled upon it with gentle flattery to appease the hairs of my head.

Another object of great value to accompany Cuthbert to the next world was an exquisite copy of the Gospel according to St John. Some think that it may have been added a while after Cuthbert's death, for the book was found lying on the inner lid when the coffin was opened in 1104, and we cannot now be quite certain that it was a copy actually used by Cuthbert. The book, which is now preserved in the library of Stonyhurst College still with its original binding, is a miniature written with the greatest care by a master scribe; testimony no less to reverence for the word of God than to the reality of men's belief in the life of the world to come (Plate 11).

The fame of a saint rested in part on his sanctity in life and in part on the miracles achieved by his relics after death, but if that fame was to be more than local, ways had to be found of spreading his reputation far beyond the range of devotees who were within easy reach of the shrine. This could be done either by taking some of the relics—a few bones or a fragment of clothing—to other places where they could be appropriately displayed, or by circulating an account of the saint's life and death. Cuthbert, though never challenged within his own kingdom, was far outstripped geographically by Oswald who won a remarkably far-flung European reputation. The martyr king, the soldier saint, may have had the greater appeal in a warring age. One of the most popular of western saints, Martin, had served for several years in the Roman army fighting along the Danube provinces as well as in Gaul before founding his monastery across the Loire from the ancient city of Tours. The church at Whithorn—the White House—was dedicated to him and the story of his life was widely read in Northumbrian monasteries. But there may have been another reason for Cuthbert's more restricted fame. His body was secured entire at the time of death and thereafter closely guarded. Oswald's, as we have seen, was dismembered on the battlefield and left for the crows. There could be no limit to the number of bones supposedly his—hence the three arms, the two heads and the body yet entire. Cuthbert's reputation was spread abroad not by the dispersal of his bones, but by the writing of an account of his life, first by the monks of Lindisfarne and later by Bede both in verse and in prose. These accounts remain with us to delight no less than to edify, particularly the one written at Lindisfarne, but at the time they were written a part of the saint himself would no doubt have been held to be more efficacious. The story of a saint's life was a guide to good living; one of his bones might cure disease.

Oswald's case was different. Men could read about him in Bede's *History*, but no separate account of his life was written until much later times. Bede relates how a piece of wood on which Oswald's head had been set, found its way to Ireland where it worked miraculous cures. Willibrord, a Northumbrian missionary who was active among the pagans of north-west Germany, had Oswald's name entered in his Calendar for the 5th of August—the Calendar itself is now in the Bibliothèque Nationale in Paris—and he himself had had experience of the miraculous power of Oswald's relics among the Frisians. It was probably through the activities of Willibrord and other Anglo-Saxon missionaries that Oswald's fame spread more widely to Belgium and France, to Germany and Switzerland, even to northern Italy. The cult prospered through the Middle Ages and there are still many European churches dedicated to St Oswald, many which celebrate his festival, many which claim some of his relics. Soon after St Oswald began the travels which took him even as far east as Prague St George was finding his way to Northumbria through, as it were, the backdoor from Iona, perhaps with a passing nod to St Martin at Whithorn.

Oswald won his great victory at Heavenfield in the name of the cross which he had erected on the night before the battle and which was to acquire a particular significance in the history of Christianity in Northumbria. Nowadays we would suppose, no doubt rightly, that the English name 'Heavenfield' was first given to the place some years after Oswald's victory, but this was not Bede's belief. He thought that the name *Cælestis Campus* in Latin had been given to it in days of old as a heavenly omen of things to come. He tells us how the brethren of the church of Hexham, which was not very far away, used to visit the place every year on the eve of St Oswald's feast to keep vigil before the celebration of mass on the following day, and how, more recently, a church had been built there. 'And rightly so,' he says, 'for as far as we know, no symbol of the Christian faith, no church and no altar had been erected in the whole of Bernicia before that new leader of the host, inspired by his devotion to the faith, set up the standard of the holy cross—*sacræ crucis vexillum*—when he was about to fight his most savage enemy.' Oswald's cross, still standing a hundred years later, was itself endowed with such healing virtue that men used to cut splinters from it, mixing them with water which then cured both men and beasts of sickness. The very moss which grew upon it healed a Hexham monk who had fallen while walking on ice one winter's night and suffered a broken arm.

Today's traveller who turns aside to visit the medieval churches within the boundaries of the ancient kingdom of Northumbria, will often find embedded within their walls, or collected in porch or crypt, sculptured stone fragments which once belonged to free-standing stone crosses. From their decoration they seem to range in date over several centuries, yet there are many which belong to what we regard as Northumbria's golden age. They abound in the churches of Yorkshire and Durham, but they may be found as far north as Abercorn on the Firth of Forth, and as far west as Whithorn and Kirkmadrine facing the Irish Sea (Plate 10). Though many of these sculptured stones are no more than small fragments, often used as building material in Norman or later times there are some, and two in particular, which still survive close to their original height. One of these stands in the open air, the weather now its greatest enemy, in the churchyard of the remote borderland village at Bewcastle where Roman camp and medieval castle are further witnesses to unwritten history (Plate 9). The other, overthrown and broken into fragments by the iconoclastic zeal of the seventeenth century, later found sanctuary in a manse garden and is now reverently housed in the church at Ruthwell hard by the northern shore of the Solway Firth. We cannot now tell how many other crosses, like those at Bewcastle and Ruthwell, could have been seen in the Northumbrian countryside, but the surviving fragments are numerous enough to suggest that they may have been a common sight.

The fame attaching to St Oswald's cross, preceding a victory which was itself followed by the Columban mission, is likely to have played an important part in the development of the cult; yet this wooden cross and its many stone successors were no more in themselves than the outward manifestation of a more profound reverence for this universal symbol of the Christian faith. The way in which Bede tells of the Heavenfield cross and of Oswald's victory reminds us, as perhaps it was intended to do, of another occasion of even greater significance for the triumph of Christianity. This was the famous vision of the cross which was seen by Constantine the Great on the eve of the decisive victory at the battle of the Milvian Bridge in 312 which led not only to his own conversion, but also to the adoption of Christianity as the approved religion of the Roman empire. Years after the battle, Constantine told of the vision to Eusebius and his work, originally written in Greek, became familiar in the west in a Latin translation. Bede knew it in the Latin account, and in his own monastery there was a sculptured monument bearing a cross and having also a Latin inscription which referred to Constantine's vision, or dream as some men called it. Furthermore, Bede also knew, and all who read his *History* could learn even if they did not know it before, that Constantine the Great was in York, the place of Edwin's baptism, when he was proclaimed emperor. After Constantine's conversion the standard carried before imperial troops was changed into the form of a cross and under imperial patronage the use of the cross spread rapidly. In later years men read how Helena, mother of Constantine, discovered the true cross itself when she was visiting the Holy Land, how the Persians seized it when they captured Jerusalem, and how it was recovered and returned to Jerusalem by Heraclius. All these stories became well known to the Anglo-Saxons. In Northumbria King Aldfrith and other men of learning read in the book *On the Holy Places* about the silver cross at Golgotha where once the wooden cross had stood, and also about a wooden cross implanted in the river Jordan where the Lord had been baptised.

Yet the learned were few. To the unlearned the cross, plain and unadorned was, like the swastika, the crescent moon or the hammer and sickle in other ages, no more than the symbol of a faith. Enriched with sculpture and written legend, it could embody much that was fundamental to that faith. Most visitors to Bewcastle will easily recognise the figure of Christ, and many will be able to identify those of John the Baptist above and John the Evangelist below, even though the sculptor chose to portray the evangelist's symbolic eagle as a falcon. They will be wise to accept the opinion of today's rune masters who tell us that the long runic inscription has suffered so much from the weather, and the attention of antiquaries, over-eager to scratch away the lichen with sharp knives, that it can no longer be read with any assurance. Fewer among the visitors will recognise the sinuous design of foliage, sometimes to be seen filling the whole of one side of a shaft, sometimes no more than a single panel. This was a pattern at which Northumbrian sculptors excelled. Though formalised and remote from its natural shape, it is yet to be recognised as deriving from the vine. On many of the Northumbrian crosses which carry this motif, birds, or other fantastic creatures of the imagination, peck at the bunches of grapes. The vine never grew in Northumbria, at least not before the days of Capability Brown (himself a Northumbrian) and glass-houses, yet it was a most fitting symbol of one who had said in the words of St John's Gospel: 'I am the vine, ye are the branches; he that abideth in me and I in him, the same bringeth forth much fruit.'

We still argue about the precise date of the Bewcastle cross and its fellows, and we still wonder why the great crosses were erected, some of them in places which nowadays seem so remote from the centres at which Northumbrian churchmen and scholars are known to have lived and worked. Some of them could have been memorials to individuals, some may have been used as preaching stations when churches were few, and some may have been intended like the paintings in the churches at Wearmouth and Jarrow to teach those who could not read. Indeed one cross could well have served all these purposes and more besides. Today we tend to look upon these crosses too much as works of art, in isolation from the doctrinal and theological teaching which they expressed in their own age. In different parts of Northumbria we can find mutilated fragments of once tall crosses portraying the miracle of the marriage feast at Cana, the feeding of the five thousand, the healing of the blind man, the ascension and Christ with the twelve apostles. There are some, too, on which the crucifixion was shown, but this was not commonly portrayed in Bede's age and never with the agonised realism bestowed upon it in the later middle ages.

The Ruthwell cross remains today, despite its mutilation as an 'idolatrous monument', the most remarkable of all in the elaboration of its scriptural scenes, in the splendour of its vine scroll and in the puzzle of its inscriptions which demand of the beholder a knowledge of Latin as well as a primitive form of his native English, and of the runic alphabet as well as the Roman. Runes were used to inscribe upon the cross some lines which seem to have been taken from a vernacular poem in which the cross told its own story from the time when it was a tree in the forest until, after bearing aloft the Lord of heaven and being buried deep in a pit, it became the symbol of creation, honoured among men far and wide across the earth. The cross bears only a few lines of this most original and moving of all Anglo-Saxon poems. That we can still read this poem in its complete form we owe to some unknown traveller, perhaps an English pilgrim to the thresholds of the apostles in Rome, who had it as travelling companion in a book of mixed and varied content which had probably been assembled in Kent. That book now belongs to the cathedral library at Vercelli in northern Italy, a reminder, like the once-desecrated Ruthwell cross itself, of how much we owe to luck for the little that we know about this Northumbrian age.

We cannot say with any certainty who wrote this great poem, now called *The Dream of the Rood*, not even where or when the poet lived, yet we may suppose that something very like it was familiar to those who designed the decoration of the Ruthwell cross. These two monuments, preserved for posterity by chisel and pen, are part, and perhaps the most inspired part, of a deep concern with the supernatural which finds expression in much of the literature of the age. Beyond all question men believed in miracles. The sick were healed by the bones of holy men. Food was provided for travellers in strange deserted lands. Fires were extinguished. The dead were restored to life. No one living in that age would have questioned the reality of the miraculous; not even the great Northumbrian scholars, men such as Bede and Alcuin. Though Bede, demanding in his approach to evidence, told only of miraculous events which had befallen others; he seems to have had no direct experience himself. Our knowledge may be greater, but in many ways our world is no less credulous than his, and we have no claim to doubt his accuracy as a historian simply because, in the very first chapter of the *History*, he countenanced a belief that scrapings from the leaves of Irish manuscripts were efficacious against snake bites. Bede has no marvels to compare with flying-saucers. Despite their condemnation by scholars down the ages, the astrologers flourish as never before. 'Dost see these fellows who own the workshops of deceit, the places where they sell their falsehoods? It is they who marvel all the while at shooting stars and then for a few pence prate of the mysteries in the heavens. They get women into their clutches, bewitch the minds of the common herd, and make their purses ripe for picking.' The invective of Cyril of Alexandria, written in the fifth century, seems not to have lost any of its relevance.

Many, and perhaps most, of the miracle stories which occupy so much space in the writings of the age, are concerned with the cure of physical ills. What else were men to believe in an age when medical knowledge was so slight? How could anyone have understood why some recovered from what we would call pneumonia and some did not, why a crisis once surmounted might be followed by deep and peaceful sleep, why some wounds healed and others led to death from septicaemia? There was a nun in a monastery in Yorkshire, daughter of the abbess. She had fallen grievously ill and had been bled in the arm, but grew worse instead of better, with her arm so swollen that two hands could not encircle it. John, bishop of Hexham, visited her and asked when it was that she had been bled. When he was told that it was on the fourth day of the moon he replied: 'You have acted foolishly and ignorantly to bleed her on the fourth day of the moon; I remember how Archbishop Theodore of blessed memory used to say it was very dangerous to bleed a patient when the moon is waxing and the ocean tide flowing.' The best medical knowledge of the day set store by moon and tide, but knew nothing of germs on a dirty knife. The bishop yielded reluctantly to the entreaties of the girl's mother that he would pray for her, and the girl recovered. So much of life in this age was inexplicable save in terms of the miraculous and of the sometimes kindly help of supernatural beings.

Men knew about the nine orders of angels—there had been ten before Satan and his followers fell from heaven—and angelic visitors frequently appeared to men. Cuthbert was favoured more than once. While still in his boyhood, he suffered from a swollen knee which made him so lame that he could not put his foot to the ground. He had been carried outside to lie by a wall in the warm sun when 'he saw a man of noble appearance and of wondrous beauty, clad in white robes, come riding up to him from afar, upon a magnificently caparisoned horse'. The angel, seemingly better schooled in medicine than Archbishop Theodore, gave him very practical advice: 'You must cook wheat flour with milk and anoint your knee with it while it is hot.' The prescription proved efficacious, as well it might. On another occasion, Cuthbert entertained an angel unawares while he was guest-master at Ripon, and was rewarded with the delicious odour of three newly-baked loaves of bread, though the angelic visitor did not stay to sample them. Angelic digestion became the subject of a nice theological problem, arising from the food which Sarah prepared for the three angels who visited Abraham. Bede supposed that angels did eat, or at least appeared to, but thought it possible to believe that their customary diet was turned instantly into an aetherial substance, just as water was instantly consumed when it was thrown on to a burning flame. Angels were sometimes the means by which souls were conveyed to heaven. Cuthbert, in a setting reminiscent of the shepherds in Palestine, was watching his master's flocks by night in the hills above the Leader Water when he saw an angel carrying a soul to heaven 'as if in a globe of fire'—Aidan's soul as it proved.

St Columba was frequently seen in the presence of angels, whose attendance might on occasion be accompanied by unpleasant consequences if their advice was not promptly heeded. Columba himself was scarred for the rest of his days by an angelic scourge, brought upon him by his refusal to obey a command contained in a book which an angel had given him. Lawrence, one of the Roman missionaries in Kent, was scourged 'long and hard' by St Peter for contemplating flight to Gaul. Birds, though lacking the varied abilities of angels, often served as carriers or messengers between heaven and earth. They came to attend upon the pious at their devotions and then flew upwards carrying the prayers to God. The soul of Paulinus made its heavenward journey in the shape of a beautiful white bird resembling a swan. After Wilfrid's death the noise of birds was heard as they settled above the monastery in which his body was lying and when they later flew away, their wings making sweet melody, men said that it was a band of angels led by the archangel Michael, that had come to take away the bishop's soul. Though angels gave stern and painful rebuke where such rebuke was necessary—cruel only to be kind in the morality of Victorian paterfamilias—they were characteristically white, shining beings, displaying great physical beauty, the apotheosis of short-lived, rheumaticky Anglo-Saxon man.

Devils, by contrast, were black and much given to making loud noises. On one occasion Cuthbert was preaching to some villagers and, foreseeing the approach of the old enemy, warned his listeners to pay particularly close attention to what he was saying. Suddenly the company was disturbed by a crackling of fire and the noise of men shouting, so that most of the audience sprang up and ran quickly to a nearby house apparently in flames. In eager search for a fire that never was, they demolished all its walls before returning in penitence to their preacher. The tale does not tell what the owner of the house thought. There was a hermit called Baldred, a man of high repute to whom Alcuin devoted a long passage in his poem about the saints of York. He lived in a place enclosed on all sides by the billowing sea, where the rocks were steep and rugged. If tradition rightly places his hermitage near St Baldred's Cradle, for which the description is equally apt today, he will have looked across the Firth of Forth to the Bass Rock and the Isle of May and the more distant coast of Fife, on guard against the approach of aerial hosts with whom he waged constant war. One day while he was at his prayers his meditations were interrupted by a fearful roaring and crashing as of hostile attack. Suddenly a soul fell at his feet, tumbling from the clouds in great terror and followed by the fearsome threats of creatures seeking to torment it. The holy man snatched the soul to his bosom and asked it who it was, why it was fleeing and what evil it had done. 'I was once a deacon,' the unhappy soul replied, 'but with evil mind I closely fondled a woman's breasts, and while I was alive in the flesh I was afraid to confess my sin.' The crime seems slight enough in the morality of a different age, but the guilt lay heavy, and for thirty days the unhappy soul had been pursued by devils who could never quite catch it, but would never let it go in peace. Even as Baldred talked with the soul, one of the devils cried out, 'Today thou shalt not escape, not even if thou art held in the arms of Peter.' But the good Baldred won a great victory and rejoiced to see the soul carried triumphantly to heaven by an angelic band. The scene would have been handled well by Hieronymus Bosch, or even Gustave Doré.

We who live in an age increasingly detached from earlier concepts of a future, as against a present, hell, must recognise the fearful realities of hell as they are described in the literature of Bede's age. There was a dissolute Mercian soldier who scorned the efforts of those who sought to persuade him towards a better life. Falling gravely ill, he was visited by two handsome men of whom one sat at his head and the other at his feet. One of them showed him a book, very beautiful, but very small. In it were written the good deeds that he had done 'but they were very few and trifling'. Suddenly the whole house was filled with an army of evil spirits, and the chief among them produced a book 'of enormous size and almost unbearable weight'. We can guess the contents and need follow the tale no further, save to observe that two of the devils stabbed the unhappy man with daggers 'one on the head and the other on the foot. These daggers are now creeping into the interior of my body with great torment and, as soon as they meet, I shall die and, as the devils are all ready to seize me, I shall be dragged down into the dungeons of hell.' And such indeed was the fate of the man who refused the brief moment of penance which might have saved him from everlasting torment.

Bede himself, and some other Northumbrian writers, made a notable contribution to that branch of medieval literature concerned with visions of the other world. The theme is usually presented in the form of a soul leaving the body of a man sick to the point of death and then returning to tell of its experiences, more often of hell than of heaven. The rational may choose to seek an explanation in the delirious sufferings of those gravely ill and with no drugs to ease their torments; certainly the modern self-inflicted counterpart is not far to seek. One of the more curious visions of this kind seems to imply that a second marriage after the death of the first spouse was regarded as sinful. The soul of a man called Merhtheof took flight from his body and found itself, accompanied by the souls of his dead children, before the judgement seat, where Merhtheof was rebuked for having married a second time. The children interceded and all were sent off to visit the first wife who dwelt in a house with lofty walls upon a mountain top. They entered the house where 'from the high-seat, flashing with radiant light, her whole body covered with gold-embroidered robes, the woman reproachfully poured disdain on the doings of her husband'. Again the children interceded and after a narrow escape from being swallowed amid the dark flames the soul was warned to be more careful in the future and then allowed to return to the body. Devotees of old numbers of *Punch* may be reminded of Mrs Caudle's Curtain Lectures. The theme is a strange one, for it was not the doctrine of the day that a second marriage was sinful.

The experiences of Merhtheof's soul were of another order compared with those of the soul of Dryhthelm, a monk of Melrose, whose delight in later years was to immerse himself in wintertime amid the icefloes of the Tweed. When his fellow monks asked him how he could endure such cold, 'he answered them simply, for he was a man of simple wit and fewer words: "I have known it colder."' He had gained his experience from an illness in which he had briefly died, returning to life at the dawning of the next day. The mourners fled in haste when his corpse sat up—all save his wife who loved him dearly. She was but poorly rewarded for her faithfulness, for Dryhthelm left her to enter the monastery at Melrose. In later years he told men of his experiences as he was approaching his final death. Guided by a man of shining countenance he came to a valley, broad, deep and infinitely long. On the left were raging fires and on the right violent storms of hail and ice and snow. On both sides were the souls of men leaping back and forth between the fierce heat and the deadly cold, but this place, he was told, was not hell.

Further on amid growing darkness he came to a great pit from which rose masses of noisome flame. Globes of fire shot upwards and then fell back, and the tips of the flames were filled with human souls, now tossed on high like sparks, now sucked downwards into the depths. An indescribable stench was accompanied by desperate lamentation and fiendish, jeering laughter. Dryhthelm himself was threatened by evil spirits holding fiery tongs, but they scattered and fled as his guide approached. Continuing their journey they came to the top of a high wall beyond which there lay a plain, fragrant with sweet flowers and flooded with light. Companies of people were sitting happily in the meadows, but this place, he was told, was not heaven. Passing onwards, they came to a yet more radiant place filled with the sweetest sounds of song, but as Dryhthelm hoped that they might enter into it, his guide turned and led him back the way he had come. And as they travelled back his guide explained that the first place—of flaming fire and freezing cold—was the place of the souls of those who had delayed confession and restitution until they were on the point of death. They would come to the kingdom of heaven on the day of judgement, and the prayers of those who were still alive, and especially the celebration of masses, would help towards some earlier escape from this purgatory. Beyond it lay the very mouth of hell itself and none who fell therein would ever escape. The first fair and flowery place was where there rested the souls of those who had lived good lives, but were not yet in such a state of perfection that they could be received immediately into heaven. Beyond this, close to where the sweet singing had been heard, lay the kingdom of heaven itself, but this place Dryhthelm's soul had not been allowed to enter. Such were the fourfold divisions of the world to come about which men read in Bede's *History*.

The imaginative detail of Dryhthelm's vision of hell may seem distasteful to some, even though its realities have continued to be outstripped by the self-tormenting genius of each succeeding age. Yet not all of these visions were scorched with the flames of hell fire; there was another, dreamed in that hour of the night when the cock announces the approach of dawn. The dreamer, his guide dressed in shining vestments and radiant of face, was led across a fair plain, rich with the sweet scents of roses, lilies and many flowering herbs. Passing through a gateway in a wall which seemed to reach the sky itself, he entered a wondrous church, its walls of smooth stone, its floors of marble. In its many chapels there were varied altars, some decked with flowers, some with crosses of gleaming gold enriched with precious jewels. As he wandered, he came to an aged man, a man whom he recognised as one of his teachers in earlier years. Behind him on a stool sat another whom the dreamer had known when he was alive, a man renowned for his learning. He moved on through the church, marvelling at the censers of shining gold, the air scented with their smoking incense, looking at the brightly shining waxen lights, at the altars aflame with gold. He came at last to a chair of greatest splendour, enriched with sapphire and beryl, and sitting peacefully upon it, he beheld his former abbot who gave him his blessing. Continuing yet further, the dreamer came to a high place in the church where, amid many glistening vessels of gem-encrusted gold, he came to a table all richly spread. There his old master took a crystal cup and 'drew with his hands the gift of sacred liquid, and gave a drink, which he blessed with pious prayers'. After he had taken the wine, of wondrous flavour, the dreamer awoke, and began to write down all that he had seen.

CHAPTER SEVEN

A Treasury of Words

POETS AND PREACHERS, writers and scholars, hold words among the greatest riches of this earthly life. They are for them as colour for the painter, sound for the musician, movement for the dancer. Men of feeling among the Anglo-Saxons saw them as precious things to be kept securely locked in the treasury of their minds, to be brought out when they were needed and to be put back under lock and key against the time when they might be needed again. The notion is helpful to us who suffer our daily battering of sound and printer's ink, so often signifying nothing, and who seek to understand a distant age to which words came as new riches to be valued no less than the gleaming gold and garnet of newly-fashioned jewels. Boniface made this equation of words with pure gold when he wrote from Germany to an English abbess in Thanet and asked her to send him a copy of the Epistles of St Peter all written in letters of gold so that the pagans to whom he preached might come to a better understanding of their worth. The value of these words, written by the chief of the apostles, was enhanced by the manner of their presentation to those who might look at them without any understanding of what they meant. The scribes gave their skills to each individual letter, progressing thence to word, phrase, sentence and ultimately the apostle's own message. Anyone fortunate enough to hold in his own hands the work of a master scribe of this age will surely sense that scribe's delight in the jewels which he has drawn out of his treasury, even if he cannot read their literal meaning. The delight, and the magic, of letters is caught by the riddler:

Numberless are we, all and each speak we, sounding in concert,
One on his own remains voiceless; black but we play upon
  white fields.
Though we converse upon high things, no sound beats on the
  ear drum;

Speak we the past and the now, foretell many things in the
future.

The silent, dancing symbols of the cinema or television screen are
suddenly stilled into meaning.

The mood has all the fresh charm of the primitive emerging
from barbarism, and herein may lie something of its golden
quality. Yet the romantic must remind himself that the riddle was
perhaps no more than an exercise in that exacting discipline
known to schoolmasters as Latin verse composition, and that in
any case this particular theme had been used by others before the
Jarrow abbot. Yet romantic and cynic alike do well to remember
that, for some at least of the Anglo-Saxons, the proper place to
keep their store of words was in the treasury. We may wonder
what Bede and his fellow-teachers thought as they read in the
Confessions of St Augustine's desire to move his school from
Carthage to Rome where discipline was stricter and students were
not allowed to rush insolently from one lecture-room to another.
Augustine had found the behaviour of the students at Carthage
quite disgraceful. They came charging into their lecture-rooms
like hooligans and upset all the arrangements which had been
made for their benefit by the master. Their reckless behaviour and
the outrages which they committed ought to have been punished
by law, but they were protected by custom.

We who teach in the mid-twentieth century can enter more
easily into Augustine's Carthage than into the schoolrooms of
Whitby or Jarrow, but the contrast is not merely between the
blustering hooligans in the lecture-rooms of Carthage on the one
hand, and the boys, indeed children, in the monastic schools on the
other. If Bede may have been surprised at some of what he read in
Augustine's *Confessions*, Augustine himself would have given poor
marks, perhaps none at all, for the Latin in which a monk of
Whitby wrote a life of Gregory the Great. And consider the
account of his meeting with Faustus, proponent of the Manichean
heresy. He was a man of high repute, but in conversation Augustine soon discovered that although he had some elementary
knowledge of literature he could make no claim to be a scholar.
Some of Cicero's speeches, a little of the work of Seneca, some
poetry and a few other books which had been written by members

of his sect—that was all his reading. What then was scholarship if
this was only elementary knowledge? Entering the schoolrooms of
Northumbria we must remember that Augustine in Carthage,
Cassiodorus in Italy, Sidonius Apollinaris in Provence and Isidore
in Spain were heirs to the learning of the classical age. Latin was
their natural tongue, an ability to read and write their natural
heritage. The Northumbrians were by classical definition barbarians, speaking a barbaric tongue, without books, without Latin
letters, but yet seeing those letters, when they came, as treasures
of great value.

Save for those few who later achieved fame, little is known
about the children of Northumbria. By count of heads we know
them mostly as pathetic skeletons in a monastic cemetery, and we
can be sure that the life-span of many was numbered in months, or
even days, rather than years. Cuthbert as an eight-year-old is said
to have surpassed all others in agility and high spirits. When his
companions had wearied he would stand triumphantly in the
playground. One day he joined some older boys at their play.
Some of them were standing naked 'with their heads turned down
unnaturally towards the ground, their legs stretched out and their
feet lifted up and pointing skywards'—the Latin for 'handstand'
perhaps eluded the author—but the scene remains familiar on
many a playground. This was the occasion when a priggish but
prophetic three-year-old rebuked Cuthbert for behaving in a
manner unseemly for a holy bishop. So far as we know Cuthbert
had no early schooling, but was brought up by a foster mother
from the age of eight until he went to Melrose at about seventeen,
though he had seen some military service. Wilfrid, troubled by a
harsh stepmother, left his home at fourteen and took service with a
nobleman who suffered from paralysis and had taken monastic
vows at Lindisfarne. Although not then himself tonsured, Wilfrid
endeavoured to live the monastic life. We are told that while he
was at Lindisfarne he learnt the whole of the Psalter by heart and
several other books as well. Bede himself was entrusted by his
kinsmen to the monastery at Wearmouth when he was seven.
Hwætbert, the abbot at the time of Bede's death, had also been in
the monastery from his earliest boyhood.

Sometimes a child might be dedicated to God in infancy. A case in point is that of King Oswy who vowed that if he were victorious over his enemy, Penda king of Mercia, 'he would dedicate his daughter to the Lord as a holy virgin'. The victory was won, the vow kept. Ælfflæd, the daughter, scarcely a year old at the time, in later years became abbess of Whitby in succession to Hilda. A mutilated inscription found at Whitby bears upon it the words *ab infant(ia)* and evidently refers to such a dedication, if not of Ælfflæd herself, then of some other. That the practice was not uncommon we may infer from the chapter of the Benedictine Rule which lays down the procedure to be followed by parents wishing to dedicate to the monastic life a child too young to make its own petition for admission. Under the old Roman educational system a child (*infans*) became a boy (*puer*) at the age of seven, and it seems a safe assumption that at least in the larger Northumbrian monasteries—Lindisfarne, Whitby, Wearmouth and Jarrow, Hexham and York—there will have been a number of boys from the age of seven upwards, and perhaps a few even younger. The nuns of Barking in Essex had a three-year-old in their care.

If the Wearmouth cemetery is representative, most boys who reached the age of fourteen had completed half their span of life. Alcuin has these youngsters in mind when he writes to the brethren at Wearmouth and Jarrow, urging them to see that the boys attend divine service and do not spend their time digging foxes out of their holes or coursing hares, for 'he who does not learn when he is young will not teach when he is old'. He urges a bishop of Hexham to make sure that the boys in his monastery are diligently taught. In his old age he writes at greater length to the archbishop of York, anxious that the school at York, of which he himself had been the master, should not fall from its high standards of scholarship. The boys are to be kept apart from the clergy. There are to be separate classes for reading, for singing and for writing. Each class is to have its own master lest the boys should take to wandering about in idleness or waste time playing foolish games. We are ill-informed about the position of young girls in Northumbrian nunneries or double houses of monks and nuns. Some, like Ælfflæd, may have been sent as infants. When Cæsarius, bishop of Arles in the sixth century, drew up a rule for nuns, he enjoined that if possible they should 'never, or at best with difficulty, let little girls be received into the monastery, unless they are six or seven years old, so that they are able to learn their letters and to submit to obedience'. The attitude seems to be one of charity only in cases of need, for he added that the nuns were never to receive the daughters either of the nobility or of common folk to be reared or taught. It is possible that there may have been some young girls in such houses as Coldingham, Hartlepool and Whitby, but we hear more often of women entering monastic life in later years, sometimes as widows or after leaving their husbands.

Alcuin writes of classes at York for reading, singing and writing, and if to these we add grammar and the elements of number, we shall have embraced all the main subjects likely to have been taught to the boys in a monastic school, remembering always that Latin was the language of scholarship and that Latin to a Northumbrian schoolboy was as foreign as Welsh to an English-man. We know something of the way in which such a boy was taught Latin from the Latin grammars of the age which still survive, but how he was taught to read and write we can only guess. There was, of course, no paper. The letters of Gregory the Great to the Roman missionaries were written on papyrus, but the stuff itself was not used in England, unless by the earliest missionaries themselves. Parchment, prepared at its best from calf skin, was too precious for common use. Books were so rare and valuable that we cannot easily envisage a schoolboy being allowed to use one save under the supervision of his master. We may guess, then, that most elementary schooling would consist of learning by heart and of endless repetition in unison. We are told that Cuthbert's memory served him instead of books. We are also told that after learning the whole of the Psalter by heart as a boy at Lindisfarne, Wilfrid learnt a different version of it at Canterbury and that later when he went to Rome he similarly learnt the four Gospels as well as other books.

Psalter and Gospels played the major part in the daily round of prayer and praise which was the essence of monastic life, and we may guess that many boys would come to know much of both by heart even before they could understand their meaning. There is a story of a boy of fourteen who in later years became abbot of Utrecht. Boniface once asked him to read a passage from a book.

He did so, but when Boniface asked him to explain the passage, he began to read it afresh from the beginning, and when Boniface interrupted, the unhappy lad had to admit that he was quite unable to explain in his own language the meaning of the Latin words he had been reading. There may still be some schoolboys who can read the passage from Caesar aloud, but yet fail at the order: 'Now, construe!'

Our best approach to the common objects of daily life in Anglo-Saxon England is often through the riddles. Among the collection which the West Saxon scholar Aldhelm sent to Aldfrith, king of Northumbria, was this:

> Of honey-laden bees I first was born;
> But in the forest grew my outer coat;
> My tough backs came from shoes. An iron point
> In artful windings cuts a fair design,
> And leaves long, twisted furrows, like a plough.
> From heaven unto that field is borne the seed
> Or nourishment, which brings forth generous sheaves
> A thousandfold. Alas, that such a crop,
> A holy harvest, falls before grim war.
>
> (*tr. Pitman*)

The writing tablet with its wax surface, leather base and wooden frame was one of the possessions which a Benedictine monk might, with his abbot's permission, be allowed to keep. Yet even this seems more appropriate to the scriptorium than to the schoolroom, as also the metal stylus used for writing on the wax. The styli found at Whitby are made of bronze, pointed at one end for writing, and spade-shaped at the other for restoring the wax to a smooth surface after use. These waxed tablets, such as Aldhelm describes, were used for taking rough notes. Adamnan, abbot of Iona, tells how he first took down the Gaulish bishop Arculf's account of his travels in the Holy Lands on such tablets before writing it in more permanent form on parchment. But did schoolboys learn to write on these tablets? Or did they perhaps use something simpler, such as a pointed bone on wet clay, or even the slate which the older of us will still remember as their first 'writing paper'?

Returning to the riddles, we find the wax of the writing tablets seen as the image of a field furrowed by the ploughshare, yet receiving no seeds, dispelling darkness, both metaphorically by the words of enlightenment which it holds, and literally by the light which it gives as a wax candle. Tablet and stylus were useful for notes and memoranda. The wax, like the modern tape, could be erased and used again and again. For a permanent record there was parchment whose preparation involved much labour in the drying, stretching and smoothing of individual skins, as well as sizeable herds of cattle. It has been estimated that the parchment used for the *Lichfield Gospels*, when they were complete, would have required the skins of more than one hundred animals. We can easily understand that the production of the parchment required for a scriptorium as active as that at Wearmouth and Jarrow would have amounted to a considerable industry. Presumably the parchment itself will have been prepared by the monks, but we do not know whether the skins came from monastic herds or from the cattle of local farmers. If the sheep, calf or goat provided the best parchment, the bull provided the inkhorn: 'Once a weapon carried on the head of a bull, it becomes a vessel holding within it bitter juices, yet when it belches it gives forth a very pleasant perfume.' For writing, a reed pen may sometimes have been used, but monks who lived by sea or river will never have lacked an abundant supply of quills from goose or swan. An abbot of Jarrow wrote:

In kind simple am I nor gain from anywhere wisdom,
But now each man of wisdom always traces my footsteps.
Habiting now broad earth, high heav'n I formerly wandered;
Though I am seen to be white, I leave black traces behind me.

The white quill-pen, and the black sweet-smelling ink, might trace their letters in one or other of two alphabets, Latin or runic, though for the latter it may be that knife or mason's chisel was the commoner writing implement. We still make discovery today of inscriptions carved during the Roman occupation of Britain, even of cursive script written on tablets. Northern antiquaries of the eighteenth and nineteenth centuries made large collections of inscriptions on stone and we may be sure that in Bede's day they will have been visible in great numbers, especially in the frontier areas and in York. Perhaps it is no more than coincidence that inscribed stones of Anglo-Saxon date (whether the alphabet used was Latin or runic) are very much more common in the military zone of northern Britain, from York and Lancaster to the Hadrianic Wall, than they are anywhere else in the country. It may be that Romano-British inscriptions on buildings or tombstones had some influence in producing, for example, the dedication stone of St Paul's church at Jarrow or the mural epitaphs at Whitby.

Even so, the common bookhands—the hands that would be taught to boys in the schoolroom—were undoubtedly themselves derived from books brought from elsewhere, either from the Mediterranean or from centres of Celtic monasticism. The stone-mason working with a chisel prefers straight lines, meeting where possible at right-angles; the scribe with his quill pen finds a curving line more natural and pleasing. From the Mediterranean, in the form of old books, there came to Northumbria that hand of stately beauty that we call uncial. The letters are each formed individually, with smoothly rounded bows and strong contrast of line flowing from the varying angle of broad-cut quill. Already an antique hand in Mediterranean lands, uncial, and its cousin the half-uncial, was developed in Northumbria to that pitch of beauty that we can see in the *Stonyhurst Gospel* (Plate 11), the *Codex Amiatinus* and the *Lindisfarne Gospels*, and whose like we cannot find again among English scribes until the revival of italic script. But these three manuscripts, and others written in the same style of hand, were intended by displaying the art of the scribe at its noblest to honour the scriptures which they contained. We may think of them as we think today of books from the Kelmscott Press, books of beauty, books to be treasured. As a living hand Northumbrian uncial had a short life since there was no way in which it could develop. Contemporary with it was the common bookhand known as insular minuscule—less formal, approaching but not quite reaching cursive, it was both easier and quicker to write. It depended little upon scribal quirks or conceits, and it remains today to offer an easy task to the reader who troubles to master the small number of shorthand abbreviations. This minuscule, we may suppose, was the 'copperplate' of Bede's schoolroom (Plate 12).

Speak to anyone of runes and he will fly at once on his mental broomstick to a magic world that never was, there to stick pins into a wax-doll. The runic alphabet was, like the Latin, Greek and Arabic alphabets, neither more nor less than an alphabet used for purposes of writing. If, on occasion, runic letters could be used for magical purposes, so also could the letters of the Latin alphabet. Most surviving Northumbrian runes are found as inscriptions cut on stones. Several of these are simple memorial stones bearing a single name such as those from the cemetery at Hartlepool. A larger inscription, now mostly illegible, is found on the Bewcastle cross, and on its fellow at Ruthwell are some lines from a vernacular poem. A bone comb from Whitby bears runes which seem to signify a mark of ownership, and runes are used for the names of evangelists on the wooden lid of the coffin in which Cuthbert's relics were placed. There are no runic texts in any surviving manuscript of Bede's age and, so far as we know, the runic alphabet was used only for short texts, not for long works.

The individual letters of the Anglo-Saxon runic alphabet in its pure form are entirely composed of vertical or diagonal lines, with no horizontals and no curves. An alphabet of this kind was well-suited for incision on wood, with the cuts running across the grain, and this has led some scholars to suspect that it may have been much more widely used for simple messages than might be inferred from the relatively small number of surviving inscriptions on wood. The excavation of one waterlogged site, in the medieval quarter of Bergen in Norway, yielded more than five hundred objects bearing runes, many of them wooden. They include not only lovers' messages and scraps of verse, but also merchants' letters dealing with business transactions. This remarkable find, almost doubling the previous total of runic inscriptions known from the whole of Norway, may lead us to wonder whether a knife, a piece of stick and the runic alphabet were a more familiar means of communication in Bede's Northumbria than we have hitherto supposed. There is an Anglo-Saxon poem, of later times, in which a message is carried between a lord and his lady on a piece of wood. Such objects would have slight chances of survival except in conditions like those prevailing near the Bergen waterfront.

We may suppose that most of the boys in the schools at Jarrow, Hexham and York would be taught to write, even though few would become scribes. One scribe known to us by name was an Irishman, called Ultan, and of him it was said that he 'made the shape of the letters beautiful one by one, so that no modern scribe could equal him'. There are some who think that the whole of the *Lindisfarne Gospels*, illuminations and text alike, was the work of one man, himself the bishop of Lindisfarne. Sometimes a long work was indeed written by a single scribe. Such was the case with the manuscript of Bede's *History* which King George I presented to the University Library at Cambridge. He was a scribe writing in a hurry, making mistakes, running his words together, spilling over into the margins, a man under pressure, eager to save space. More often a piece of work would be shared among several scribes whose hands, though writing a common script, are distinctive enough for separate recognition. An example of such a work is offered by another manuscript of Bede's *History* which an eighteenth-century Russian diplomat took from Paris to Russia and which is now housed in Leningrad. The words are separated, there is a modicum of punctuation, each page has two columns, there are one or two ornamental initials; a manuscript written with care and providing an accurate text.

Nowadays a parson may write his sermons by hand, a lecturer his notes, but he will not expect anyone save himself to be able to read them. In Bede's age it was of the first importance that a book written by hand should be easily legible by anyone who had been taught to read. In the Preface to his *History* he writes of 'the thoughtful listener', of 'the devout and earnest listener or reader', of 'those who listen to or read this *History*'. His conception of a book is not of something which men will normally read to themselves in silence, though this would sometimes happen, but of something which will be read aloud to a listening audience. A book, then, was certainly and primarily a work of instruction, but it was also a work of entertainment which demanded narrative power in its author and dramatic qualities in its details so that its audience might be held. Such a book was the *Life* which Eddius wrote of Wilfrid, full of stirring incident and dramatic settings. Where in Bede's country today could we find an audience capable of understanding his *History* if it was read aloud to them in Latin? Perhaps only now, and probably only then, in a monastery.

The importance of reading was recognised by the inclusion of the office of *lector* among the minor orders of the Church. The *lector*, as we may learn from Isidore of Seville, was not merely someone who read a book aloud, the medieval equivalent of radio's 'Book at Bedtime' soporific. Since so much of what was read came directly from the Bible or from commentaries upon it, he was regarded as announcing or preaching the Word of God. His voice must be clear and virile, not sounding like the voice of a woman. He must be sure that his appeal was to the ear of those who listened, not to the eye of those who watched. He must avoid the mistakes of inexperienced readers who could falsify the meaning of a particular passage by a wrong stress or a misplaced pause. We may recall a modern church tower with an inscription running round its four sides and so spaced that the visitor reads on one face 'Heaven and Earth are Full', and we may wonder what were the other hazards which brought blushes to the cheeks of nervous lectors. As a help to such readers, manuscripts were sometimes written in double columns with very short lines, each containing perhaps no more than three or four words grouped as nearly as possible to form phrases.

Visitors to Durham, wandering through the cathedral precincts or meditating in the cloisters, may often hear the song of the choristers against the harsher notes of the jackdaws in the great towers. Where so much that is beautiful of painting, sculpture and literature has survived from Bede's age, we cannot but feel sad that all its music has been lost beyond the possibility of its recovery. Pictures of David in manuscripts, of which we may see one from the eighth century in the library of the dean and chapter at Durham, sometimes show him plucking a stringed instrument. There is another in the British Museum that comes from explicunt Capitula.

At Intfato Inpugnae eoumoị
puincia illeȝōn ȝ̄rr propria
filiuspatruis aelfrici uocab
linif: ioȝ ȝ̄ratsacram ōrtir Inbırtar
hardua ypuinciar ȝōn nordan hị
cōpıtfiluraedilfridi qui deillaȝ
dıxȝ̄rat nomine eanfrid. sıḡdōn tōn
filni p̄fatı̄r ȝ̄raedilfridi quiam
nobilium luuōrate apud protcori
docơmam protcori ōath ōrpatı @
Quı uōmoptuor ȝ̄elnimı̄ co pat̄r
mur eor quōn dıximur eanfrid yı̄
tōr ōn ręȝni Insular yortturẹỵ
Inttatur ȝ̄rat anathōnattzandoị
yordıb. pollučhdum ydōhdum qị
brōtonum ceadualla Impıamar

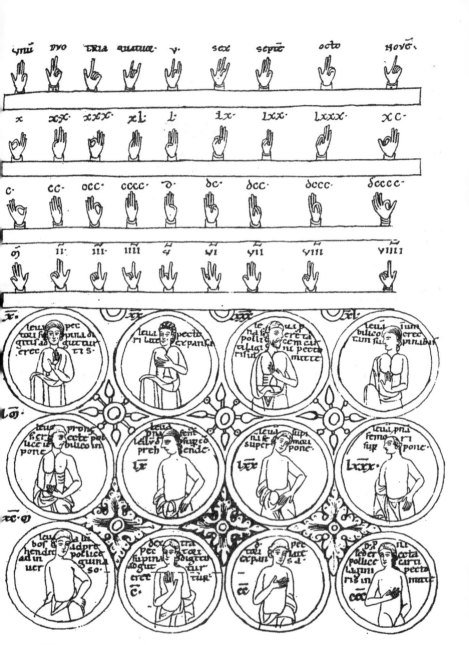

13 Finger Counting: from a manuscript of Bede's *De Temporum Ratione*

Canterbury. We are all familiar with the story of Cædmon who watched with increasing apprehension as the harp was handed from one to the other of his companions at table, and left the room before his own turn came to entertain. Among the discoveries at Sutton Hoo were the remains of a small musical instrument with six strings. The fragments themselves, with the remains of similar instruments from a grave in Buckinghamshire and others in Germany, have enabled a reconstruction to be made, not of a harp, but of a lyre. In the hands of a skilled musician this instrument is capable of a wide range of expression with a surprising degree of resonance.

Shortly after Bede's death, there was a harp or lyre of some sort in his monastery, but unhappily nobody knew how to play it, and the abbot, shyly hesitant, concluded a long letter to an English missionary in Germany with a request that he would send someone who could. 'I beg that you will not scorn my request nor think it laughable.' It would be pleasant to think that there was a teacher ready to make the long journey, but the records are silent. We have no direct evidence of any other musical instruments from Northumbria, though we might have expected trumpets and bells, if no more. Aldhelm (Bede's older contemporary, but a West Saxon) has been taken to be riddling upon an organ when he writes:

> Buglers may blow curved horns of hollow brass,
> And harps twang loud, and noisy trumpets blare,
> But from my vitals burst a hundred strains;
> My mighty voice makes mute the sounding strings.
>
> (*tr. Pitman*)

Whatever the instruments, there can be no doubt that singing—the Psalms and some hymns—played a very important part in the daily round of monastic life and that a great deal of time was devoted to this art. We recall Alcuin's insistence that there should be separate classes for reading, for writing and for singing. James the Deacon taught the Roman chant in Northumbria after Paulinus had returned to Kent, Wilfrid brought two singing masters from Kent to Northumbria, Acca was renowned as a singer at Hexham and found a new teacher when standards were falling, Wearmouth received as visitor none other than the chief cantor of St Peter's church in Rome. Antiphonal singing with double choirs was well established in the Northumbrian church. One of the great difficulties faced by the singers of this age was that there was no system of musical notation. As Isidore wrote; 'Unless the sounds are retained in man's memory, they perish because they cannot be written down.'

A story in Bede's *History* shows us a glimpse of the way in which boys were taught to read. The scene is an oratory about a mile and a half from Hexham, perhaps where Warden now lies. In Bede's time the oratory was dedicated to St Michael, as is Warden church today, with some of its fabric of Anglo-Saxon date. To this place John of Hexham used to retreat, and while he was there he was visited by a youth who was dumb. Let Bede tell the rest of the story:

> On the second Sunday in Lent, he ordered the poor man to come in to him and then he told him to put out his tongue and show it him. Thereupon he took him by the chin and made a sign of the holy cross on his tongue; after this he told him to put his tongue in again and say something. 'Say some word,' he said, 'say *gæ*', which in English is the word of assent and agreement, that is, yes. He said at once what the bishop told him to say, the bonds of his tongue being unloosed. The bishop then added the names of the letters: 'Say "A",' and he said it. 'Say "B",' and he said that too. When he had repeated the names of the letters after the bishop, the latter added syllables and words for the youth to repeat after him. When he had repeated them all, one after the other, the bishop taught him to say longer sentences which he did.

> (*tr. Colgrave*)

We seem close enough to the schools of yesteryear. Daily repetition of the *Pater Noster* and the *Credo*, the chanting of the Psalms and all the other elements of the liturgy would quickly give familiarity with at least the sounds, if not always the meaning, of the Latin words, yet for those who were expected to master the language, there was no escape from grammar. The late imperial

equivalent of Kennedy's Latin Grammar was the *Ars Grammatica* of
Ælius Donatus. Indeed so long and widely was his grammar used
that, like Cardigan and Macintosh, Wellington and Macadam, his
own name was transferred to the object associated with him. A
'Donatus' meant 'a Latin grammar', and a 'Donatus Anglice' an
'English grammar'. Those who learnt their Latin grammar from
Kennedy were luckier than Bede, in that Kennedy was at least
written in English, whereas the grammar used by Bede, and all
other schoolboys of his times, will have been written entirely in
Latin. The direct method of language teaching is not so new as
some may suppose.

Bede himself, as a teacher, may have written his own Latin
grammar for use in his school, though none has survived and he does
not mention such a work in his list of his writings. Some Anglo-
Saxons did write Latin grammars, perhaps because an English boy
would face difficulties different from those confronting his Spanish
or Italian contemporaries. One such grammar was written by a
Mercian priest called Tatwine who became archbishop of
Canterbury and died the year before Bede. A pupil who used this
grammar would have found it divided into eight sections dealing
respectively with nouns, pronouns, verbs, adverbs, participles,
conjunctions, prepositions and interjections. As an example of the
kind of material which he had to learn, we may take a short
passage from the section dealing with the noun. We read here (in
Latin of course):

> Everything designated by the word 'noun' is either a solid
> substance (*corpus*) or pertaining to such a substance (*corporale*) or
> lacking such substance (*incorporale*); a substance is something that
> can be felt and seen like 'earth'; what pertains to such a substance
> can be felt but not seen, like 'wind'; what lacks such substance
> can be neither felt nor seen, like 'wisdom'.

From such materials pupils would pass on to matters of gender,
case, number and several other aspects of the noun. There can be
no doubt that the task was hard, the discipline exact. The easy
fluent Latin written by Bede and his contemporaries was the
reward for many years of schoolroom grind.

Yet for some at least the task was not all grind. Words, we recall, were kept in the treasury. They were precious, but they could do strange things. Consider the oft-heard 'Alleluia'. The father of Edwin, first Christian king of Northumbria, was called Ælli —remove the 'e' and put it in place of the 'i' and we have *alle*, the English for 'all', and did not Christ say, 'Come unto me *all* ye that labour and are heavy laden'? And take Edwin's own name —written Eadwine and pronounced with three syllables— which surely signified the mystery of the Trinity. This fascination with playing upon words, new-found toys, finds its most familiar expression in the puns attributed to Gregory the Great who supposedly met some youths of Anglian race from the kingdom of Deira which was ruled by Ælle, causing Gregory to rejoice with Alleluias that these young men—more like Angels than Angles—might yet be rescued *De Ira Dei*. Whether Gregory would have been ready to accept the authorship of these puns is questionable. So also with the occasion when he himself had set out from Rome towards England. After three days a locust (*locusta*) settled on his book. He took the message—*Sta in loco*—and stayed where he was, until messengers from Rome caught up with him and summoned him back.

The scribblings and the trivialities of schoolroom and scriptorium have naturally perished, but those who delighted in riddles, puns and the intricacies of interwoven patterns on stone as well as parchment, are likely enough to have indulged in other forms of word play. Good tradition associates the West Saxon Boniface with the introduction of different forms of secret writing to his monastic foundation at Fulda in Germany. Boniface, called Bonifatius in Latin, could have disguised his name in the simplest of codes as:

B :: N . F : T . :·: S

where five patterns of dots are correlated with the five vowels. A variant of this simple device was the use of the next following consonant in place of each vowel, yielding:

B P N K F B T K X S.

A third method was to use an abbreviated version of the first five ordinal numbers for the five vowels, yielding:

BQUARNTERFPRITTERQUINS.

The result is not immediately recognisable and the method seems rather extravagant of space. Yet there was an Anglo-Saxon nun who did use this last method to disguise her authorship of the lives of two Anglo-Saxon missionaries, calling herself:

HQUINGSECDBQUINRC.

Her proper name was Hugeburc. We may prefer the simpler charm of Acton and Currer Bell to these Brobdignagian contortions. No such Northumbrian codes now survive, but it would be surprising if the scholars, or at least the schoolboys, of York did not sometimes indulge in such frivolities. Bede himself was far from scorning exercises in verbal gymnastics. One such, a hymn in praise of virginity, he included in his *History*. The hymn was composed in elegiac couplets and in each couplet the first part of the first line is repeated as the last part of the second line, and as if this were not ingenious enough, the opening letter of each couplet forms a complete alphabet from A to Z. The first two and the last two couplets read thus in an English translation which preserves the form of the Latin original:

> All-bounteous Three in One, Lord of all time,
>   Bless mine emprise, all-bounteous Three in One.
> Battle be Maro's theme, sweet peace be mine;
>   Christ's gifts for me, battle be Maro's theme.
>
> Yields to those holy weeds each frightful plague;
>   Disease aghast yields to those holy weeds.
> Zeal frenzied tears the foes that conquered Eve;
>   Triumphs the saint, zeal frenzied tears the foes.
>   (*Tr. Colgrave*)

This curious piece has as *envoie* another four couplets whose initial letters spell A M E N. The genre was familiar to its age, akin to that 'Austrian army awfully arrayed (that)/Boldly by battery besiegèd Belgrade'.

Letters were the foundation, the means by which men could learn the thoughts of others long dead and pass on their own thoughts to others far distant or yet unborn, but there were some for whom knowledge and understanding was to be found in number. Isidore of Seville could write, in a much-quoted passage: 'Take away number in all things and all things perish.' Number was constant in a seemingly fickle world, and perhaps herein lay its appeal for those who sought the unchanging eternals. How was this subject presented to pupils in the monastic schools? Number seemed to be of such fundamental importance to Bede that he devoted the whole of the first chapter of the larger of his two works on chronology to this subject. He entitled the chapter, 'On Counting or Talking with your Fingers'. Children, and some others not adept at figures, still count on their fingers, and children, as well as the deaf and dumb, still use their fingers for an alphabet. Yet today's method of counting on the fingers, simple and obvious though it seems, was not the method used in Bede's schoolroom.

Finger-counting, or the *computus digitalis* as the would-be learned may like to call it, has a long history stemming from the classical and late antique worlds and reaching to the Middle Ages. The system familiar to Bede begins thus: 'To say one you bend the little finger of the left hand and place it in the central part of the palm. To say two you bend the finger next to the little finger and place it similarly. To say three you put the next finger in the same position.' So far all is simple, but then comes the unexpected. 'To say four you raise the little finger and to say five you similarly raise the one next to it.' As the illustration will show, the antique method of expressing five with the fingers was to our eyes much more difficult than the modern (Plate 13). Bede continues with a detailed description of how to show the other numbers up to nine, followed by the tens up to ninety-nine. All the figures from one to ninety-nine were expressed with the left hand, with one hundred the right hand was used, and by repeating with the fingers of the right hand the signs for the 'tens', given on the left, one achieved the numbers from one hundred to nine hundred. For example the sign for twenty on the left hand—placing the top of the thumb between the junction of the forefinger and the middle finger—signified two hundred when it was made with the right hand. The system continues through the thousands—to say ten thousand you place the left hand flat in the middle of the chest with the fingers turned upwards towards the neck—as far as one million, expressed by clasping both hands together with the fingers interwoven alternately.

A method so complicated as this is not very easy to follow, even from a modern printed edition of Bede's text, and we shall certainly be right in thinking that the pupils would learn to use it directly by following the actions of a teacher who knew the system well. But other methods were also used. Several of the museums of western Europe possess numbers of circular discs made of bone or ivory, somewhat resembling the pieces used for the game of draughts, though a little smaller. On one side they show a hand with the fingers held in such a position that they represent the number (in the Latin form) shown on the other. Such discs or counters would be an excellent means of helping pupils to associate the number with the appropriate position of the fingers. In addition to these, several manuscripts have drawings either of complete human figures or of hands alone with the fingers appropriately placed for the different numbers.

The method of speaking with the fingers was quite simply to correlate the letters of the alphabet with the signs for the numbers from one onwards. Today's schoolboys—or at least yesterday's—used to call '*kayvee*' (before they learnt to spell it *Cave*) on the unwelcome approach of a master who threatened to interrupt some illicit activity. Bede told his own pupils how to do the same, perhaps sensing that a little light relief would be welcome at the end of a rather difficult first chapter. 'If a friend of yours is placed among enemies and you want to warn him to be careful, make the finger signs for the numbers three, one, twenty, nineteen and five, and for one, seven and five, and this will mean, "Be careful" (*Caute age*).' There may well have been occasions of real danger when the ability to convey a secret message with the fingers would have been a valuable accomplishment. But at other times, as Bede points out, a schoolboy could enjoy himself, at the expense of his less knowledgeable companions, by sending a message to someone standing far away from him and so gaining for himself a reputation for wizardry. Behind these severe Latin texts, now seeming so forbidding in their appearance that not many read them, we can still see the boys playing tricks on their fellows (with Bede's evident approval), or at other times running off to dig out foxes or course hares with their dogs.

Man's fascination with number is most strikingly revealed in the development of number symbolism, a notion whose origins lie in the remote past. There was something that might be said about virtually every number. One enjoyed the position of principle of numbers because it had neither middle nor end, but only beginning. Uneven numbers were good, even numbers bad, the reasoning being that two is evil because it moves from unity towards multiplicity. Six was a perfect number because it is composed of the sum of its parts, a sixth being one, a third being two, a half being three, and these added together bring us back to six. No other number in the units behaved in this way, and its perfection became related to the six days of creation and to the six ages of the world. Seven had a great many qualities: it represented the day of rest after the creation; the seventh age was when the saints would pass from earth to heaven; and there were the seven gifts of the spirit.

We can see the application of some of this number symbolism, taken to considerable extremes, in Bede's account of the flood. Noah's age was six hundred at the time of the flood and this was made up of six—the days of creation—multiplied by one hundred whose special quality consisted in the fact that when men used finger counting they passed from the left hand to the right hand when the number one hundred was reached; and men knew well enough the Biblical significance attaching to the distinction between those on the left hand and those on the right hand. Sinister still carries its connotation of evil. The forty days of the flood represented the ten commandments multiplied by the four gospels. The ark itself came to rest in the seventh month on the twenty-seventh day, and this latter number enjoyed the distinction of being the cube of three—a simple three itself was no more than a straight line, but when multiplied by itself it achieved squareness, and when cubed it achieved depth and solidity; so representing the perfection of faith. And so we might continue; ourselves feeling something of the fascination. There are still with us those who like to foretell the future from the measurements of the great pyramid; but others may wonder why it was that a man of such great scholarship as Bede indulged so extensively in this kind of symbolical elaboration. Yet it is not difficult for us to understand why men came to be fascinated with something that seemed to behave according to unchanging rules in an age when all else was subject to such rapid change and decay, a theme to which Anglo-Saxon poets constantly returned. Number could be seen to have about it a quality of permanence which it shared with God, and there may have been those who in search of the eternal found some comfort in this thought.

Reading, writing, counting and singing; these, with much time spent on Latin grammar, were the labours which turned some at least of the schoolboys in Northumbrian monasteries into scholars of distinction, with Bede and Alcuin as the giants among them. Pupils would pass from these fundamentals to more advanced topics—metrical composition in all its varieties, astronomy and the mathematics needed for mastery of lunar and solar cycles, natural philosophy, rhetoric and law, a widening knowledge of Latin enabling men to correspond easily in the language and eventually to appreciate the works of such as Cicero, Virgil and Boethius when copies reached them. A few, Bede among them, may have learnt a little Greek.

We can only guess at much else that we would gladly know about the schoolrooms. What part, we may ask, was played by the vernacular English? We are told that Bede was familiar with English poetry. We know that the scholars of Whitby produced, through Cædmon, a large body of vernacular religious verse, but if there was any vernacular literature dealing with secular themes, none has survived, though scenes on the Franks Casket, as well as Alcuin's rebuke to the monks of Lindisfarne for listening to such pagan tales, hint at its former existence. A favourite method of teaching in medieval schools was by means of the Colloquy or Disputation between master and pupil. Again no examples survive from any Northumbrian schools. Perhaps the nearest approach we can make is through the Latin Disputation between Alcuin and the young Pippin, of which a part runs thus:

Alcuin: A certain man unknown spoke with me without tongue or voice, a man who never was before, nor will be afterwards, and whom I neither heard nor knew.

Pippin: Did a dream trouble thee master?

Alcuin: I have seen the dead create the living and the dead were consumed by the breath of the living.

Pippin: From the rubbing of sticks fire is born and the fire consumes the sticks.

Alcuin had once been master of the school at York. He, no less than his pupils, delighted in drawing riddling words from the treasury of his mind.

CHAPTER EIGHT

He could ornament Books with fair Marking

Living within my shell I used to be clothed and protected.
No food then did I taste; my eyes were totally sightless.
I find my food in the pastures now that I'm stripped of my
  vestment,
Though I had no life when I left the womb of my mother.

THE RIDDLE, ONE of those composed by Abbot Hwætbert,
affords adequate excuse for evading the ancient conundrum about
the priority of chicken and egg, as we turn away from the
schoolboys declining nouns and counting with their fingers,
towards the scholars by whom the schools were established. If we
seek to learn how it came about that a small band of men of
barbarian ancestry, handicapped in almost every imaginable way,
contrived to turn themselves into scholars of a stature unrivalled in
their age, we shall in the end find ourselves filled more with
wonder at their achievement than with knowledge of how it was
done. We shall find it difficult to imagine the impact of these new
things called books upon Northumbrian society in the seventh
century. No doubt men marvelled at the new skills which enabled
architects to build fine churches of white stone, enriched with
sculpture, coloured glass and paintings. This we can understand.
But can we imagine what it was like when intelligent men in
Northumbria first discovered that in written books they could
learn about the deeds, the thoughts, the teaching of others who had
lived in distant lands and in ages long past? The sudden, infinite
enlargement of man's capacity for acquiring knowledge now
seems to lie beyond our comprehension.

There are many questions that we need to ask. How in the
conditions of this age did you create a library? Where did you find
the books? What sort of books were they? By whom had they been
written, and when? And after acquiring adequate knowledge,

what sort of books did you want to write yourself? Who would read them? And how many of them have survived into our own times? We shall try to find answers to some of these questions, but before doing so we might be wise at the outset to remind ourselves how recent had been the overthrow of the western empire by unlettered barbarian peoples whose arrival in Britain, Gaul, the German provinces and even Spain had been accompanied by much destruction. So far as we know literacy was totally destroyed in all those parts of Britain which were heavily occupied by the Anglo-Saxons during the fifth and sixth centuries. Doubtless there had been books in Roman London, Roman York and many other towns, but papyrus is fragile material and no British book has survived from that age. We have only inscriptions, mostly on stone, a few on metal, and that rare treasure of documents, preserved by lucky accident and compressed bracken, on the floor of a room at the abandoned Roman site at Vindolanda, not far from Hadrian's Wall. Some books, notably books of the Bible, may have travelled westwards, but in eastern Britain the currency of literacy, like the currency of money, ceased.

Augustine reached England a few years before 600 to preach to a people among whom paganism was deeply rooted, and the work of eradication was far from being completed even by the middle of the seventh century. Yet, before the end of that century had been reached, there were English men and women who were writing fluent Latin, there were some in Kent who were said to be as familiar with Greek as they were with their own native English, and English monasteries were nurturing scholars whose achievements could rank among the greatest of the European middle ages. The suddenness of the change from destructive barbarism to creative literacy, from the pagan Penda to the scholarly Aldfrith, is one of the most remarkable aspects of this age. With time past somewhat foreshortened, we seem at one moment to have little else to contemplate save those crudely made clay urns, the 'sad sepulchral pitchers' in which many of the Saxon dead had the misfortune to be buried, albeit after their bones had first been reduced to ashes. For the inspiration which they gave to Sir Thomas Browne we may forgive their makers, and then turn away to contemplate monastic libraries filled with books which were read, and had sometimes been written, by English scholars.

The first steps towards the transformation were taken by the missionaries who came from Rome to Canterbury and from Iona to Lindisfarne. Augustine and his companions, likewise Aidan and his, would bring with them at least those books that were necessary for Christian teaching in its most elementary form. We know from Bede that a second group of Italian missionaries, arriving a few years after Augustine, brought a great many books—*codices plurimos*—with them, but no one has told us what books they were. Now in the care of the librarian of Corpus Christi College at Cambridge, among the many notable books presented to that college by Archbishop Matthew Parker, there is an incomplete copy of the Gospels which is written in a hand claimed by palaeographers to stem from a Mediterranean country, probably Italy itself, and to date from the sixth century. There is a good Canterbury tradition that this copy of the Gospels had once belonged to Augustine himself. Another good tradition tells that Augustine brought with him a copy of a work which came to be widely read in England. Bede was familiar with it and commended it to others for frequent reading. This was Gregory the Great's own book *On Pastoral Care*. Of the books which Aidan brought to Lindisfarne or those which were used by James the Deacon we know nothing at all, but at the very least they will have included copies of the Gospels and of the Psalter.

Outside Canterbury the earliest signs of a growing interest in learning come rather surprisingly from East Anglia. A king called Sigebert began to reign here *c.* 630, three years after the conversion of Edwin of Northumbria. Sigebert had passed a time of exile in Gaul and while he was there he had been baptised. When he returned to his own kingdom 'he at once sought to imitate some of the excellent institutions which he had seen in Gaul, and established a school where boys could be taught letters, with the help of Bishop Felix, who had come to him from Kent and who supplied him with teachers and masters after the manner in Kent.' Sigebert is described as a man very learned in all things, perhaps a forerunner of Northumbria's Aldfrith, but we know nothing of the books which he read nor even the location of the school which he founded. Soon after his death the daughters of another East Anglian king were attracted to Gaul by the high reputation of nunneries where they were able to get the kind of education which they could not find in England. Hilda herself had wanted to go as well. There are scattered hints that more was afoot in East Anglia than we have commonly supposed. It may be that we undervalue both the achievements of East Anglian scholars and the importance of Gaulish intellectual influences.

We are less likely to underestimate Irish influences on English, and more particularly Northumbrian, scholarship. There is a familiar passage in Bede's *History* : 'At this time, in the days of Finan and Colman the bishops, there were many people there of English race, nobles as well as lesser men, who left their island home and went to Ireland either for the sake of Scriptural studies or for a more rigorous way of life. And indeed some of them presently gave themselves faithfully to the monastic way of life, while others, choosing rather to visit the cells of teachers, rejoiced in devoting themselves to the tasks of study. All the Irish welcomed them most gladly, giving them their daily food without any charge and also freely providing them with books for reading and with instruction.' It would be easy enough to compile a long list of those who went in search of learning among the Irish, whose influence extended widely over England as well as Gaul and other countries.

Fresh impetus came from outside with the arrival of Theodore as archbishop of Canterbury in 669. Himself a man of great learning and the mature wisdom of old age—he was sixty-nine when he reached Canterbury—he was accompanied by another learned man, Hadrian, a monk from North Africa. Let us listen again to what Bede has to say: 'And because they were both, as we have said, men abundantly taught in sacred and secular letters, each day they used to pour forth streams of saving knowledge to water the hearts of the assembled concourse of students, seeking thus to give their hearers instruction in the arts of metre, astronomy, and ecclesiastical computation while they studied the books of holy scripture. As evidence of this there are some of their students even to this day who know the Latin and Greek languages as well as their own tongue spoken since birth. Never since the English first sought out Britain had there been happier times.' Here surely was an age of gold when all who wished to be taught could find teachers ready to hand, yet let us remember that when Theodore arrived in England Bede was not yet born and that when Theodore died Bede was only about seventeen years old.

Meanwhile from a school at Malmesbury, founded originally by an Irish scholar, there emerged a remarkable West Saxon man of learning, Aldhelm. Two of his letters enliven for us the rapidly changing scene. In one of them he welcomes the return to England of a friend who had studied in Ireland for six years. Praise of his scholarship, Aldhelm writes, rolls like thunder in the ears of the English—the scholars are travelling back and forth between Ireland and England carrying their knowledge even as bees carry honey to their hives. But why, he asks, is it necessary for all these seekers after learning to go to Ireland? Are there not teachers enough in England now, men learned in both Greek and Latin? Why cross the sea to Ireland when you can be taught in Canterbury? There was point to Aldhelm's questions, because he himself had been to Canterbury to learn, and in another letter, written to a bishop of Winchester, he complains at the lack of time for the many subjects which he was trying to study—Roman law, literature, both prose and verse, all the complexities of metrical rhythm, music, arithmetic and all the mysteries of the stars in the heavens. From his pen too comes the striking picture of their great teacher Theodore, among his pupils 'like an angry boar surrounded by a pack of grinning Molossian hounds'. We may guess that the boar was more than a match for the hounds, and that his tusks were much sharper, for Theodore was one of the greatest scholars of his times.

There were close links between Theodore and Northumbria. His guide from Rome to Canterbury was Benedict Biscop, Bede's first teacher, and founder of both Wearmouth and Jarrow. Aldhelm had once been a close companion of Aldfrith, the learned king of Northumbria, to whom he sent his collection of riddles. Another of Theodore's pupils was a man called Oftfor, whose earliest studies had been in Northumbrian monasteries at Hartlepool and Whitby, and who, after visiting Rome, became a bishop in the west midlands. Yet another of Theodore's pupils was Albinus who became abbot of St Augustine's monastery in Canterbury and was chief among those who urged Bede to write his *History*. We know that Theodore visited Lindisfarne where he rededicated the church to St Peter, and that he intervened on the battlefield to bring peace to Northumbria and Mercia, whose royal families were threatened by a damaging blood feud.

The learning of all scholars who worked in Britain, whether they were Celtic or Saxon by race, had its roots in the countries which surround the Mediterranean. Perhaps, then, before we return to the questions which we posed at the outset, it may profit us to make a hasty visit to those countries, seeking out the homes of men whose books were widely read in Northumbrian centres of learning. Our tour may well begin in Africa, rather than in Italy, for near Africa's northern coast was born at Tagaste the Augustine who became bishop of Hippo Regius and who died there in 430 while the city was under siege. This Augustine, though some two centuries ahead of his namesake of Canterbury, had some indirect contact with Britain because his doctrine of divine grace was powerfully attacked by Pelagius, a native of Britain who maintained that man had within himself the capacity to move towards salvation without the need for divine grace. Augustine was well able to defend himself, but Bede, who was widely read in Augustine's writings, still had frequent occasion to denounce the heresy preached by Pelagius. We would do well to extend our African visit eastwards to Alexandria because more was known about mathematics in Alexandria than in Rome, and when men came to argue about the proper date for the celebration of Easter, as they often did, and by no means only at Whitby, the men of Alexandria were more likely to reach a mathematically correct answer than the Romans themselves.

Leaving the Alexandrians to their cycles, indictions, epacts and other mysteries of sunshine and moonshine, we perhaps do best, out of an abundant choice, to visit Jerusalem, the home in his later years of one of the greatest of biblical scholars, Jerome; alive to the imagination of Dürer who lets us see him as a desert hermit guarded by his fiercely protective lion, or as an old man at work in his study, the lion now sweetly smiling and happily at rest. He was born near the Danube provinces of the Roman Empire at a time when the military commanders in Britain were strengthening the island's defences against increasing Saxon attack, and in Rome he was taught by Donatus, the great grammarian whose name later became familiar at Jarrow. While travelling in northern Italy, on his way to Gaul, he fell in with Rufinus, another name to become familiar to Anglo-Saxon scholars, for it was this Rufinus who translated into Latin the ecclesiastical history which was written in Greek by Eusebius and which, in its Latin version, was read by Bede. Bede knew the story of Jerome's vision, how, at the point of death, he found himself before the judgement seat and how when he claimed to be a Christian, he was told: 'Thou liest; thou art a Ciceronian, not a Christian.' Though Jerome never lost his interest in the authors of classical antiquity, his later years were mostly devoted to biblical studies, and in particular to that revision of the Bible which he had been urged to undertake by Pope Damasus. Jerome's revision of the Gospels, known to us as the Vulgate, was widely used in Northumbria. Anyone who looks at the *Lindisfarne Gospels* will find there, among some other preliminary material, Jerome's letter to Pope Damasus explaining how he had come to undertake this great work.

Jerome's biblical revision was done mainly in Jerusalem, a city of whose appearance Bede was well informed. From Palestine we may turn back towards the west, visiting Cilicia wherein lay the city of Tarsus, known to all as the birthplace of St Paul, but perhaps only to a few as the birthplace of Archbishop Theodore. He had been educated at Athens and we may think of him as a Greek by both race and learning. From Asia Minor and Greece we may take ship westwards across the Ionian Sea coming to land by the Gulf of Squillace on the coast of Calabria. A few miles inland, at Squillace, Cassiodorus founded a great monastic institute, designed partly as a school of theology, partly as a place where scribes could be trained for the copying of manuscripts. The place was called *Vivarium*, after the fishponds which were among its many delights. The great library which was collected at Vivarium included three copies of the Bible, and one of these, known to scholars as the *Codex Grandior*, eventually reached Northumbria where it was seen by Bede. One of the great works achieved by Cassiodorus himself—he died shortly after 560—was a commentary on the Psalms. Visitors to the library of the dean and chapter at Durham may see a manuscript of this work produced at Jarrow or Wearmouth in the eighth century.

Travelling northwards again we might call in at Naples to pay our respects to one or two Neapolitan saints whose feast days were noted in the *Lindisfarne Gospels*, and thence to Rome to find the man whose writings were perhaps more widely read in Northumbria than those of any other scholar—Gregory the Great. Continuing northwards from Rome, and then westwards along the Côte d'Azur to the Bay of Cannes, we might pay a brief visit to the Isles de Lérins, wondering what Benedict Biscop would think of the Riviera were he able to return to the island monastery where he spent two years before the foundation of Wearmouth and Jarrow. Before his day the monastery had been frequented by churchmen and scholars from the ancient Roman cities in Provence, notably Arles, where there were men who felt kindly towards the doctrines of Pelagius. Bede may have read some of their works, but he had no forgiving words to say of Pelagius himself or any of his teachings. From Provence we go south again into Spain and complete the circuit of the Mediterranean by calling on Isidore of Seville, the great encyclopaedist whose many works were widely read and copied in Ireland as well as in England. Bede was translating one when he died.

Against this background with its increasing flow of book learning towards England, sometimes direct from Italy, sometimes in a more roundabout way, perhaps from Spain and Gaul to Ireland, we may return to our questions about books and how they were collected. A letter written in a comfortable study produced in quick response a photograph of the title page of a Northumbrian gospel book now in the safe keeping of a librarian at Utrecht in the Netherlands (Plate 15); another letter to a librarian in the Vatican City produced the illustration of finger-counting in a manuscript of one of Bede's works (Plate 13). Since the obvious can so easily be forgotten, it is worth reminding ourselves that the only way to secure books in the age of Bede was to go and get them. Imagination may conceive something of the physical hardships and dangers (there were wolves as well as brigands) endured by those who set out to travel hundreds of miles by foot, horse and boat in search of the books from which the Northumbrian libraries were made. Yet the affluent may value their prize the less, and if imagination can see no more than the shadow of the hardship, neither can it share the joy of the traveller safely returned with his book satchels well filled with precious volumes.

Only imagination can enlarge the detail of Benedict Biscop's several journeys to Rome from one of which 'he brought back many books on all subjects of divine learning which had either been bought at an acceptable price or given to him by the generosity of his friends. And as he was returning home, when he came to Vienne, he recovered the books which he had bought and left in the safe keeping of friends.' This brief glimpse shows us that there were booksellers in at least one of the cities of the Rhône valley, even if it leaves us with curiosity unsatisfied about the nature of the haggling before that 'acceptable price' was reached. The phrase is Bede's and one would like to read into it an implication that Benedict had picked up some good bargains such as were not to be found in later days when books were in much greater demand.

The high price of books was a matter of concern to Bede. One of the reasons why he wrote his own commentary on Genesis was that, although a great many books had been written on this topic, only the wealthier could afford to buy them. We are told that while Ceolfrith was abbot of Wearmouth and Jarrow he increased the library established by Benedict Biscop to double its former size. Another abbot, Hwætbert, the composer of the riddles, had spent no small time in Rome in his earlier years and while he was there he copied everything that he thought might be useful and brought it all back with him. There was a priest of the church in London who went to Rome and brought back with him copies of some of the letters of Gregory the Great which Bede was able to use in his *History*. At Hexham Acca 'built up a very large and most noble library, assiduously collecting histories and the passions of the martyrs as well as other ecclesiastical books.' Unhappily we must content ourselves with general statements of this kind. None of the book collectors has left us a list with the titles of the books which he found. In one case, Whitby, we know that there was a good library, but we have no hint of the way in which it was collected.

During the middle and later years of the eighth century, after Bede was dead, we can see how Northumbria had itself become a source for books needed by Anglo-Saxon missionaries working among the Germans. The letters which they wrote, and the replies which they received, sometimes give us a little of the detail that we lack for the earlier period. Boniface asks Abbot Hwætbert if he will 'be so kind as to copy and send us some of the treatises of that keenest investigator of the Scriptures, the monk Bede, who, we have learnt, shone forth among you of late as a beacon of the church'. He sends a similar, but more specific request to Egbert, archbishop of York, asking particularly for Bede's lectionary for the year (this would consist of a series of homilies) and also for his commentary on the Proverbs of Solomon. Abbot Cuthbert (successor to Hwætbert) writes to Lul saying that he has got his scribes to make him copies of the account of Cuthbert's life, one which had been written in verse and another in prose. He would gladly have done more had it been possible, but because of the extreme severity of the winter the scribes had not been able to copy a large number of books. An archbishop of York writes to Lul in response to some request he had made about books dealing with the tides of the sea, but the archbishop was not able to help him; he had some cosmographical books, but they were in bad shape, and although he had meant to have them copied he had not been able to get scribes to do the work.

The evidence of letters such as these, amplified by that of many manuscripts now widely scattered in the libraries of western Europe, testifies to the copying and exchanging of books on a considerable scale especially in the eighth century. What sort of books did these Northumbrian monks want to have in their libraries? As we have seen, the book written by Adamnan *On the Holy Places* came to Northumbria from Iona, and King Aldfrith possessed a book of *Cosmographers*, but it is very rare for a particular book to be named by title and author, and no early catalogue survives from any Northumbrian library of this age. Yet we are not wholly without means of forming at least a general idea of the books which Bede would have been able to consult. For example, his *Martyrology* contains information about no fewer than one hundred and fourteen martyrs and it is probable that he had used the material collected by Acca for the Hexham library. When we find that in his relatively short commentary on Genesis Bede cites Augustine's *City of God* on no fewer than a hundred and twenty occasions, and that in his commentaries on Luke and Mark, he cites Gregory the Great's *Homilies on the Gospels* some seventy-five times, it is a fair inference that both of these works were in Bede's library. Yet, if 'spotting the quotation' can be a satisfying intellectual exercise, it can also be a dangerous foundation upon which to reconstruct the content of a library. When a man welcomes us with the cry: 'This is Liberty-Hall, gentlemen', we do not assume that he has read the works of Oliver Goldsmith.

The library of a monastery large enough to have a school would need a number of books dealing with secular topics, even though these would represent only a small part of the total. Latin grammars were essential and there is evidence that the works of several grammarians were widespread, in addition to those of Donatus, the most famous of them all. Books on ancillary subjects were also needed, notably such as dealt with metrical scansion, with figures of speech and how they should be used, as well as with other matters of importance for those wanting to write good Latin. Books of this kind had such titles as *De Arte Metrica*, *De Schematibus et Tropis*, *De Orthographia*. There were no grammars of the English language at this period. Although there was nothing closely corresponding with a modern Latin dictionary, word lists and glossaries with English and Latin equivalents would certainly be needed by those learning Latin and we may presume that there will have been many of them. Men were also interested in the meanings and definitions of words. Among the writings of Isidore of Seville which were known in Northumbria was a large work entitled *Etymologiae*, almost to be regarded as a kind of encyclopaedia. There were also some books dealing with the natural world. Another of Isidore's works was entitled *De Natura Rerum,* and Bede himself wrote a work with this title. We know that Bede had at least a substantial part of Pliny's *Natural History*. As well as books about words and grammar, men needed books about number. A good library would certainly have had many treatises dealing with what we call the *computus*, the field of study concerned with the apparent movement of the sun about the earth, with the ages of the moon and with all else that lay at the foundations of the annual calendar and of chronology in general. Bede wrote two works on the theme of chronology and we know that he was able to draw on a large body of earlier literature, much of it Irish, dealing with this same subject.

Supposing that we had been able to visit the Northumbrian libraries about the year 730, we would not have found there any of the works of classical antiquity, with the exception of some of Pliny's *Natural History*. Bede knew enough Greek to be able to use a copy of *Acts* written in Greek and to correct a faulty translation of a saint's life from Greek into Latin, but it is certain that he knew nothing of Homer, Herodotus, Thucydides, Aristotle or any other of the great Greek writers. Plato's name was known to him, but not his writings. Similarly with the authors of classical Italy, though with some difference. Then as now, the Latin grammarians illustrated their points with quotations from the great writers and most notably from the works of Virgil. In this way many people, Bede among them, might become familiar with a number of single lines or couplets written by Virgil, but I do not believe that there was a copy of the *Aeneid* in Northumbria during Bede's lifetime.

Bede himself was uncompromisingly hostile towards pagan classical literature, much more so than Gregory the Great. He could not deny that St Paul himself had used material drawn from pagan authors in his own writings. 'But,' Bede tells us, 'we must use greater care in plucking the rose amid its sharp thorns than in gathering the lily in its soft foliage, and it is much safer to seek wholesome advice in the writing of the apostles than in the pages of Plato.' He condemned, no less than he condemned Christian heretics, all the seductive allurements of rhetoric, dialectic, philosophy and astrology, equating them with the tapestries and fine linen with which the prostitute decked her bed. If then we had walked through these Northumbrian libraries during Bede's lifetime in search of evidence that Northumbrian scholars were in some ways intermediaries between classical antiquity and medieval Europe, we would have been disappointed.

Had we been able to visit the York library some fifty years after Bede's death, we would have found some interesting changes. Even if Bede had never read his Virgil at first hand (a proposition which may not be acceptable to all scholars), it is quite certain that Alcuin had. There is a tale, reminiscent of Jerome's dream, that Alcuin was visited by a supernatural being who rebuked him with the charge that he loved Virgil more than he loved the Psalms. It is equally certain that he had read the rhetorical work of Cicero and was very familiar with it; he himself was highly practised in the rhetorical art. Alcuin gives us in a poem which he wrote about York a list of the authors whose work was to be found in the library there. It is by no means to be regarded as a catalogue of the library, yet it has much of interest to tell us, for in that list we find the names not only of Virgil and Cicero, but also of Aristotle, Lucan and Statius, and perhaps most interestingly of all, of Boethius, author of that work *The Consolation of Philosophy* which has held the interest of men of letters all down the ages, one of the books translated into English in the time of Alfred the Great. The York scholars knew no Greek so presumably such works of Aristotle as they had were in Latin translations. In his old age Alcuin looked back to his own early manhood at York as to a golden age, the age when, as we may suspect, at least some of the treasures of classical antiquity found their way to Anglo-Saxon England. The twelve books of the *Aeneid* would have been a rare treasure indeed. Long after Alcuin's death an eminent Carolingian scholar wrote to York in the hope that he might be able to borrow from its library the twelve books of Quintilian's work on *Rhetoric*. By this date, less than twenty years before its destruction by the Danes, York had grown into one of the great libraries of early medieval Europe.

Bede's Jarrow is more widely famed today than Alcuin's York, yet we may guess that a modern scholar would have found York the more congenial place in which to work, not because it was more sheltered from the east winds blowing across the North Sea, but because its intellectual rigours were softened a little by some touch of classical humanism. For Bede's generation there was no place for secular knowledge in its own right. Our imagination already stretched to the limit to understand the power of the written word upon barbarians, may find it no less difficult to perceive the effect upon these same barbarians of the revelation of ultimate truth. No Northumbrian scholar of the seventh or eighth century would ever have questioned the absolute and literal truth of the word of God as it was expressed in the Bible. Our understanding of this attitude of extreme fundamentalism may be helped a little by Cassiodorus whom we visited in southern Italy. In one of his books he gives advice to scribes on the correcting of mistakes which they might find in manuscripts which they were copying. An approach which might be regarded as legitimate where secular authors were concerned, he says, would be quite inappropriate when they were dealing with books of holy scripture. In the latter case it would be wrong to alter the inflections of nouns so as to adapt them to current human usage. Preference must rather be given to the idioms of divine communication. A phrase which was known to have been pleasing to God must not be subjected to alteration by mere humans. In a very real sense, then, Cassiodorus regarded a scribe as the guardian of the words which had been spoken literally by God.

Out of this fundamentalist attitude there arose a difficult problem. What, in fact, had God said? The cynics of this modern age may say—what indeed? Yet we must realise that a generation of Northumbrian scholars, unshakeable in their faith, devoted their talents to finding the answer to this question. Turning to recent times, the eighteenth and nineteenth centuries, most English Protestants would not have been aware that such a problem could exist. The word of God was expressed in the King James Bible. What the Bible said was not a matter for argument—the writing was plain to see on the printed page. Many of those of simple faith even supposed that God had spoken English. But in distant Northumbria there was no Authorised Version of the text, nor anywhere else in western Europe. It was even exceedingly rare for a man to be able to find anywhere a single book called a Bible. Instead there were a great many manuscript books of widely varying origins, and men who looked carefully at them and compared one with another found that they sometimes said different things on matters of great importance. A glance at the Latin Vulgate in the Clementine revision of 1592 shows that the contents page lists forty-six separate books in the Old Testament, and in the New Testament the four Gospels, the Acts of the Apostles, the Book of Revelation and twenty-one catholic Epistles. Even if we count the Epistles as one, we have a total of fifty-three books. About the year 700 in Northumbria most of these would be literally separate books not bound together into a single volume; and these were the books which above all others were needed for the monastic libraries, together with the volumes in which Christian scholars had expounded their meaning.

The task to which the scholars of Wearmouth and Jarrow devoted much labour was the reconciling of the many different readings which they found in the various texts which they had in front of them. They would have several different versions of the Psalter, and different versions of the Gospels, and the problem of reconciliation was not an easy one. We may take an example from Bede's commentary on the Book of Genesis. He writes that 'in our text' it says that the Garden of Eden was planted there 'in the beginning', but in the 'old translation' it says that the garden was planted 'towards the east'. This immediately raised a problem about the Flood. Bede says that those who accepted the second reading sometimes argued that the Garden of Eden lay in the eastern part of the earth, separated by wide expanses of sea and land from all those parts of the earth which were inhabited by the human race. But if this had really been so, how could the water of the Flood which overwhelmed the inhabited part of the earth have been able to reach the Garden of Eden? Even more difficult was a problem about creation. Bede writes that the 'other translation' said that God had completed his work on the sixth day, but 'our text' says that he did so on the seventh even though it did not say that he created anything new on that seventh day, unless it was to be supposed that he had created the seventh day itself. Nowadays it is difficult to feel ourselves able to be exercised by problems of this kind, but we must recognise that they were of vital importance to the biblical scholars of Northumbria, and indeed to biblical scholars everywhere.

Why should complete copies of the whole Bible in one single book have been so rare? Nowadays anyone who so wishes can possess himself of the Authorised Version in one easily legible volume containing more than 1,100 pages of print, and the whole, weighing less than seven ounces, will fit comfortably into a not very large pocket. Yet this book would not have brought much solace to the ageing Boniface who wrote to Daniel, bishop of Winchester, asking him to send a book which had once belonged to his former teacher and which contained six of the Prophets in one volume 'in clear letters written in full. . . . With my fading sight I cannot easily read writing which is small and filled with abbreviations.' Boniface might well wish to read from the Bible himself, but most men would listen while others read, and this demanded large and clear writing. We still possess one complete copy of a Northumbrian Bible which was written about the year 700. It contains 2,060 pages, not of India paper but of stout vellum, and it weighs seventy-five and a half pounds, the equivalent of a sack of potatoes containing about five and a half stones, the weight of a seven year-old child, the weight of about one hundred and seventy copies of a handy modern Bible printed on India paper. Each page is twenty-seven and a half inches high and twenty and a half inches wide, and the book is ten and a half inches thick. The handwriting is clear and distinct, the margins are ample, yet it is not extravagant in the use of space. A modern scholar has left us a vivid impression as he waited for the great book in Michael Angelo's reading-room in the Laurentian Library in Florence. 'One watches with awe two attendants, with a third to open the door, staggering in under the load. Half-a-dozen fat volumes have to be placed on the table, to take the strain off the binding, before one can open its covers.' We can understand why complete Bibles were not common.

The Northumbrian Bible now preserved in Florence is known to scholars as the *Codex Amiatinus*. Itself a remarkable achievement, there were once two other copies like it, both of them made in Northumbria. One was intended for the church at Wearmouth and the other for the church at Jarrow. These two copies have perished save only for a few fragments. Early in this century a single leaf was found by a canon of Durham cathedral in a bookseller's shop in Newcastle not many miles from where the manuscript had originally been written. It had been used as the cover of an eighteenth-century account book. A few other fragments have been found as covers for deeds relating to certain Yorkshire estates. The survival of the third copy, the *Codex Amiatinus*, can seem hardly less than astonishing when we consider the hazards which it faced. We owe that survival to its chief begetter, the Abbot Ceolfrith who, at the age of seventy-four, perhaps prompted in part by a sense of his failing physical strength, decided to lay down his abbacy and travel to Rome, where he hoped that he might die at the thresholds of the apostles. Keeping his intention closely secret, he made all the necessary preparations for an embassy to Rome—such an expedition as had been sent more than once before. A ship was prepared and a list with the names of those who were to go. On the very day appointed for departure the aged abbot to Bede's great distress, so great that he had to lay aside the work on which he was engaged, revealed that he himself was determined to be of the company.

Taking farewell of all the brethren both at Wearmouth and Jarrow he set off on 4 June of the year 716 (see above, p. 97). Among the gifts which he took with him was the great Bible, amply wrapped and encased, as we may suppose, against the hazards of the long journey. Progress was slow. The sea-voyage was stormy, with a whole day passed amid the tossing of wild waves, and the old abbot became increasingly fatigued by the rigours of travel. Others joined the company which numbered as many as eighty as they crossed northern France, but when they reached the city of Langres in Burgundy Ceolfrith died, barely half-way to Rome. He was buried in a monastery outside the city, but later his body was brought back to Wearmouth. Some of his companions returned home to take news of his death, but others continued on their way, carrying the great book with them.

We lose sight of the book for a while and its real identity was lost for close on 1,200 years. There is no letter from Rome telling how the Jarrow monks had reached their destination, no letter of gratitude from the pope, but in circumstances of which we know nothing the book came into the possession of the monastery at Monte Amiata, some ninety miles to the north of Rome. When it left Northumbria it had at its beginning a dedicatory inscription written in Latin verse and mentioning Ceolfrith by name, describing him as an 'abbot from the farthest ends of England.' When the book was in Italy someone tampered with this inscription. He erased the words *Ceolfridus Anglorum* and inserted in their place the words *Petrus Langobardorum*. It was not until late in the nineteenth century that the forgery was detected as a result of work done by several scholars, chief of whom was Anthony Hort, the great Cambridge biblical scholar. The codex is now recognised by all for what it is, a Northumbrian book produced by the scribes and artists of Wearmouth and Jarrow at some date shortly before 716. It embodies the attempt, unrivalled anywhere in western Europe in its own age, to establish a new, authoritative version of the Bible, and it was to this end that most Northumbrian scholarship had been devoted in the decades before and after 700.

We have seen that a good monastic library would have needed a small number of secular works, mostly such as were concerned with grammatical studies and with the computus; and that it would also need as many copies as it could get, wherever they might be found, of the various books of the Bible. Among these latter, some would of course be more highly prized than others, especially the book of Psalms from the Old Testament and the four Gospels from the New. Since no man doubted the historical truth of all that was recorded in the Bible from the days of creation down to and beyond the resurrection, there would be great interest in anything else that could be learnt about the past that seemed to bear directly or indirectly upon the history of Christianity. The Jewish historian, Josephus, was born a few years after the resurrection and was himself present at the siege of Jerusalem by Titus, an episode which is portrayed on the Franks Casket. Eusebius, bishop of Caesarea who died *c.* 340, wrote a history of the Christian church extending from the apostolic age down to his own times. Bede knew the works of both of these writers. He read Eusebius's history, originally written in Greek, in a Latin translation, but in it he found the model which guided him in the writing of his own *Ecclesiastical History of the English Nation*, a work which is to be viewed both in the setting of England and in the far wider setting of the whole Christian church. Several other historical writings found their way to Northumbrian libraries, including the work of the Frankish historian, Gregory of Tours, and of the British historian, Gildas. Nowadays we make a sharper distinction than would have been made in earlier times between hagiography, or the *Lives* of saints, and history. The Hexham library, as we have seen, was well supplied with works concerned with the saints, but the genre was extremely popular and widely distributed throughout the Christian world. It was the great popularity of this kind of literature, together with the need for Christian propaganda, that led some English writers to write lives of their own saints. Those of Cuthbert and Wilfrid are the most notable Northumbrian instances, but there were many others. To these several categories of books we may add the writings of some of the early Christian poets, such men as Juvencus, Paulinus of Nola and Sedulius, all of them living in the fourth or fifth centuries.

We may now have some impression of the range of books that might have been found at Whitby, Wearmouth and Jarrow, or Hexham, though naturally we shall not suppose that the smaller monasteries had equally good libraries. We have also seen that in the middle and later years of the eighth century, after Bede's death, the range of books in the library at York was significantly widened, notably by the addition of some of the Latin classics and of the famous philosophical work written by Boethius. We have yet to take account of what may well have been the largest single element in all of these larger libraries—the books which we call patristic literature. When we speak of the writings of the Fathers we are usually referring to the works of those who wrote theological treatises from the end of the first century down to the end of the eighth. Bede had certainly read widely in patristic literature especially in the writings of Augustine of Hippo, Jerome and Gregory the Great. Here and in the works of many other writers, he could find commentaries, explanatory and doctrinal expositions, the exposure of heresies, the defence of orthodoxy, and all else that lay at the foundation of his own mighty contribution.

If we are right in thinking that during the decades preceding 700 Northumbrian scholars were mainly concerned with studying the Bible itself and seeking to establish a uniform text, there can be no doubt that during the next thirty years the emphasis shifted from the Bible towards the writing of commentaries upon it. This was both the task and the achievement of Bede himself, standing out as a giant among his fellows. Bede's theological commentaries, of such great importance to himself, to his contemporaries and to his successors, are not widely read today, save perhaps by theologians, to whom must be left the task of giving him his rightful place in the long line of distinguished scholars who have devoted their lives to theological studies. Laymen can still read Bede's *History* with no less pleasure than profit for it has in it qualities of immortality. They cannot be expected to read his commentaries, yet they should know that men in the Middle Ages looked upon Bede not as a historian, but as a great theologian. More than a hundred of the libraries of medieval Europe contained copies of Bede's theological writings, and this may give us some small idea of the strength of his influence. Even now scholars are at work producing new editions.

Bede tells us that in its earliest shape his *Life of Cuthbert* was cast in the form of rough notes and that when these had been checked by men who had known Cuthbert, a fair copy was made on parchment and sent to Lindisfarne where it was studied for two days before being finally approved. As we have seen, Adamnan's book *On the Holy Places* was first taken down from Arculf on wax tablets and then transferred to parchment. However, it is unusual for us to be told anything about methods of writing or copying. Ultan is the only Northumbrian scribe known to us by name, a name which tells of his Irish origin, but we know that a large scriptorium would have several scribes. Sometimes a manuscript might be written entirely by one scribe—such as the Moore manuscript of Bede's *History* now in Cambridge—but it was more usual for the work to be shared among several who could then work simultaneously in the copying of a manuscript which itself was separated into several parts. The Leningrad manuscript of Bede was written by four scribes, while as many as seven worked at the huge *Codex Amiatinus*. Recalling that this last had two companion volumes of similar size, we can see that scribing will have played an important part in the life of Wearmouth and Jarrow, but we cannot say whether this work was concentrated at one of the two or shared between both.

Scribes are likely to have spent much time in the copying of two works in particular—the Psalter and the Gospels.

> It is a good thing to give thanks unto the Lord,
> and to sing praises unto thy name, O most high.

The Latin for this, the opening verse of the 92nd Psalm,

runs—*Bonum est confiteri domino et psallere nomine tuo altissime*. We can read the words on a single dark brown sheet of vellum now in the university library of Cambridge (MS. Ff. 5. 27, flyleaf), a sheet badly stained with the glue by which it had been stuck to the board of a binding. The membrane is so thin that the writing shows through clearly from one side to the other, and all is peppered with worm holes, product of that tiresome creature, a gift to riddlers in all ages, who swallows the words of men working like a thief in the night but becoming no whit the wiser for his meal. In his commentary on the *Song of Songs* Bede tells us that the 'resin of cedarwood is useful for preserving books, for when they are smeared all over with it, they are not attacked by bookworm nor do they age with time'. Palaeographers think that the handwriting of this fragment is that of the Wearmouth/Jarrow scriptorium and that the sheet was probably written when Ceolfrith was abbot. Slighter clues lead them to suspect that the scribe had bungled his work on this particular sheet which was then placed on one side, not for destruction but to be kept against some other need at a later date. Parchment was too valuable to be wasted. That use was eventually found four hundred years later when it came to serve as a flyleaf of a manuscript written at Durham in the twelfth century. It was fastened upside down to a board, but it has since been released from this indignity and is now placed the right way up, an evocative relic of Bede's Jarrow.

We may guess that most of the works copied in Northumbrian scriptoria were plain serviceable texts, but once again we have to remind ourselves of how little we know. There is no single manuscript of which we can say for certain that it was written in York or in Whitby or in Hexham before 850. Taking all the Northumbrian monasteries together, and there may well have been twenty or thirty, there are only two from which there survive to the present day a small number of manuscripts which we believe to have been written in one or other of them in the seventh or eighth centuries. One of these is Bede's own monastery and the other is Lindisfarne. With less than a dozen manuscripts (and some of these incomplete) surviving out of a total which must surely have run into some hundreds, it is difficult for us to know how far scribes were concerned with plain copying, how far artists were engaged in more elaborate embellishment, whether particular monasteries were renowned for their special skills in one or other form of manuscript art. The *Codex Amiatinus* which we know to have been a Wearmouth/Jarrow book, contains a number of illuminated pages. There is one which shows a scribe seated on a stool, pen in hand as he writes on a book balanced on his knee. About him lie the instruments of his craft, and in the background there is an open cupboard on whose shelves lie nine volumes. All is coloured, with reds, russets and browns predominating. Elsewhere in the same book there is a picture of Christ seated between two angels, all three figures being enclosed within a framework of concentric circles. Outside this central medallion are small figures of the four evangelists, each with his particular symbol, man or lion, calf or eagle.

Now in the university library at Utrecht there are a dozen disconnected leaves from a Gospel Book whose title page (Plate 15) is written in the same characters as are used for the dedicatory verses of the *Codex Amiatinus*. The lettering is enclosed within an ornamental scalloped border wherein there is written in small, neat lettering a short prayer in Greek: 'Holy Mary help the scribe.' Palaeographers also recognise the capitular script of the *Codex Amiatinus* in the copy of St John's Gospel called the *Stonyhurst Gospel*, a miniature of perfection, the achievement of a man who gave the best of his great skill, as well as his love, to making 'the shape of the letters perfect one by one' (Plate 11). Another book now attributed to the Wearmouth/Jarrow scriptorium is the Leningrad manuscript of Bede's *History* which contains two ornamental initials but no full-page illuminations. Stemming from some Northumbrian scriptorium is a manuscript of the commentary which Cassiodorus wrote on the Psalms. It contains two pictures of David; in one of them he is standing, robed in a severely classical style, while in the other, a much more elaborate composition, he is seated upon a throne and playing a small harp or lyre.

Ripon, as we have seen, once possessed a copy of the Gospels written in letters of gold on parchment dyed purple. This book may have been of foreign origin, but none of it survives. Whether a book of such splendour might have been found at Jarrow we

14   *The Lindisfarne Gospels:* a detail from the beginning of St Luke's Gospel

In cip
IN NOMINE ÐNI
NI IħU XPI EUANGE
LIA NUMERO IIII
SEC MATTHEUM
SEC MARCUM
SEC LUCAN
SEC IOħANNEM

15　Title page from a Gospel Book

16　The Franks Casket: Weland in his Smithy; the Adoration of the Magi

cannot now tell, though its production would have been within the capacity of the scribes and artists who worked there. Many churches in Britain are likely to have sought to do honour to God's word by embellishing it with all the art at their command, and several richly illuminated copies of the Gospels still survive. There are some in the library of Trinity College Dublin—notably the *Book of Durrow* and the *Book of Kells*. There is another in the library of Lichfield cathedral, sometimes called the *Chad Gospels*, though the book has no known connection with St Chad. In Paris we may see the *Echternach Gospels* which are believed to be of Northumbrian origin, some might say from Lindisfarne. In Stockholm there is the *Codex Aureus*, of southern English origin. And there are others, complete or fragmentary.

Only one of these splendid books can now be securely located in time as well as place on acceptable historical evidence, the one which we know as the *Lindisfarne Gospels*, now preserved in the British Museum. When this book was with St Cuthbert's community at Chester-le-Street in the tenth century a priest of that community wrote a brief note on a blank space at the end of St John's Gospel saying, among other things, that: 'Eadfrith, bishop of the Lindisfarne church, originally wrote this book, for God and St Cuthbert and, jointly, for all the saints whose relics are in the island.' This Eadfrith became bishop in 698 and died in 721. Most scholars accept the attribution to him and most scholars would accept a date for the writing of the book within a decade or so of the year 700, perhaps later rather than earlier. The most detailed study of this book has led its author to conclude that it was completed within a relatively short period of uninterrupted work and that the whole of it—the text and all the elaborate illuminations—was the work of one man in whom, if the argument be sound, we must recognise one of the greatest masters of his craft.

It is the task of the art historian to examine and analyse facets of ornament and to relate them in historical sequence to similar facets in other books; similarly it is the task of the biblical scholar to examine textual details and to relate them to the general transmission of the Bible text as a whole. Let us rather imagine a man in somewhat humbler guise, a pilgrim *pro amore Dei et Sancti*

Cuthberti, picking his way cautiously across the treacherous sands that surround the island of Lindisfarne. Had he visited the monastery shortly before 740 he would have found there the former king, Ceolwulf, to whom Bede had dedicated his *History*. Holding office as bishop there would have been Ethelwald who would have been able to explain to our pilgrim the exact part which he himself had played in making the cover for the Gospel Book. He might also have met (though we can only guess) an anchorite called Billfrith who had adorned the cover with gold, silver-gilt and gems. In the church, formerly dedicated by Archbishop Theodore to St Peter, he would have seen the relics of Saint Cuthbert lying within a wooden coffin of pale oak, all sharply incised with the figures of Christ, the Virgin, Apostles and Archangels. It is likely (though again we guess) that the great Gospel Book itself would have been lying on the high altar, for it was not a book intended to be in regular daily use.

No ordinary pilgrim would have been allowed to handle this book, but one who was specially privileged and allowed to turn its pages would have been astonished, even overwhelmed, by the brilliance of its variegated colouring, by the intricacy of its designs, and by the notion, likely to be new to him, that the portrait of a man might be placed upon the page of a book. Looking at these portraits of the four Evangelists, each with a page to himself at the appropriate place, he would surely have looked at them as paintings of real men, of Matthew and Mark, of Luke and John; not for him the sophisticated eye of the modern scholar seeing these portraits as stylised copies made by a man who worked from a pattern book with a long Mediterranean ancestry, infinitely remote from a painting of a living man. Our pilgrim would not have been troubled by any awareness that there might be something not quite as it should be with the cushion on Matthew's bench or with the carpentry of John's bench; that in one or two places the attributes of perspective had not been fully understood; that in the fall of the drapery the patterns of light and shade were not as an artist of later times would have shown them.

Turning from the portraits our pilgrim would surely have looked very closely at the several pages of abstract design in which the background to an over-riding cross was filled with almost unbelievably intricate patterns. The elements of these patterns would have been familiar to him if he had travelled much in England or Ireland—simple lines complexly turned in regular repetitive designs, whirls and coils in spiralling curves, beasts and birds with beaks and bodies, legs and wings, all reduced to a state of apparently total confusion, yielding on closer study to complete order. These patterns were not fundamentally new. Craftsmen in metal or stone had used them for a long time. The newness lay not in the pattern but in the explosively burgeoning growth —like wild bryony in a country hedge—as varying colour flowed easily from pen or brush on to the smooth surface of vellum (Plate 14).

Pilgrims of this modern age may need to go no further than to a good library where they may be able to find the whole of the *Lindisfarne Gospels*, and others of similar background, skilfully reproduced in faithfully coloured facsimile. They too are likely to be a little bemused by the more ornate pages, wondering at the skill which enabled men of these times to produce such complex designs. They should remember that generations of smiths had made similarly complex, if smaller, designs in less tractable materials such as gold, bronze and stone. They should remember, too, one of the instruments to be seen lying in a prominent position on the floor at the foot of the scribe portrayed in the *Codex Amiatinus*—a pair of dividing compasses with metal points, such as a schoolboy finds in his first set of geometrical instruments. Some schoolboys may still remember the enchantment of discovering how to use a pair of compasses to describe an exact circle, and how easy it was to enrich that plain circle with one, two, an infinite number of overlapping circles, semicircles or lesser arcs. There was no end to the variation of pleasing design that might be produced. This was the magic that came, with the magic of letters, to the scriptoria of Northumbria. With circle, curve and diagonal line men built up these complex patterns, repetitive and mechanical in their execution, but still conveying something of that eager, one ventures even to say boyish, delight that may sometimes spring from the new. In some of these illuminated manuscripts we can still see the holes which were left by the compasses used for laying out these patterns, simple in their elements, infinitely complex in their outcome, approaching though not quite reaching, the beauty of frosted crystals upon a pane of glass.

CHAPTER NINE

The Fortunes of Men

THE READER MAY find himself refreshed by the passages which follow. They have been selected from works written in Northumbria during the seventh or eighth centuries.

Lege feliciter!

A DRAGON

A horrid beast, I lie in the ghastly gloom of a cavern, aroused, I rise fluttering into the lofty air and fly with my crest displayed, the fair air whirling. My crawling body is stronger than that of all snakes or of any monsters dragging their excessive weights. Though uncouth and savage, I feed through a tiny mouth, my chest through narrow pipes is filled with breath, and not to my teeth do I owe my sinister power, nay, the seat of my impetuous strength is in my tail.

Aenigmata Eusebii, XLII
(*Tr. E. von Erhardt-Siebold*)

PORTENTS

There appeared in the air flashes of fire such as mortals of that time had never seen before; and they were seen almost all night, that is on the first of January.

Symeon of Durham, *Historia Regum*, A.D. 745

Flashes of fire were seen in the air, such as formerly appeared during the night of the first of January, as we mentioned before.

Ibid., A.D. 765

Fearful prodigies terrified the wretched nation of the English. Horrible lightnings and dragons in the air and flashes of fire were often seen glittering and flying to and fro. And these signs indicated the great famine and the terrible and indescribable slaughter of a great many men which followed.

Ibid., A.D 793

What is the meaning of the rain of blood which, during the season of Lent, in the city of York we saw fall threateningly from the summit of the roof on the north side in the church of St Peter chief of the Apostles which is the head of the whole kingdom, though the sky was clear?

Alcuin to a king of Northumbria (*c.* A.D. 793)
(*ed. Dümmler No. 16*)

STORMS

A great many ships were wrecked by the violence of a storm in the British sea. They were shattered and broken to pieces or sunk with a great multitude of men.

Symeon of Durham, *Historia Regum*, A.D. 799

At this same time, before the Nativity of the Lord, on 24 December, a great gale arose from the south-west or west. By its indescribable force it destroyed and flattened to the ground towns, many houses and a great number of villages in various places. Also countless trees were torn out by the roots and thrown down to the ground. In this year a surge of the sea flowed onwards beyond its bounds, forgetful of what the psalmist says—'Thou hast set a bound that they may not pass over.'

Ibid., A.D 800

A HARD WINTER

Deep snow hardened into ice unlike anything that had ever been known in previous ages and oppressed the land from the beginning of winter until almost the beginning of spring. By its severity the tress and plants mostly withered and many creatures of the sea were found dead.

Symeon of Durham, *Historia Regum*, A.D. 764

Now since you asked me for some of the works of the blessed father Bede, for your love I have prepared what I could with my young pupils, to the best of their ability. In accordance with your wishes I have sent you the little books written in verse and prose about that man of God, Cuthbert. And if I had been able I would gladly have done more. But during the past winter the island of our race has been very savagely oppressed with cold and ice and with long and widespread storms of wind and rain, so that the hand of the scribe became sluggish and could not produce a very large number of books.

Letter from Cuthbert, Abbot of
Wearmouth to Lul. *(ed. Tangl, No. 116)*

FIRE

When Aidan was bishop: a hostile army of Mercians, with Penda as their leader, spread cruel devastation far and wide over the lands of the Northumbrians and eventually reached the royal stronghold which is called after the name of a former queen, Bebba (Bamburgh). Because he could not capture it either by assault or by siege he tried to destroy it by fire. He pulled down all the homesteads which he found in the neighbourhood of the stronghold and dragged there a huge pile of beams, planks, partitions, hurdles and thatch from rooves and he surrounded the stronghold with them to a great height on the side next to the land. When he saw that the wind was favourable, he set it all alight in an attempt to burn down the stronghold.

Bede, *Ecclesiastical History*, III, 16

The wind veered in response to Bishop Aidan's prayers.

The minster in the city of York was burned on Sunday, the twenty third of April.

Symeon of Durham, *Historia Regum*, A.D. 741

Catterick was burnt by the tyrant Earnred, and by the judgement of God he himself perished miserably by fire in the same year.

Ibid,. A.D. 769

FAMINE

For three years before Wilfrid's arrival in the land (of the South Saxons) no rain had fallen in those parts, and thereby a most acute famine attacked the people and destroyed them with a cruel death. Indeed they say that often forty or fifty men together, wasted with hunger, would go to some cliff or to the seashore and with their hands joined in their misery they would all leap down together either to be destroyed by their fall or to be overwhelmed by the waves. But on the selfsame day on which that people received the baptism of faith, there fell a gentle but abundant rain. The earth blossomed once more and as the fields turned green a joyous and a fruitful season followed. And so when they had cast off their former superstition and extinguished their idolatry the hearts of all and the flesh of all rejoiced in the living God, for they understood that He who is the true God had by his heavenly grace enriched them with both inward and outward blessings. When the bishop had first come into that land and saw such dire affliction of famine, he taught the people to get food by fishing, for the sea and their rivers abounded in fish, but the people had no skill in fishing save only for eels. And so when they had collected all their eel-nets together, the bishop's men cast them into the sea and with the help of divine grace they soon caught three hundred fish of various kinds.

Bede, *Ecclesiastical History*, IV, 13

PLAGUE

In the same year of our Lord 664 there was an eclipse of the sun on the third day of May at about four o'clock in the afternoon. Also in that year a sudden pestilence first depopulated the southern parts of Britain and then attacked the kingdom of the Northumbrians as well. Raging far and wide for a long time with cruel devastation it struck down a great multitude of men. . . . This same plague oppressed the island of Ireland with equal destruction.

Bede, *Ecclesiastical History*, III, 27

When Cedd had for many years both held the bishopric in the aforesaid kingdom and been in charge of this monastery (Lastingham) whose rules he had established, he happened to arrive at this same monastery in the time of the plague, and there he was smitten with bodily sickness and died. . . . When the brothers who were in his monastery in the kingdom of the East Saxons heard that the bishop had died and been buried in the kingdom of the Northumbrians, they came there from their own monastery, about thirty men, desiring to live beside the body of their father, if God so willed, or to die and be buried there. They were gladly received there by their brethren and fellow-soldiers, but when an attack of the aforesaid plague came upon them there, they all died, saving one small boy who is said to have been preserved from death by the prayers of his father.

Ibid., III, 23

When the kingdom of the East Saxons was being oppressed by the disaster of the aforesaid mortality, Sigehere, together with his part of the people, abandoned the sacraments of the Christian faith and turned to apostasy. For both the king himself and a great many of the common people and of the nobles, loving this life and not seeking a future life, or even believing there to be one, began to repair the temples which had been abandoned and to worship images, as if by them they could be defended from the plague.

Ibid., III, 30

Now whilst he [Benedict Biscop] was tarrying in places beyond the sea, behold, a sudden tempest of pestilence laid hold of Britain, and wasted it with widespread disaster. In which visitation many persons from both his monasteries passed away, and the Abbot Eosterwine himself (honoured and dear to God) was suddenly taken to the Lord. . . . Furthermore in the monastery over which Ceolfrith presided all those brethren who could read or preach or recite the antiphons and responds were taken away, with the exception of the abbot and one little lad, who had been reared and taught by him, and who is at this day still in the same monastery, where he holds the rank of a priest, and both by written and spoken words justly commends his teacher's praiseworthy acts to all who desire to know of them.

Life of Ceolfrith, 13–14
(*Tr. Boutflower*)

It is commonly believed that 'the little lad' was Bede himself.

BREAD

Two tales of St Cuthbert.

Coming from the south to a river which is called the Wear, on reaching a place called Chester-le-Street, he crossed it and turned aside on account of the rain and tempest to some dwellings used only in spring and summer. But it was then winter time and the dwellings were deserted, so that he found no man to succour him and his horse, wearied as they were by their journey and by lack of food. So he unsaddled his horse and led it into the dwelling-place and, fastening it to the wall, he waited for the storm to cease. As he was praying to the Lord, he saw his horse raise its head up to the roof of the hut and, greedily seizing part of the thatch of the roof, draw it towards him. And immediately there fell out, along with it, a warm loaf and meat carefully wrapped up in a linen cloth.

Anon., *Life of Cuthbert*, I, 6
(*Tr. Colgrave*)

When the signal was given at the third hour of the day and prayer was over, he at once set out a table and spread thereon such food as he had. Now by some chance there was no bread in the guesthouse, save that he had placed some crumbs on the table as a blessed gift of bread. Thereupon the man of God went back to the monastery to seek a loaf; but failing to get any (for they were still baking in the oven) he returned to the guest whom he had left eating alone; but he did not find him nor even his footprints although there was snow over the surface of the ground. He was amazed and removed the table to the storehouse, realising that it was an angel of God. And immediately at the entrance, his nostrils were filled with the odour of the choicest bread and, finding three warm loaves, he gave thanks to God.

Anon., *Life of Cuthbert* II, 3
(*Tr. Colgrave*)

Abbot Ceolfrith.
Yet neither by consideration of his priestly degree, nor by that of his learning, nor even by that of his birth, did he choose, as some men do, to abandon his attitude of humility; nay rather in all things he took pains to submit himself to regular observance. For instance, whilst he held, and that for no short time, the office of baker, in the midst of his duties of sifting the flour, lighting and cleaning the oven, and baking loaves in it, he was diligent not to omit the learning and practice of the rites of the priesthood.

Life of Ceolfrith, 4
(*Tr. Boutflower*)

FEASTING

Dedication of the church at Ripon.
Then, after the sermon was finished, the kings began upon a great banquet which lasted for three days and nights, rejoicing with all the people, showing forgiveness to their enemies and being humble with the servants of God.

Eddius, *Life of Wilfrid*, Ch. 17

Wilfrid was not submerged by the wave of feasting, neither did the wave of fasting cast him down in pride, for at seasons of festival he used to live with such abstinence that when he thirsted with the heat of the sun in summer or was wearied by the cold of winter, he never drained the cup by himself alone, were it never so small a vessel.

Ibid., Ch. 21

Two days ago, most beloved brother, a messenger came to me
from your holiness bringing from you most joyful words of
peaceful greeting. But presently he brought all into a state of
grievous confusion by adding that you had heard my name being
chanted among those of the heretics by licentious boors in their
cups. I confess that I was horrified and I grew pale as I asked of
which heresies I was being accused.

Bede, *Letter to Plegwine*

It is said of some bishops that they so serve Christ that they do not
have with them any men of religion or restraint, but prefer those
who are given to laughing, joking, story telling, feasting and
drinking, and daily fill their bellies with feasting rather than feed
their souls with heavenly sacrifices.

Bede, *Letter to Egbert*

Never give up the study of letters, but have such young men with
you as are always learning and who rejoice more in learning than
in being drunk.

Alcuin, Letter to a bishop of
Lindisfarne *(ed. Dümmler No. 285)*

SPIRITUAL COOKING

We are being nourished on food roasted on a gridiron when we
understand literally, openly and without any covering, the things
that have been said or done to protect the health of the soul; upon
food cooked in a frying pan when by frequently turning over the
superficial meaning and looking at it afresh, we comprehend what
there is in it that corresponds allegorically with the mysteries of
Christ, what with the condition of the catholic church and what
with setting right the ways of individuals; and afterwards we
search in the oven for the bread of the Word when by exertion of
mind we lay hold of those mystical things in the Scriptures, that is

upon matters concealed aloft, which as yet we cannot see, but which we hope to see in the future.

Bede, *I Samuel*
(ed. Hurst p. 87, ll. 815–24)

BUILDING

Bishop Finan built in the island of Lindisfarne a church suitable for a bishop's see, yet he constructed the whole of it in the manner of the Scots, not of stone, but of hewn oak, and covered it with reed; in later times the most reverend Archbishop Theodore dedicated it in honour of the blessed apostle Peter. But Eadbert, bishop of the same place, took away the reed and had it covered entirely with sheets of lead, that is to say both its roof and also the walls themselves.

Bede, *Ecclesiastical History*, III, 25

For in Hexham, having obtained an estate from the queen, St Æthelthryth, the dedicated to God, Wilfrid founded and built a house to the Lord in honour of St Andrew the Apostle. My feeble tongue will not permit me to enlarge here upon the depths of the foundations in the earth, and its crypts of wonderfully dressed stone, and the manifold buildings above ground, supported by various columns and many side-aisles, and adorned with walls of notable length and height, surrounded by various winding passages with spiral stairs leading up and down; for our holy bishop, being taught by the spirit of God, thought out how to construct these buildings; nor have we heard of any other house on this side of the Alps built on such a scale. Further, Bishop Acca of blessed memory, who by the grace of God is still alive, provided for this manifold building splendid ornaments of gold, silver and precious stones; but of these and of the way he decorated the altars with purple and silk, who is sufficient to tell?

Now while the masons were constructing the highest part of the walls of this building, a certain young man among the servants of God slipped from a pinnacle of enormous height, fell to the ground and was dashed upon a stone pavement. His arms and legs were broken, all his limbs were out of joint and he lay breathing his last; the masons thinking he was dead, quickly carried him outside on a bier in obedience to the commands of the holy bishop who was tearfully praying.

Eddius, *Life of Wilfrid*, Ch. 22–3
(*Tr. Colgrave*)

The young man, whose name was Bothelm, recovered with the aid of Wilfrid's prayers and the skill of the physicians who bound his broken limbs.

For when we in our human frailty have some task to perform, for example when we are building a house, we begin the work by preparing our material and after this beginning we dig deeply. Next we put stones into this foundation and then we place walls upon it in rising courses of stones, and so little by little we reach completion in accomplishing the task upon which we have set out.

Bede, *In Genesim*, I, ll. 8–14
(*ed. Jones*)

The bitumen which the builders of Babylon used in place of cement, and which was taken out of the earth or from pits, assuredly represents a tendency towards that earthy and base pleasure with which men of this world surround all their works. . . . In wholesome contrast with this we read that the temple of the Lord was made by *caementarii*. For cement is made from stones which have been burnt and turned into ash. These stones, which were previously strong and firm, each one by itself, are worked upon by the fire in such a way that when they have been softened by the addition of heat and when they have been joined together in a better way, they are themselves able to bind other stones which have been placed in position in a wall. Thus they soon receive again in a better way the strength which for a little while they seemed to have lost.

Bede, *In Genesim*, III, ll. 631–46
(*ed. Jones*)

Commenting on the passage in Genesis xi. 3 which refers to the building of
the tower of Babel and which reads:'Go to, let us make bricks, and burn
them thoroughly. And they had brick for stone and slime (bitumen) for
mortar,' Bede writes:

Perhaps they used bricks instead of stones and bitumen instead of
cement because those districts lacked a sufficient quantity of stones
for the completion of so great a work or because they knew that a
wall built of brick offered greater resistance to the danger of fires.
Bitumen is made from trees; it is also made from earth or waters.
Wherefore it is written later of the lands of Siddim (Gen. xiv.
10)—'The wooded vale had many wells of bitumen'—and the
Dead Sea is called in Greek 'the lake of Asfalt', that is of bitumen
because bitumen floating on top is wont to be gathered there.

Bede, *In Genesim*, III, 389–98

(ed. Jones)

Bitumen is an exceedingly hot and powerful glue whose virtue is
that wood which has been smeared with it cannot be consumed by
worms nor by the heat of the sun nor by the blowing of the winds
nor can it be dissolved by immersion in waters.

Bede, *In Genesim*, II, 1168–71

(ed. Jones)

GLASS

When the work was approaching completion (the building of the
monastery at Wearmouth) he sent messengers to Gaul to fetch
glassmakers, for craftsmen of this kind had hitherto been unknown
in Britain, so that they might lattice the windows of the church
and its chapels and upper storeys. They arrived and this was done;
not only did they complete the work which was asked of them, but
they also taught and instructed the English race in their skill. Their
art was exceedingly well adapted both for the enclosed lamps of
the church and for vessels of various different uses.

Bede, *Historia Abbatum*, 5

And I pray you that you will not spurn my request and my need—if there is anyone within your own diocese who is good at making vessels of glass, that you will deign to send him to me when the time is favourable. But, if, perhaps, there is one outside your boundaries, beyond your diocese and in the control of some other person, I beg your brotherly kindness to urge him to come here to us, because we are ignorant and without knowledge of this art.

Letter of Abbot Cuthbert to Lul, 764
(ed. Tangl No. 116)

JET

Britain is rich in veins of metals, of copper, iron, lead and silver and has a great deal of excellent jet. This is black and glossy. It burns when it is put in the fire and when it is lit it drives serpents away. When it is warmed by rubbing it holds what is applied to it, just as amber does.

Bede, *Ecclesiastical History*, I, 1

BLACKSMITHS

The king is Ecgfrith and the bishop Wilfrid.
The king, angered by what he had heard, ordered the bishop to be taken into his stronghold at Dunbar in charge of an officer called Tydlin, seemingly a more cruel man. He gave him orders that even this man who was so great a bishop was to be bound hand and foot and kept by himself, apart from men. The officer, compelled by the king's command, ordered blacksmiths to make iron chains. They set about their task with eagerness, measuring the limbs of our holy confessor, although they had no cause to do so, for God was against them.

Eddius, *Life of Wilfrid*, Ch. 38

The chains always proved to be too small to encompass the bishop's limbs, or so large that they fell off.

The speaker is Bede himself.

I myself knew a brother (and would that I had not) who was placed in a noble monastery, but himself lived an ignoble life. I could give his name if it were any use. The brethren and elders of the place often rebuked him and admonished him to turn towards a more chaste way of life but although he would not listen to them, nevertheless they suffered him patiently because they needed his outward service; for he was a smith of remarkable skill. He gave himself much to drunkenness and the other pleasures of a loose life. He preferred to remain in his workshop by day and by night rather than take part in singing psalms and praying in the church and listening with the brethren to the word of life. And so it befell that man, as some people are accustomed to say, that he who does not wish to enter the gate of the church in humility and of his own accord is bound to be led against his will into the gate of hell as a man condemned.

Bede, Ecclesiastical History, V, 14

On his deathbed this blacksmith was vouchsafed a vision of the hell to which he was bound. He died without the viaticum and was buried in the remotest corner of the monastery.

Let me recall with wondrous tales a brother, who could control and shape metals of the iron variety. His hammer under wise guidance crashed on to the iron placed under it in different positions on the anvil, while the forge roared. He had been called Cwicwine by his father in solicitude. In his lifetime God endowed him with the grace due to his merits, and crowned him with great honour, as a man noble in the eyes of his friends.

Æthelwulf, De Abbatibus, 278 and ff.
(Tr. A. Campbell)

The soul of this blacksmith was carried to heaven by an angelic host.

HORSE RACING

In the early days of my youth I was living among the bishop's clergy, devoting myself to the study of reading and singing, but with my mind not yet wholly restrained from its youthful pleasures. It happened one day as we were travelling with him on a journey that we came down on to a level track that was broad and suitable for galloping horses. The young men who were with him, mostly laymen, began to ask the bishop if he would allow them to try their horses against each other in a longer gallop. At first he refused, saying that what they wanted was idle folly, but eventually he was persuaded by the unanimous determination of the many. 'Do so if you wish,' he said, 'but Herebald is to have absolutely no part in this competition.' I begged him all the more earnestly to give me leave to compete with them for I believed that the horse which he himself had given me was the best, but I could in no way prevail upon him. The bishop and I watched as they turned back and forth, spurring their horses to a gallop, and I myself was so overcome by my wanton spirit that I was no longer able to restrain myself. Despite his prohibition, I mingled with the competitors and began at the same time to put my own horse to the gallop. While I was doing this I heard him behind my back saying with a sigh: 'Oh, what great grief you cause me by riding thus.' Although I heard him I went on against his bidding. And straightway as my fiery horse took a great leap across a hollow place in the track, I lost my balance and fell. At once I lost consciousness and all power of movement, as though I were dead. For in that place there was a stone level with the ground and covered with thin turf and no other stone could be found in the whole of that stretch of level ground. So it happened by chance, or rather by divine intervention as a punishment for my fault of disobedience, that I hit the stone with my head and with my hand which I had placed under my head as I fell. My thumb was broken and my skull fractured and, as I have said, I lay like a dead man.

Bede, *Ecclesiastical History*, V, 6

Herebald made a good recovery.

BARBAROUS CUSTOMS

You wear your garments according to the fashions of the Gentiles whom with God's help you drove out of your country by arms. It is an astonishing and senseless thing that you should follow the example of those whose way of life you have always hated. By a shameful custom you also mutilate your horses by slitting their nostrils and fastening their ears together. Indeed you also make them deaf and cut off their tails. Although you could have them uninjured you do not want this, but you make them repulsive to everybody. We have also heard that when there is a lawsuit among you, you draw lots after the fashion of the Gentiles. In these times this is held to be altogether sacrilegious. There are also many among you who eat horse, a thing which no Christians do in the east. Avoid this too and strive to make all that you do becoming and according to the Lord.

Report of the Papal Legates, A.D. 786

A CORRUPT PRIEST

If a priest or a deacon shall be found after examination to be corrupt, how shall the watchfulness of pastors guard against those who have been removed from office seeking to minister in another diocese, and so bringing scandal upon some others?

If a priest or a deacon who is renowned for his crimes and has been driven out by his own bishop, shall have ventured to officiate in another church, as soon as it shall have become known, let him be driven out by the bishop whose diocese it is. And so, never settled in any diocese of the church, let him remain ever wandering and fugitive, until humbled by long suffering he returns to submit himself to the laws of the church.

Archbishop Egbert's *Dialogue*

PENANCE

If a cleric has committed murder and has killed his neighbour, if he does it with hatred in his heart, he shall do penance for ten years. If a layman has committed murder in anger and with hatred in his heart, he shall do penance for four or five or six years; if in a quarrel, he shall do penance for three years; if he has unwillingly killed by accident, he shall do penance for one year.

Those who sacrifice to demons in great matters, if they are in the habit of doing so, shall do penance for ten years; in small matters for one year.

Those who practise auguries and divinations shall do penance for five years.

Those who send forth storms shall do penance for seven years.

If anyone drops the host negligently on the ground, he shall sing fifty psalms.

If anyone has neglected the host so that there are worms in it or it has become discoloured and lost its taste, he shall do penance for twenty or thirty or forty days. The host shall be burnt in the fire and its ash concealed beneath the altar.

Anyone who eats and drinks what has been tainted by a domestic animal, that is a dog or a cat, and is aware of it, is to sing one hundred psalms and fast for two days; if he is not aware of it, he is to sing fifty psalms and fast for one day.

If anyone shall have given to another a drink in which a dead mouse or other small creature are found, if he is a laymen he shall do penance for seven days. Anyone who afterwards discovers that he has drunk such a drink shall sing three hundred psalms in the monastery.

If a dead mouse or other small creature are found in flour or in any food or in drink or in curdled milk, what is in contact shall be thrown outside, but what is left may be eaten.

> Egbert's *Penitential*

This penitential, like others of the age, devotes much space to sexual aberrations. There are no Northumbrian civil law codes corresponding with these ecclesiastical penitentials.

MARRIAGE

If, however, the human race increases and is multiplied with the blessing of God, how greatly do they deserve to be cursed who prohibit marriage and condemn the following of a divine ordinance as if it had been discovered by the devil. And so marriage, which God established with the grace of his heavenly blessing for the propagation of the human race and the filling up of the earth, is not to be condemned. But more to be honoured and worthy of greater blessing is that virginity which, after the earth has been filled with men, desires with pure mind and body to follow the lamb whithersoever he shall have gone, that is the Lord Jesus in heaven.

Bede, *In Genesim*, I, 855–64
(ed. Jones)

EXHORTATION TO GOOD LIVING

We have remarked what noble fathers you had. See that ye be not degenerate sons to such forefathers. Look at your treasure of books. Consider the splendour of your churches, the beauty of your buildings, your way of life according to the Rule. Remember again how blessed is that man who passes from these most beautiful dwellings to the joys of the heavenly kingdom. Let the boys be present with praises of the heavenly king, and not be digging foxes out of holes or following the fleeting courses of hares. How wicked it is to let slip the services due to Christ and to follow the tracks of foxes. He who does not learn when he is young does not teach when he is old. Reflect upon that most noble teacher of your age, the priest Bede, how eager he was to learn when he was young, what praise he has now among men and what much greater glory of reward with God. Therefore stir up sluggish minds by his example. Be attentive to those who teach, open your books, look closely at what is written, understand what it means, so that you may succeed both in nourishing yourselves and in offering the food of spiritual life to others. Avoid secret feasts and furtive drinkings like the snare of the devil.

Alcuin, Letter to the Monks of
Wearmouth and Jarrow *(ed. Dümmler No. 19)*

Let the word of God be read in the company of priests. It is fitting for the reader and not the harpist to be heard there—the writings of the fathers, not the songs of the Gentiles. What has Ingeld to do with Christ? Narrow is the house. It will not be able to hold both. For the Kingdom of God will have no communion with profligate kings. This everlasting king reigns in heaven while that ruined pagan laments in hell. Let the voices of those who read be heard in your houses, not the uproar of those who laugh in the streets.

Alcuin, Letter to Bishop Higbald
of Lindisfarne *(ed. Dümmler No. 124)*

FOXES AND HERETICS

The nature of foxes accords well with the ways and the words of heretics, for they are exceedingly deceitful creatures who lie hidden in caves and in dens, and when they do come out they never run on a straight course but follow devious paths.

Bede, *In Cant. Cant.*
Pat. Lat. 91, 1114 D

AN ANECDOTE ABOUT BEDE

It is certain that those who were the first founders of your community very often visit the places where you dwell. And they rejoice with those whom they find living honourably and keeping their statutes, and they never cease to intercede for them with the holy judge. And it is not to be doubted that visitations of angels occur in holy places. For men say that our master and your patron the blessed Bede said: 'I know that angels visit the canonical hours and the congregations of the brethren; what if they do not find me among the brothers? Will they not say—"Where is Bede? Why does he not come to the appointed prayers with the brothers?"'

Alcuin, Letter to the Monks at
Wearmouth *(ed. Dümmler No. 284)*

MNEMONICS FOR SCHOOLBOYS

February First is the day of Policarpus.
  On the Second there is Christ in the Temple.
Agatha belongs to the Fifth of the month.
  On the Fourteenth we remember Valentinus.
Sixteen February is the day of Juliana,
  While Matthias consecrates the Twenty-Fourth.
Next we come to Gregory who takes the Twelfth of March,
  But the Twentieth we always keep for Cuthbert.

York Metrical Kalendar

ADAM

The name contains four letters—'a' and 'd' and 'a' and 'm', and from these four letters the four quarters of the earth take their beginning when they are named in Greek. Among the Greeks the east is called *anatole*, the west *disis*, the north *arctos* and the south *mesembria*. It is very right that the name of the first man, by whose progeny the whole world was to be filled, should contain mystically within itself all the four quarters of the world.

Bede, *In Genesim*, II, ll. 729–34
(*ed. Jones*)

SINGING

Now Paulinus had left in his church at York James, a deacon, a true churchman and saintly. For a long time afterwards he remained in the church and seized much prey from the ancient enemy by teaching and baptising. The village near Catterick in which he used chiefly to live is still called by his name to this day. Because he was very skilled at singing in church, when peace had been restored to the kingdom and the number of the faithful was increasing, he also began to teach ecclesiastical singing to many people in the manner of the Romans and of the men of Kent. He himself went the way of his fathers old and full of days, as the Scriptures say.

Bede, *Ecclesiastical History*, II, 20

From this time also men began to learn throughout all the churches of the English the way of singing in church which they had hitherto known only in Kent. Excepting James about whom we have spoken above, the first singing master in the churches of the Northumbrians was Æddi, surnamed Stephen, who had been invited from Kent by the most reverend man Wilfrid, the first among the bishops of English race who learnt to deliver the catholic way of living to the churches of the English.

Ibid., IV, 2

There was in the monastery of this abbess [Hilda] a certain brother who was specially marked by divine grace in that he used to compose songs which were suitable for men of religion and piety. And so it was that whatever he learnt from the holy Scriptures through translators, he himself soon afterwards turned into poetic words of the greatest sweetness and humility in his own language, that is English. . . . He had lived in the secular habit until he was well advanced in years and had never learnt anything of poetry. And so it sometimes happened at a feast, when it had been decided that for the sake of entertainment each should sing in turn, he would get up in the middle of the feasting when he saw the harp approaching himself, go out and make his way home.

On one occasion when he did so, he left the place of feasting and went to the cattle-byres which had been entrusted to his care for that night, and there at the proper time he composed himself for sleep. While he slept someone appeared to him, greeting him and calling him by his own name: 'Cædmon,' he said, 'sing me something.' But he replied, 'I don't know how to sing; this is why I left the feasting and came here.' Then the man who was speaking with him said: 'But you must sing to me.' 'What must I sing?' And the man said: 'Sing about the beginning of creation.' When he had received this answer Cædmon immediately began to sing verses which he had never heard before in praise of God the Creator. This is their general sense: 'Now we must praise the maker of the heavenly kingdom, the power of the Creator and his counsel, the deeds of the Father of glory; how He, since He is eternal God, became the author of all marvellous works, who being the almighty guardian of the human race first created heaven as a roof for the children of men, and next the earth.' This is the meaning but not the exact order of the words which he sang as he slept; for songs, however excellently composed, cannot be literally translated from one language into another. When he woke from his sleep, he retained in his memory everything that he had sung while asleep and soon added more verses in the same way in song worthy of God.

Ibid., IV 24

Under the guidance of his teachers Cædmon later turned many passages from Scripture into English verse, singing so sweetly that his teachers became his audience.

Benedict also contrived to bring the aforesaid abbot John to Britain so that he might teach in his monastery the full year's cycle of singing as it was practised at St Peter's in Rome. Abbot John carried out the instructions of the pope and taught the singers of the aforesaid monastery [Wearmouth] the order and manner of singing and reading aloud, also committing to writing everything that was necessary for the celebration of festal days through the whole course of the year. These writings are still preserved in that monastery and have now also been copied by many others round about. Not only did John teach the brothers of that monastery but from almost all the monasteries of that kingdom those who were skilled in singing came flocking to hear him, and there were many who invited him to teach in other places.

Ibid., IV, 18

Bishop Acca invited an excellent singer called Maban who had been taught the harmonies of singing by the successors of the disciples of the blessed Pope Gregory in Kent, to teach himself and his people. He kept him there for twelve years so that he might not only teach them those ecclesiastical chants which they had not known before, but also restore to their original form those which they had once known but which had begun to deteriorate by long use or neglect. Bishop Acca himself was a singer of the greatest skill.

Ibid., V, 20

When the revered festivals of God's saints came round, and when between two choirs in the church he sang the verses of the psalms among the brothers, they rendered in song the sweet-sounding music of the flowing antiphon. And the lector, a man very learned in books, poured forth song to the general delight, singing in a distinct voice. And, when as the day went on, they completed the singing of mass, the brothers accompanied their spiritual father to the table with harmonious song. Moreover no man could describe fittingly how earnestly he desired to celebrate sacred solemnities with his monks at festivals, how the clergy rejoiced within their bounds: shaking the church they filled it with loud song.

Æthelwulf, *De Abbatibus,* 495–506

(*Tr. A. Campbell*)

The abbot was Sigwine, but we do not know the site of his monastery.

THE ACTIVE AND THE CONTEMPLATIVE LIFE

To live the active life is to devote oneself to just works as a zealous servant of Christ, and especially to keep oneself unspotted from this world, restraining mind, hand, tongue and all the other members of the body from every kind of pollution by sinful temptation, and to submit always to the service of God. And then to help one's neighbours to the best of one's powers with the necessities of life by giving food to the hungry, drink to the thirsty, clothing to the cold, and by receiving the destitute and the wanderers into one's home, by visiting the sick, by burying the dead, by snatching the helpless out of the power of the stronger, and the destitute and the poor from those who lay hold of them. And also by showing the way of truth to those who err and submitting oneself to the demands of brotherly love, and especially by striving for justice, even unto death.

The contemplative life is when a man who is thoroughly taught through the long practising of holy living and who is instructed by the sweetness of daily prayer and often goaded by remorseful tears, has learnt to set himself free from all the affairs of the world and to direct his gaze towards the one true love, and has begun in the heat of his desire to taste beforehand the joy of everlasting bliss which will be experienced in the life to come, and sometimes even, as far as is right for mortal men, to gaze upon the divine in the rapture of his mind. This life of divine contemplation comes especially to those who, after long trial of monastic discipline, have learnt to live apart from men, with minds so much the freer to meditate upon heavenly matters as they are set apart from earthly disturbances.

Bede, *Homiliae*, I, 9, ll. 151–74
(*ed. Hurst*)

PRAYER

Citizens of the heavenly fatherland who are pilgrims upon earth are not forbidden to pray unto the Lord for times of peace, for bodily health, for abundance of crops, for fair weather and for the necessities of life—that is, if these things are not sought to excess, and if they are sought only in order that, with life abounding in the present, we may reach out the more freely towards the gifts that are to come. There are some, however, who demand temporal peace and prosperity from their creator, not in order that they may obey that same creator with greater dedication of spirit, but in order that they may have all the more opportunity for feasting and drunkenness, in order that they may the more easily and freely become slaves to the allurements of fleshly desires. Of such men it is rightly said that they pray in evil fashion. Truly, none of those who pray in this way deserve to receive what they seek in this evil manner. And so, my beloved brethren, let us strive both to pray well and to become worthy to receive that for which we pray.

Bede, *Homiliae*, II, 14, ll. 112–25
(*ed. Hurst*)

CHAPTER TEN

A Whirlwind came out of the North

'IT IS NOT always night, neither is it always day, but each takes its turn; so also with times of suffering and times of good fortune in this world. Today the storm may threaten, but tomorrow fair weather will shine.' Alcuin, courageously seeking to give consolation to others for the evils of the time which lay so heavily upon himself, was aged about seventy when he wrote these words in a long letter to the archbishop of York in 801. He continued: 'Let the anchor of our hope be fastened in Christ. Let him who rejoices in times of prosperity be fearful for times of adversity; and let him who is wearied with misfortune hope that better times will come soon.' Alcuin died in 804, more than twenty years after he had left York to join the palace school of Charlemagne at Aachen; but he wrote many letters to kings, bishops, abbots and others who were among his friends, and as we read these letters today we cannot fail to be impressed with a strong sense of his continuing affection for his native Northumbria to which he was never able to return. His greatest love was for his own school at York, whose library contained some rare treasures of books that he had not been able to find among the Franks. He sent young scribes from his monastery at Tours to make copies and bring them back; and by his messenger, Cuculus (the little bird of spring), he sent wine for the archbishop, a hundred pounds of tin for such repairs to the church as might be needed, and four latticed railings. 'It seems only right that the belfry should be covered with a roof, for beauty's sake, as well as for the fame of the church ... Cuculus will tell you of my illness. I am a little better, praise be to God, but I do not recover the health I used to have.'

Alcuin's letters tell us much about these later years of Northumbria's history, even if they may prompt greedy historians to wish for more. In particular they allow us to share, at least in a small way, the shock and grief by which he was afflicted when he heard the news which was briefly recorded by an annalist in these words: 'In that same year 793, on 8 June, the ravages of heathen men miserably destroyed God's church on Lindisfarne, with plunder and slaughter.' Another writer later enlarged the detail, telling how 'pagans came to Britain from the north with a flotilla of ships, like stinging hornets. Like fierce wolves they overran the country on all sides, plundering, tearing, killing, not only beasts, the sheep and the oxen, but even priests and deacons, companies of monks and nuns. They came to the church of Lindisfarne and laid all waste with fearful plundering, they trampled upon the holy places with unhallowed feet, dug up the altar and carried off all the treasures of the holy church. They killed some of the brethren and took some away with them in chains. They drove out many of them naked and loaded with insults, and some of them they drowned in the sea.' In the following year, we read, 'the aforesaid pagans, ravaging the harbour of King Ecgfrith, destroyed the monastery at the mouth of the river Don (thought to be Jarrow). But St Cuthbert did not allow them to depart unpunished. Their leader was put to a cruel death there by the English, and after a short while a violent storm shattered, destroyed and broke up their ships, and the sea swallowed up a great many of them. Some of them were cast ashore and quickly slain without mercy. And these things befell them rightly for they had deeply injured those who had done them no wrong.'

There are some nowadays who say that we exaggerate the damage done by the Vikings, that we pay too much heed to the lamentations of monastic chroniclers written by men whose tale was coloured by their misfortunes. Assuredly they would have found it hard to see the Vikings' point of view. Yet each new changing age, whether it be Roman, Anglo-Saxon, Viking or Norman, was undoubtedly initiated with much violence, and we do not belittle the stature of later achievements by recognising the violence of these beginnings. The monks of Lindisfarne saw the altars of God splashed with the blood of those whose only weapon was prayer. They could not have the consolation, nor could their companions who were carried off in chains, of knowing that posterity would come to marvel at the great ships of Gokstad and Oseberg, to rejoice in the writings of Snorri Sturlason, to cherish the sagas of the Icelanders.

There can be no mistaking the impact of the news upon Alcuin;

it was one of horror amounting almost to disbelief: 'We and our forefathers have lived in this most lovely land for almost 350 years and never before has there appeared in Britain such terror as we have now suffered from a pagan race. Behold the church of the holy Cuthbert bespattered with the blood of God's priests, robbed of all its ornaments, the most venerable place in all Britain given over as a prey to the pagans.' The blow was felt to be all the harder because it had fallen on the very place where Christianity had been reborn among the English after Paulinus had left York. 'What assurance can there be for the churches of Britain if even St Cuthbert defends not his own?' The same anguished tone colours Alcuin's letters to the monks of Wearmouth and Jarrow—'you who live by the sea whence the plague first fell upon us'. Men might read in this disaster the fulfilment of the word which the Lord had spoken to the prophet Jeremiah: 'Out of the north an evil shall break forth upon all the inhabitants of the land.'

Alcuin is unlikely to have known the full tale of the last decade of the eighth century, when the whirlwind came out of the north. Had he been able to read all the records still preserved in our own times, he would have learnt that by the end of the century the Vikings had visited Iona itself, the island of Lambey, off the Irish coast by Dublin, and Morganwg in south Wales. They had raided islands lying off the coast of Aquitaine and had rounded Land's End to enter the English Channel. A West-Saxon record tells how in these days 'suddenly a not very large fleet of the Danes arrived, speedy vessels to the number of three; that was their first arrival. At the report the king's reeve, who was then in the town called Dorchester, leapt on his horse, sped to the harbour with a few men (for he thought they were merchants rather than marauders) and admonishing them in an authoritative manner, gave orders that they should be driven to the royal town.' Unhappily for the reeve and his men the intruders did not take kindly to being admonished in an authoritative manner; they killed the reeve and his companions 'on the spot'. On the Dorset coast, as on the Northumbrian, men were taken aback by the sudden, by the unexpected, by what seemed almost beyond belief.

These were not great fleets of invaders, only two or three ships skilfully handled, swift to come and swift to go, ships carrying

men armed with sword, axe and spear. They came in search of
loot, and perhaps of slaves, and were surely astonished to find that
both were there for the taking, not secure in remote fortresses, but
lying close by the very sea itself and completely defenceless.
Anglo-Saxons had often fought each other and were still doing so,
but they had never been themselves attacked from the sea since
their own coming to Britain. We have no need to follow the
further unfolding of the Viking Age, nor could we, even if we
wished to, trace in detail the destruction of the Northumbrian
kingdom. Historical records were kept by monks and when these
were attacked, the keeping of records ceased. We cannot find a
Northumbrian writing history again until after the Norman
Conquest. It is from a West Saxon, not writing in Latin but in his
native English, that we learn about the conquest of York by the
Danes in 867, an event which may be taken to mark the final
destruction of the Northumbrian kingdom. With continuing
Scandinavian pressure in the south, and growing Scottish pressure
in the north, the old Northumbria gradually shrank northwards
from Humber to Tyne and southwards from Forth to Tweed,
while her old British enemy on the west, the ancient kingdom of
Strathclyde, recovered something of its former strength.

Bede knew that there were many in his own day who were
bringing monastic life into disrepute, but he also knew that there
were many others who strove to live a life of Christian virtue.
During the two centuries which separate the Danish capture of
York from the Norman victory at Hastings, Northumbrian
monasticism, once the creative spring of all that was greatest in
Northumbrian civilisation, was totally destroyed. We cannot
follow the process of destruction, but no doubt there were failures
within as well as attacks from without. Shortly after 1070 the prior
of Winchcombe in Gloucestershire, a monk called Aldwin, was
prompted by reading Bede's *History* to visit the places where there
had once been so many companies of monks. He and two
companions set off, intending to live a life of poverty and solitude.
They came eventually to Jarrow where they found only roofless
walls, nothing left of those splendid treasures of books and
buildings which had been familiar to Alcuin three centuries
earlier. They put up a roof of rough-hewn timber and thatch, and

built inside a small hut where they lived in cold and hunger. Jarrow, we may suppose, was in no worse plight than Lindisfarne, Melrose, Hexham, Whitby, York and many other places where there had once been fine buildings and precious books. It may have been in the days of the Danish attack that the great Roman column now lying beneath York Minster was overthrown.

Bede's *History* served as one reminder of happier days in the past, but there was another link, one which had never been quite broken. After the fall of York, much of southern Northumbria, the old kingdom of Deira, came under Danish or Norse rule. Further north the community at Lindisfarne became anxious for the safety of their most precious possession—St Cuthbert. The story of his fate is not told by those who witnessed it, but grew from tradition richly embroidered by Symeon for the greater glory of Cuthbert's final home, the cathedral church at Durham. The tale tells how the community left Lindisfarne in the year 875, taking their treasures with them, but it may be that a move had already been made somewhat earlier to a less exposed site at Norham on the mainland. We cannot now distinguish the truth of the matter, but must rest content with the legend, telling how the congregation, including seven men specially chosen to guard the saint's body, wandered about for seven years. When they tried to take ship to Ireland a storm drove them back, and they lost overboard a treasured copy of the Gospels, adorned with gold and precious stones. It was later found lying on the sand three miles out from the shore when the tide fell to an exceptionally low level, and (as those who read hagiographies would naturally expect) the book showed no sign of damage from being immersed in the salt waters. The congregation, diminished by privation, found itself at one time in Yorkshire and later at Chester-le-Street, an old Roman site in the county of Durham. Here St Cuthbert stayed, the focus of the community, for almost a hundred years, until the final move was made to Durham in 995. Whatever the legend, whatever the truth, Cuthbert's relics, the *Lindisfarne Gospels* and one or two other books were faithfully guarded in times of great danger, and we may be thankful to the guardians that they remain still in our possession.

The Normans gave Cuthbert a place of honour at the east end of their new cathedral. The tale of Bede's bones is less heroic. There was a priest of the church of Durham whose name was Alfred. He was a pious man, greatly devoted to St Cuthbert and a jealous guardian of the relics. He visited the sites of the ancient monasteries and raised from the grounds the bones of many saints. Among them, as Symeon would have us believe, were the bones of Baldred (he who had once comforted a soul in peril), of Acca, bishop of Hexham (though Hexham would not admit this claim), of the murdered Deiran king Oswine, of Æbbe, the abbess of Coldingham. They were all gathered to Durham, a city:

> renowned throughout all Britain,
> Set on steep slopes and marvellously built
> With rocks all round. A strongly running river
> Flows past enclosed by weirs, and therein dwell
> All kinds of fishes in the seething waters.
>
> *(Tr. Hamer)*

But Alfred was ambitious for his church. He used to go each year to Jarrow where he knew that Bede had lived, died and was buried. Once when he was there he left very early and returned alone to Durham. Although he lived for many more years afterwards, he never again went back to Jarrow. His friends used often to ask him about the resting-place of Bede's bones, and he would answer, speaking promptly as a man who knew what he was talking about, 'No one knows better about this than I do.' Today's visitor may go to the tomb in the Galilee Chapel, at the west end of the cathedral, and read upon the marble top: *Hac sunt in fossa Bedae venerabilis ossa.*

The kingdom of Northumbria, like the reign of one of its warrior kings, was born and died in violence. It grew upon the ruins of one empire built by land, and it fell before the onslaught of another whose strength lay upon the sea. The power of Rome stretched north and south, east and west, as far as men could march, not readily entrusting themselves to the storms and tides of ocean

waters. The Viking ships, with the great rivers and all the wide
expanses of the sea for their highway, were not hindered by
mountain or forest. They could reach the southern shores of the
Caspian whence their traders might join the camel trains to
Baghdad. They could cross the Black Sea to Byzantium. Their
crews carved runes upon an ancient Grecian lion by the harbour of
Piraeus, a lion whose home is now in Venice. They knew the coasts
of Africa and Spain. They went to Iceland, Greenland and North
America. Needing only wind and a strong arm they could come
and go where they pleased. As the map of Europe, some of Asia,
some of Africa and some of North America unfolds in the mind's
eye, the little kingdom of Northumbria seems to grow less and less
until it almost vanishes from sight, like those rafts driven down the
Tyne and so far out to sea that they seemed no larger than small
birds floating on the waves. How then, can we claim for a
kingdom so small, with a history so short, those qualities which go
towards the making of a golden age? There is at least one ready
answer—the city of Athens was smaller.

Seen against the background of the great European migrations—the movements of Ostrogoths and Visigoths, Lombards
and Burgundians, Franks and Alemanni—the kingdom of
Northumbria seems no more than a very small patch in the great
variegated European quilt. It was one of almost a dozen kingdoms
established in Britain by the Anglo-Saxons. Three of its kings
achieved sufficient strength to win themselves a rewarding
supremacy over those who ruled as their contemporaries in central
and southern England, but the ground was lost by their successors;
and we cannot say that the rulers of Northumbria made any great
contribution either to the political unification of England or to the
means by which the country was eventually to be governed. They
established no lasting boundary to the north, they left no codes of
law to their successors. The rulers of Mercia in the eighth century,
and of Wessex in the ninth and tenth centuries left to posterity a
greater legacy of unity and strength. Yet, within their narrower
limits, the kings of Northumbria in the seventh century fulfilled
the duty of a Germanic king to keep a firm hold upon his kingdom
and in so doing they brought necessary peace and security after a
season of great violence. Bede recognised what this achievement

had meant for his own age, and he embodied it in the tale of the woman alone with her newborn babe crossing the land in perfect safety. It may be that Æthelfrith and Edwin, Oswald, Oswy and Ecgfrith fought for no more than the victory which would bring them the spoils of war—'an incalculable and incredible store of royal treasure and gifts'. Yet the outcome of victory was the peace and stability which were the necessary foundation of other achievements.

Upon the protection, or at least the tolerance, of strong kings there depended the success of the monks who came from Italy or Iona to preach the Christian faith to the pagan English. This was no less the case in other Anglo-Saxon kingdoms—Kent, Wessex, East Anglia—than it was in Northumbria. Just as the Northumbrian kings who protected the monks have seemed in some ways to be characters in a book, rather than men whom we have been able to know more directly, so also with the missionaries. We gain nothing by pretending to greater knowledge than we have, much more by pondering a little upon the extent of our ignorance. Saving only a couple of letters from Gregory the Great, there is no contemporary written evidence about the conversion of the Northumbrians. Neither Paulinus nor Aidan, neither Hilda nor Cuthbert, have left us so much as one line written by themselves. We may read the entries in the diary of Samuel Pepys for but a single month, and wonder what we might have learnt if Paulinus had written as much to cover all the six years of his Northumbrian mission; if Ceolfrith had written about the plague at Jarrow as Pepys wrote about the plague in London. If we recognise Bede's account of the conversion for what it is, we by no means lessen its value for posterity, indeed we may perhaps discern herein a little of that elusive golden quality; that there was a man found with the vision to see what inspiration others might derive from the story of how Christianity came to a pagan race. Yet the vision is now to be found more in the telling than in the fact. The saints stand more clearly before us than the men, not speaking for themselves, but drawn only as others saw them. Cuthbert compelling all by his gentleness, Wilfrid repelling some by his vigour. We can share a little more directly in their countryside, for neither Tweed at Old Melrose, nor Holy Island, have changed so much that we cannot still see them much as Cuthbert saw them. We can envisage the monasteries in which these men and women lived, descending the steep stairs beneath the church at Hexham to enter Wilfrid's crypt and finding it much as he left it. Bede's own account of Wearmouth and Jarrow, detailed in several ways, has now been given increased depth and colour by excavation. He must indeed be insensitive who can go there and enter the church of St Peter or the church of St Paul without any awareness of a past still continuing into the present. Yet when we try to look beyond the saints and the scholars, it is hard to catch sight of any others. The little church at Escomb stands almost complete from this age, but we can say so only because of the way it was built, not because of its history, for it has none. All the detail is lost and when only achievement remains, the real may be heavily suffused by the romantic, until we remind ourselves how young were most of the people who were buried in the Wearmouth cemetery.

Should anyone be more interested in learning about the countryside than about the religion professed by its inhabitants, he will find the answer to his every question obstructed by lack of evidence adequate for even the most general reply. Skilful excavation now offers a foundation upon which the imaginative can build his own impression of the royal township at Yeavering. We can envisage a town at York with almost all its buildings of Roman origin; a place busy enough to attract a colony of Frisian merchants, ships bringing North Sea cargoes to the old Roman wharves. Occasionally we can catch a glimpse of a village—but how many people would be living in it, what did their houses look like, did they own their land or rent it or work it as serfs, what kind of plough did they use, what sort of corn did they grow, how many beasts did they have? And so we might go on, piling question upon question, but finding no answers. Some day excavation may tell us more, but so far, those who have dug have been less fortunate in their excavations than Trimma was when he went off to an old battlefield in search of King Edwin's bones. Though aerial photography may tell us much, celestial shafts of light are less helpful than they used to be. Even at Yeavering which had belonged to some of the most powerful and probably the wealthiest of the Nothumbrian kings, the only hint of former treasures was a single gold coin. Yet if, as seems likely enough, most villagers were poor, there were certainly some men who acquired great wealth, men who could give rich endowments to churches and monasteries, so rich that Bede was fearful lest the whole church might be corrupted. Was this wealth acquired merely as the spoil of war or were there any rich merchants, like the wool merchants of East Anglia in the later Middle Ages? Whence came the gold for the great cross and for the chalice which Edwin gave to the church at York? How was *lapis lazuli* brought to the scriptorium at Lindisfarne?

The Northumbrian nobility, the farmers, the traders, the slaves remain unknown, and we must turn back from the countryside towards the church again. Even in this field we must enlarge the boundaries of our ignorance, and take care lest we be too free with our labels—barbaric and pagan, civilised and Christian, remembering that Virgil and Æthelfrith were both pagans. Bede would condemn the writings of Aristotle and Plato, of Virgil and Ovid, no less than he would condemn the unwritten tales coming out of the Germanic past. Was there a bard at Æthelfrith's court and did he sing in ancient forms about the great battle at *Degsastan*, that most celebrated place, at which the English king defeated the Scots? It is worth our while to ask the question if only to elicit the answer that had there been such a pagan battle-poem the church would not have allowed it to survive. We know nothing about the virtues most highly prized by Bede's grandparents. Neither Tacitus writing about the German races nor Bede telling of the destruction of a pagan temple in Yorkshire enable us to compare the older pagan values with the newer Christian virtues. We can see the new, but we shall never recover the old. Even so, it would surely be unwise to envisage any sudden, complete, total replacement of the old by the new. Christian books laid down the penance for those who stirred up storms by witchcraft.

Those who ponder upon the greatest achievements of Northumbrian civilisation may turn their thoughts towards Bede's own *History*, to the richly-coloured pages of the *Lindisfarne Gospels* or to the dignity of Christ's effigy on the Bewcastle cross, all of them symbolic of seemingly triumphant Christianity. Yet there is another face to Northumbria, less sharply cut, perhaps more powerfully suggestive. Anyone who looks closely at the little casket made from the bone of that stranded whale will find much to stir the imagination. Carved upon it in miniature—the whole casket is no more than nine inches in its greatest dimension—they will see a picture of Titus capturing Jerusalem, and another with the she-wolf feeding Romulus and Remus, two scenes from the Mediterranean, one of pagan and one of early Christian times. Two other scenes are more difficult to interpret. One of them shows a fight in which an archer is defending his house against a vigorous attack by a group of armed men. Among the several figures in the other scene is a curious seated creature with wings and the head of a beast, but seemingly human hands and feet; there is a horse with head drooping over a small hunched human figure who seems to be placed within a mound or perhaps a cave; and elsewhere in the same scene there is an armed man and three figures in conversation. We may suppose that both of these scenes, now obscure to us, tell stories about heroes familiar to the age in which they were carved. There have been many attempts to relate these scenes to stories about Egill, brother of Weland the Smith, and to Sigurd and his wife, Sigrun, but none of them has yet succeeded in winning the approval of all scholars. They remain enigmatic and tantalising reminders of our ignorance about so much of Northumbria. There are still two more scenes, and since they are placed side by side on the front panel, the designer may have regarded them as of special importance. To one side are the three kings of orient bringing their gifts and bowing down before the infant Christ, held by the Virgin Mary. Balancing this Christian theme, there is a scene from the tale of Weland the Smith (Plate 16). Luckily this tale came to be widely spread, in slightly differing versions. It tells how Weland avenged himself on a king who had injured him, by killing the king's two sons and turning their skulls into drinking cups—and there on the casket we can see Weland in his smithy, with all his tools around him, a cup held in his tongs, a headless body lying by the anvil. What was the philosophy of the man who had this casket made for his delight? Barbaric Christian? Civilised pagan? Why did he choose to place Weland and Christ side by side? What treasure might we have found in this little box had it not been opened by some Pandora?

As we learn more, so, in paradox, we become increasingly aware of our ignorance; where so much must remain unknown we hesitate to reach any conclusion, to move towards any judgement. Those who have studied the great ages of creative achievement in the past, in Greece or Italy, in Shakespeare's England, may smile with some condescension at the conceit which dares to bestow upon Northumbria's history any of the qualities of a golden age. Standing upon the Athenian Acropolis, entering St Peter's in Rome or crossing St Mark's Square in Venice, a man, even if he have any awareness of Northumbria's existence, will see it only as an infinitely remote, barbaric land, irrelevant to his own surroundings. In some ways this judgement will be a right one, but of course it is coloured by its maker's point of view. Certainly Northumbria was both remote and barbaric, its inhabitants speaking neither Greek nor Latin. In July of 598, a year after the arrival of Augustine in Canterbury, Gregory the Great wrote joyfully to a bishop in Alexandria, telling how Christianity had reached the English race who lived in a far corner of the world and who had hitherto worshipped only sticks and stones. Several hundred years later William of Malmesbury described his own birthplace as lying in the most distant corner of the world, on the furthest shore of an island which some people called 'another world', because there were not many geographers who had ever heard of its existence: Bede would have been entirely in sympathy with this point of view; for him the centre of the world lay in Jerusalem, as men might know from the tall pillar which stood there and cast no shadow at the season of the summer solstice. Read what he says in his commentary on the *Song of Songs*. 'I urge the reader of this work not to think that I have laboured in vain in having wanted to discuss at greater length the many things which are contained in this book about the nature of trees and aromatic herbs, and which I have learnt from books written in ancient times. I have not done this with any sense of my own conceit, but out of regard for the ignorance of myself and of my fellow men who have been born and bred in an island of the Ocean so far outside the world.'

This sense of remoteness, and the increased challenge which it brought to men seeking knowledge, perhaps brings us closer to the heart of the matter. Northumbria, nowadays greatly loved by those who belong to it, was a harsh land for men of earlier times, well served by the sea, but not offering any easy means of livelihood. Ireland, thought Bede, was a gentler land where the snow seldom lay upon the ground, where there was no need to cut hay in summer for winter use, nor any need to build stables for the protection of beasts. The vine could be made to grow in Northumbria only under the skilled hand of the stone-mason who carved its intricate patterns upon the great crosses. Yet in this remote corner of a remote island, seeming so bleak until the Romantic poets with comfortable homes and plenty of wine taught us to see it otherwise, there was born out of barbarism a civilisation which, for a brief century or so, itself gave the lead to others in the struggle to create something new upon the ruins of the old. We can, if we wish, dismiss it as credulous, naïve, barbaric. We can see in it all the unfeeling intolerance of prejudice and bigotry. Even so, those who study its achievements will find it hard not to sense an invigorating freshness that blows as keenly as the winds of spring along the Bamburgh shores. There is nothing here of that accumulated dust which sometimes lies upon an antique world. We in this present age no longer share that unshakeable faith which moves mountains in its powers of creation, as well as of destruction, but we can look back, with gratitude, at what was achieved by those to whom certainty was given. We can still, if we make sufficient effort, share a little in the childlike trust and in the eager delight which a few of these sons of barbarians used to find, to borrow the words of the greatest among them, in learning or teaching or writing.

Advice to a Pilgrim

WE HAVE IMAGINED an Anglo-Saxon bard travelling northwards from southern England or a pilgrim slowly passing his years on a southerly journey from Iona. What may be said to the fast-moving traveller of a modern age? It should be said first that he could travel far and wide without seeing anything at all that Bede might have looked upon, save for the countryside itself. Therefore it is to the countryside that the traveller should first look—to the Yorkshire Wolds, the Pennine Chain, the Lakeland hills, the southern uplands of Scotland, the river estuaries and the long stretches of seashore on both eastern and western sides of the country. Northumbria—in its widest extent from Humber and Mersey to Forth and Clyde, and not to be confused with the much smaller Northumberland—remains a thinly-peopled country outside the dense concentrations of modern industry. Those who have learnt to know this countryside, especially by walking its moors and hills, will understand how different were the problems facing a Northumbrian king from those confronting a Mercian king whose dominion embraced the flat plain of the English midlands. Though lacking the barren ruggedness of the Scottish Highlands, Northumbria is predominantly an upland country. It was not easy to travel between east and west, save where the path had been smoothed by a Roman road. Its people looked outwards towards the sea, not inwards towards the empty hills; perhaps this was why its remoteness was no barrier to its intellectual and artistic growth. A land such as this, kept apart by its central hills, could not easily be turned into a firmly-controlled political unit, as London governments down the ages have had to learn. Authority will have depended less upon the elaboration of local government, such as Alfred later achieved for Wessex, than upon ability to lead a warband to victory upon a distant battlefield or to defeat a sudden intrusion from without. Yet today's traveller should remember that Bede's Northumbria had for centuries been part of the Roman Empire. The visible remains of Roman roads and Roman forts are much more striking today than any remains of the Anglo-Saxon period—how much more impressive will they have been in Bede's time.

The traveller will be greatly helped by two maps, both of them published by the Ordnance Survey: the *Map of Roman Britain* (3rd Ed. 1956, scale 1 : 1,000,000) will reveal the impact of the Roman occupation upon the Anglo-Saxon countryside; and the *Map of Britain in the Dark Ages* (2nd Ed. 1965, scale 1 : 1,000,000) marks Anglo-Saxon and Celtic antiquities of the period *c.* 410–*c.* 870.

The area formerly included in the kingdom of Northumbria at its greatest extent is now covered by Sheets 6–11 of the Quarter-Inch series published by the Ordnance Survey (1 : 250,000). For places which strangers may find difficulty in locating, national grid references are given to these sheets to the nearest kilometre. The same references can of course be used on the One Inch Series.

A motorist approaching Northumbria from the south has a choice of two obvious routes and one less obvious, and in all three cases he will be following, with greater or lesser deviation, the general line taken by the old Roman roads. He may take the M6 to the west of the Pennines or the A1 to the east; the former, offering more spectacular scenery, passes through country in which Celtic influences probably remained strong, while the latter approaches more closely to Northumbrian sites and antiquities of Bede's age. Those who choose the A1 will cross near the beginning of their journey the rivers Trent, Idle and Don close to which some of the great battles of the seventh century were fought. This is the area known in earlier times as Hatfield Chase, where Northumbria's southern Marches lay, flat, low-lying country, marshy and liable to heavy flooding before modern drainage. We may recall the battle in which Penda was defeated and killed in 655 near the river *Winwæd*. The identity of this river has been lost but Bede tells us how owing to heavy rains it 'had overflowed its channels and its banks to such an extent that many more were drowned in flight than were destroyed by the sword in the battle'.

Crossing the river Aire, the traveller moves into country which had once belonged to Elmet, the British kingdom conquered by Edwin in the seventh century; the observant may notice signposts pointing to Barwick-in-Elmet, west of the A1, and Sherburn-in-Elmet to the east. Before these are reached another signpost points to Ledsham (S E 4529); here the church of All Saints embodies some interesting and important remains dating from before 800. Relatively close to Ledsham are the churches of Otley (S E 2146) and Collingham (S E 3946) both of which contain sculptured crosses of the Anglo-Saxon period. Since York must not be missed the traveller might turn from the A1 to the A64, and if he does so he will pass through Tadcaster. This is believed to be the site of a Roman station known in Bede's time as *Kælcacæstir*; to it, says Bede, retired Heiu, believed to have been the first woman in Northumbria to have taken the nun's veil.

A traveller at leisure might choose the third route to the north, going first to Lincoln, visited by Paulinus, and then following the Roman road, now called Ermine Street, northwards to Humber. This part of the country belonged to the kingdom of Lindsey, subject to the domination at one time of Northumbria and at another of Mercia. At Barton-on-Humber (T A 0321) there is a small Anglo-Saxon church of the greatest interest, and although it is tenth or eleventh century in date, no traveller interested in Anglo-Saxon antiquities should miss an opportunity of seeing it. Even though the open sea is some twenty-five miles away to the east, the Humber is still almost two miles wide at the point where the car-ferry crosses from New Holland to Kingston-upon-Hull, and the voyager who uses it cannot fail to see how formidable was the barrier offered by this estuary. Imagination may even induce a sense of arriving in a foreign land after a sea-crossing, a sense no doubt more keenly present to the travellers of Bede's age. A further gain from the Humber crossing is that it leads directly to the Yorkshire Wolds, the heartlands of the kingdom of Deira, the lands chosen by the earliest Anglo-Saxon settlers north of Humber. The *Map of Britain in the Dark Ages* will show where Anglo-Saxon cemeteries have been discovered; such places as Driffield (T A 0358) and Sancton (T A 9039), though the visitor should not expect to see any superficial remains on the ground.

Close by Sancton lies Goodmanham (T A 8943). the site of the heathen temple desecrated by the priest Coifi after Edwin and his councillors had accepted Christianity. The exact whereabouts of the temple is unknown, but those with an eye for topography may wonder if it might not be the same as the site now occupied by the early Norman church.

York was the scene of Edwin's conversion, the seat of the Northumbrian archbishopric from 735 onwards, the home of Alcuin's library and school. There are now no visible Anglo-Saxon architectural remains dating from before *c.* 800 and we do not even know the exact site of either Edwin's church or Alcuin's monastery. York Minster, lying east and west, cuts diagonally across the street plan of the Roman fortress, but it seems probable that the Roman orientation continued in use for most, if not all, of the Anglo-Saxon period. The York of King Edwin and Bishop Wilfrid would be much closer in its general appearance to the Roman than to the medieval city. There are Anglo-Saxon antiquities to be seen in the museum and visitors may now see the results of the recent extensive excavations beneath York Minster itself.

Places to be visited in the more northerly parts of Yorkshire include Ripon (S E 3171), where the crypt of Wilfrid's church, built in the seventh century, may still be seen, Lastingham (S E 7290) whose medieval church houses many fragments of Anglo-Saxon carved stone, and Whitby (N Z 9011), the site of Hilda's monastery.

Neither of the old names Bernicia or Deira has survived in any modern place-name, nor do we know whether the boundary between them was ever sharply defined. If any such boundary was recognised in Bede's time, it probably lay along Tees rather than Wear or Tyne, since the monasteries at Wearmouth and Jarrow looked towards Hexham for their bishops rather than towards York. Yet today's traveller who crosses Tees enters the patrimony of St Cuthbert. Many of the churches in the county of Durham contain material, either architectural or sculptural, of Anglo-Saxon date, though not all of it is as early as Bede's age. If the choice of places to be visited were to be limited to four, these four should include Escomb (N Z 1830) with an unparalleled example of a church which is almost entirely of seventh or eighth century date; the churches at Wearmouth and Jarrow both of which preserve architectural features and sculptured monuments dating from the lifetime of Bede; and the cathedral at Durham, with Cuthbert's shrine at the east end beyond the high altar, and Bede's tomb in the Galilee chapel at the west end. Visitors to Durham are admitted to what was formerly the monks' dormitory which contains a large collection of sculptured stones (mostly originals but some of them casts), as well as the relics of St Cuthbert, including his pectoral cross and the carved coffin in which his body was placed. The library houses a number of important manuscripts of this age, including more than one copy of the Gospels and also a copy of the commentary by Cassiodorus on the Psalms. Some of these manuscripts are usually displayed in show cases.

Crossing into the former county of Northumberland (its former boundaries lately modified for the needs of government), Hexham offers a good base to visit both the former Roman frontier works, still so prominent in Bede's days, and also churches of Anglo-Saxon date in the Tyne valley. At Hexham itself may be seen Wilfrid's crypt, the abbot's chair and the so-called 'Acca' cross, as well as other sculptured fragments. There are early architectural features to be seen at Corbridge (N Y 9864) where much of the fabric consists of re-used Roman material probably taken from the nearby Roman town at *Corstopitum*. Both of the two neighbouring churches at Bywell (N Z 0461) contain architectural features of Anglo-Saxon date, though the remains at St Peter's are of earlier date than those at St Andrew's.

There are objects of Anglo-Saxon date to be seen in the Museum of Antiquities in the University of Newcastle upon Tyne.

From Hexham a motorist could visit on a single day's excursion the remarkable crosses at Bewcastle in the Cumberland fells (N Y 5675) and at Ruthwell on the northern side of the Solway Firth (N Y 1068). These two are the most notable surviving examples of Northumbrian sculptured crosses; while their date is open to dispute, the eighth century seems generally favoured by modern scholars.

The most important sites in Northumberland are clustered in the
north-eastern parts of the county—Bamburgh (N U 1935), the
Farne Islands (N U 2737) and Lindisfarne which is alternatively
known as Holy Island (N U 1241). There are no visible structural
remains of the seventh or eighth centuries at any of these places, but
they lie at the heart of much of Northumbria's history—and all
should be visited. The rock at Bamburgh, crowned by a medieval
castle, is an impressive sight visible from afar. Visitors are taken to
the Farne Islands from Seahouses in small fishing-boats and are
usually able to land on two of the islands. The whole excursion
takes about two hours, with a voyage of some twenty minutes each
way. The boats do not go in rough weather, but even in calm
weather the tidal race may make the journey both choppy and
wet. The experience greatly enriches understanding of Cuthbert's
life. Visitors to Holy Island (Lindisfarne) drive across the sands on
a metalled causeway. The times when it is safe to cross are
prominently displayed on noticeboards and they should be strictly
observed. The cost of ignoring these notices can be very high in
money as well as time. In no circumstances should drivers stray
from the causeway on to the sands which are extremely dangerous
in places. There is a small museum on the island with many
interesting antiquities from the Anglo-Saxon monastery. Some
sixteen miles inland from Bamburgh, within the Northumberland
National Park, lies the site of the royal township at Old
Yeavering, visited by Paulinus who baptised in the river Glen
close by. There are no visible remains but a roadside monument
shows where the site lay (N T 9230).

South-eastern Scotland, like the northern parts of Northumberland, remains a sparsely populated countryside, but
there lie here several places associated with episodes in the history
of the kingdom. Cuthbert visited Coldingham (N T 9067), a house
of monks and nuns close beside the Berwickshire coast. Further
north Dunbar (N T 6979) was the scene of Wilfrid's imprison-
ment, and across the estuary of the Haddington Tyne lies
St Baldred's Cradle (N T 6482). West of Edinburgh and close
beside the Forth Bridges lies Abercorn (N T 0879), site of church
and monastery, and for a short while a Northumbrian bishop's

seat; there are sculptured monuments of early date. Inland the Teviot and the Leader Water both have associations with Cuthbert. The site of Cuthbert's monastery at Old Melrose lies in private grounds and is best viewed from Bemersyde Hill (N T 5934), preferably before the sun has moved too far towards the west. This was Walter Scott's favourite view and those who yield to its romantic beauty will be further rewarded if they follow the footsteps of Wordsworth westwards from Melrose along the Yarrow Water to Yarrowkirk (N T 3528); the church and cemetery here may well be successors to a British Christian community which flourished in the fifth and sixth centuries, long before Paulinus reached York.

A zealous pilgrim may wish to continue his northern journey to Stirling (N S 8993), the probable site of the place which Bede calls *Urbs Giudi*, and then turn north-east into Fife and across the Tay in order to savour the country which lay in the kingdom of the Picts. It was at Dunnichen Moss in Forfar that Ecgfrith, last of the warrior kings of the seventh century, was killed in 685. Returning towards the west, the great rock at Dumbarton, on the north bank of Clyde, was the chief stronghold of the kingdom of Strathclyde. It was taken by King Eadbert in 756, but most of his army was destroyed on the way back. Southwards from Clyde, the country was more often controlled by British than by English kings, but nothing is known in detail about the history of this area until we reach the shores of the Solway Firth. Several places near the firth have yielded early Christian antiquities, most notably Kirkmadrine (N X 0949) and Whithorn (N X 4936) which was the seat of a Northumbrian bishopric in the eighth century. There are important collections of sculptured and inscribed monuments at both places. Travelling east the pilgrim may return to Ruthwell (N Y 1068), and thence to Carlisle whose Roman buildings were shown to Cuthbert who also used to visit the anchorite called Herbert whose cell lay on St Herbert's Isle in Derwentwater (N X 2622). There are very few early documentary references to particular places in north-western England, but several of the churches contain collections of sculptured monument of various dates, among them are Dacor (N Y 4627), Kendal (N Y 5293), Heversham (N Y 5083) and Lancaster (N Y 4763). When he reaches the Ribble the traveller will have completed his pilgrimage. We do not know if the boundary was ever closely defined on this western side of the Pennines, but the endowments of Wilfrid's church at Ripon included lands lying near the Ribble.

Travelling companions which are light in the pocket (as well as on the purse) might include two volumes of the Penguin Classics—Bede's *History of the English Church and People* (L. Sherley-Price, revised ed.), and *Lives of the English Saints* (J. F. Webb); the latter contains Bede's *Life of Cuthbert* and Eddius' *Life of Wilfrid*. Anyone who prefers to read Bede's own Latin will find the *Ecclesiastical History* in the Loeb Classics (J. F. King) and in *Bede's Ecclesiastical History* (B. Colgrave and R. A. B. Mynors); both editions provide the Latin text with a facing English translation. Should anyone wish to read more deeply in Northumbrian history of this age he may be helped by *The World of Bede* (Peter Hunter Blair) which contains a long Select Bibliography. He should also use the collection of studies assembled under the title *Saint Wilfrid of Hexham* (ed. D. P. Kirby).

APPENDICES

INDEX

Chronology

THE DATES WHICH follow are intended to help a reader unfamiliar with the period, but it is not always possible to be precise. The familiar modern era of the *Annus Domini* did not come into regular use in Northumbria until the late seventh or early eighth centuries. The dates of earlier events were calculated in various different ways and the adaptation of these ways to the Christian *Annus Domini* could lead to error. We may be told that a king reigned for, say, fifteen years, but we may not have any direct evidence even for the year, let alone the day of the month, at which the reign began or ended. The years have to be calculated from indirect evidence. Those who kept records were often content with figures rounded off to whole numbers of complete years. We do not know whether account was taken of any interregnum between the death of one king and the accession of another. It is only very rarely that we can establish a date of birth with accuracy. I do not believe that we can now improve upon Bede's own chronology for the main events, but some scholars will not agree.

Events

547   Ida began to reign at Bamburgh
593   Æthelfrith began to reign
597   Columba died
       Augustine reached Canterbury
603   Æthelfrith defeated the Scots at *Degsastan*
616   Æthelfrith killed in the battle at the Idle
       Edwin succeeded
627   Edwin baptised at York on Easter Day, 12 April
633   Edwin killed in Hatfield Chase
633–4   Cadwallon ravaged Northumbria
634   Oswald defeated Cadwallon at Heavenfield and began to reign
635   Aidan came to Lindisfarne
642   Oswald killed at *Maserfelth* on 5 August
       Oswy succeeded
655   Penda killed at the river *Winwæd*
664   Synod of Whitby
670   Oswy died on 15 February
       Ecgfrith succeeded
673–4   Founding of the monastery at Wearmouth
       Ripon and Hexham churches being built in this decade
681   Founding of the monastery at Jarrow
685   St Paul's church at Jarrow dedicated on 23 April
       Ecgfrith killed at Dunnichen Moss
       Aldfrith succeeded
705   Aldfrith died
       Osred succeeded
716   Osred died
       Cenred succeeded
718   Cenred died
       Osric succeeded

729	Osric died
	Ceolwulf succeeded
731–2	Bede's *Ecclesiastical History* finished
737	Ceolwulf resigned, going to Lindisfarne (where he died in 764)
738	Eadbert succeeded
758	Eadbert resigned, going to a monastery in York (where he died in 768)
765–74	Alhred reigned
778–88	Ælfwold reigned
793	Lindisfarne attacked by Vikings
867	York taken by Danes

Men and Women prominent in the Church

	Born	Died
Hilda	c. 614	680
Eanflæd	626	after 685
Benedict Biscop	c. 628	689
Wilfrid	c. 633	709
Ceolfrith	c. 633–4	716
Cuthbert	c. 634	687
Ælfflæd	654	c. 713
Bede	c. 674	735
Alcuin	c. 730–5	804
Paulinus	Left Rome for England 601; ordained bishop 21 July 625; went to Northumbria 626 and baptised Eanflæd; baptised Edwin 627; returned to Kent 633; became bishop of Rochester; died 644	

Index

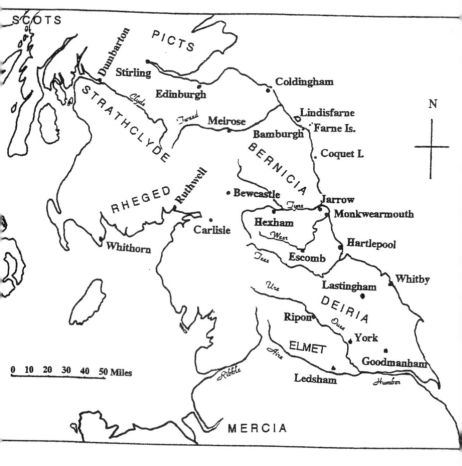